Anastacia Kurylo, Ian Reifowitz
Riling Up the Base

De Gruyter Series in Race, Ethnicity, and Political Communication

Edited by
Stephen Maynard Caliendo and Charlton D. McIlwain

Volume 3

Anastacia Kurylo, Ian Reifowitz

Riling Up the Base

———

Examining Trump's Use of Stereotypes
through an Interdisciplinary Lens

DE GRUYTER

ISBN (Paperback) 978-3-11-142566-5
ISBN (Hardcover) 978-3-11-142692-1
e-ISBN (PDF) 978-3-11-142627-3
e-ISBN (EPUB) 978-3-11-142632-7
ISSN 2942-6618

Library of Congress Control Number: 2025935656

Bibliographic information published by the Deutsche Nationalbibliothek
The Deutsche Nationalbibliothek lists this publication in the Deutsche Nationalbibliografie;
detailed bibliographic data are available on the internet at http://dnb.dnb.de.

© 2025 Walter de Gruyter GmbH, Berlin/Boston, Genthiner Straße 13, 10785 Berlin
Cover image: Robert Llewellyn / Photodisc / Getty Images

www.degruyterbrill.com
Questions about General Product Safety Regulation:
productsafety@degruyterbrill.com

Acknowledgments

Researching and writing a book can be a solitary journey. Happily, and for the first time in my career, on this journey I had an incredible co-author and partner, Dr. Anastacia Kurylo. I want to thank her for her wonderfully collaborative spirit, her creative approach to the development of this project, and, not least importantly, her hard work in producing this book on a tight timeline in order to accommodate the timing of my research sabbatical. To say that I could not have done this project without her is the literal truth—the project would not have existed without her. The complementary nature of our scholarly background means that this book would have been impossible without her.

I am also grateful to my colleagues at SUNY-Empire State University for supporting this project, in particular History Department Chair Paul Miller and Dean of the School of Arts and Humanities Nicola Allain, both of whom have graciously championed my work and my various applications for institutional support. Empire State provided me with the aforementioned research sabbatical, without which I could never have had the time to research and write my parts of this book, and so I truly appreciate my university's support of my work. Great scholars and friends Steven Beller, Volker Berghahn, and Aviel Roshwald have heard much about this project, and shared their invaluable wisdom with me, which I treasure.

As always, I want to thank my family. My wife, Jane Kaufman—who was asked (note the subjectless passive voice) far too often whether a particular phrase sounded right—is always the person my work impinges on the most. I hope she knows how much I appreciate her help and support, editorial and otherwise. My mother, Helaine Mazur, Mike Mazur, and my uncle and fellow scholar of politics, Professor Leslie Schuster, also offered their support for me in various ways, for which I am grateful. Finally, our two daughters, Lauren and Kate, who were not even born when my first book came out, are now young adults, and I could not be prouder of them. I thank them for their patience while I was working and not doing something else that might have helped them more directly—like getting their meals ready exactly when they wanted to eat. I dedicate this book—or my half, at least—to them.

–Ian Reifowitz

https://doi.org/10.1515/9783111426327-001

It's been an honor to work with Ian on this project and I am grateful for his extensive contributions and continual efforts to finetune the manuscript. It is an understatement to say we worked together well and Ian's attention to detail and ability to capture the perfect example for the point I was trying to express is uncanny. Our collaboration bolstered my occasionally wavering faith in humanity. The ability to disagree with respect, talk about topics that matter even when such discussion is hard, and persevere with mutual respect retained is a wonderful foundation to have built this book upon. For many reasons, this book at this time in my life was not an easy book to write but it was an easy book to write with Ian.

My greatest debt and appreciation is reserved for my husband Mike and my children Anna and Lincoln from whom I am always learning. As a magician, Mike practices constantly and pushes through difficulties to produce magic that entertains as well as makes his audience think. This provided a metaphor for my work on this book. Similarly, my children are navigating high school to find their paths with high grades balanced with fun and their own unique creative and perpetually inspiring projects. They provided a consistent reminder throughout my work on this book that through adversity, we can learn, grow, and create.

This book spanned my time at two colleges: St. Joseph's College and Brooklyn College, where I found and continue to find great support among my colleagues and the institutions themselves. I am grateful to Sharona Levy for her enthusiasm and encouragement to get students involved in this important project. She reinforced that the college environment is about more than learning in a classroom. The pre-professional and research opportunities that take place on a college campus are what feed the professional scientific research community. Without support for colleges and without colleges' support of their teachers, the ability for today's college students to be tomorrow's leaders will become nothing more than a legend. Among these future leaders are my research assistants on this project for whom I am eternally grateful, including the amazing students from St. Joseph's College that took my Stereotypes and Communication course, especially Nicole, and my equally fantastic Brooklyn College students Cody Butler, Kaleb Cheek, Isabella Crawford, and Jake Mooney.

–Anastacia Kurylo

Finally, this is from both Anastacia and Ian: At De Gruyter, we want to thank Ze'ev Sudry, for believing in this project and for providing invaluable guidance throughout the process of submitting and revising our book proposal, prior to signing a contract. Content Editor Annika Friedrichs, also at De Gruyter, has been a wonderful help as well throughout the writing and editing process. Our series editors, Stephen Maynard Caliendo and Charlton McIlwain, gave us incredibly productive and helpful feedback that made this book stronger, more cohesive, and, frankly, better-written than it otherwise would have been. And a sincere thank you to Jennifer Mercieca, for writing such an insightful and expertly crafted Foreword.

Foreword

Ours is a moment of crisis—a new "age of catastrophe," like the one historian Eric Hobsbawm described as existing in the first half of the 20th century.[1] Our age of catastrophe is characterized by crisis levels of distrust, polarization, and frustration as well as the erosion of democratic governments around the world. "Nearly 3 out of 4 persons in the world – 72% – now live in autocracies," according to the 2025 Varieties of Democracy (V-Dem) report. "This is the highest since 1978." Liberal democracies—once stable and plentiful—have become scarce. And it's happening here too. According to the Democracy Index, the United States has been a "flawed" democracy since 2017.[2] The public seems to agree: according to an October 2024 NYT/Siena survey, 76% of Americans believe that democracy in America is "under threat."[3] Like the political catastrophes a century ago, ours is also enflamed by authoritarian leaders who use communication as a weapon.

How did we get here? Part of our age of catastrophe is that we are vulnerable to democratic backsliding. As Robert Putnam explained in *Bowling Alone*, over the past several decades a lot of us have stopped associating, thinking, and communicating democratically.[4] As we have withdrawn from public life, we have lost bridging social capital and trust in the political process. Scholars of democratic legitimacy, democratic erosion, and democratic deliberation have explained that a healthy and stable government requires trust—governments are only seen as legitimate so long as their citizens trust institutions, practices, and people to behave according to "the democratic rules of the game."[5]

Within such a crisis, a typical presidential candidate would attempt to bridge political divides and unite the public in a common national vision, but that was not Donald Trump's strategy. We know, for example, that Trump frequently used *ad hominem* attacks—a strategy of avoiding accountability by attacking the people

---

1 Hobsbawm, Eric, *Age Of Extremes: The Short Twentieth Century, 1914–1991.* (1994). Abacus, London.

2 https://www.economist.com/graphic-detail/2017/01/25/declining-trust-in-government-is-denting-democracy (accessed April 21, 2025); https://www.washingtonpost.com/business/2020/09/18/united-states-is-backsliding-into-autocracy-under-trump-scholars-warn/ (accessed April 21, 2025).

3 https://www.nytimes.com/interactive/2024/10/27/us/elections/times-siena-poll-crosstabs.html (accessed April 21, 2025).

4 Putnam, Robert D. *Bowling Alone: The Collapse and Revival of American Community.* (2000). Simon and Schuster.

5 Levitsky, Steven, and Daniel Ziblatt. (2019). *How Democracies Die.* Harlow, England: Penguin Books.

https://doi.org/10.1515/9783111426327-002

who made arguments against him, rather than refuting their arguments.[6] Trump got a lot of attention for deploying nicknames like "Low Energy Jeb" or "Crooked Hillary," but traditionally those kinds of attacks would signal to audiences that a political candidate like Trump was unqualified to hold high office. Typically, *ad hominem* attacks would be seen as unstatesmanlike and disqualifying—why did they work for Trump? Why did his audience not just tolerate his childish taunts, but celebrate them? Why did they go to Trump's rallies and chant his childish taunts and post them on social media?

While many books have explained what communication strategies Trump used and how they helped him to win elections, few (if any) books have explained how Trump's communication strategies worked on the cognitive processes—the minds—of his audience. This important question is answered in *Riling Up the Base: Examining Trump's Use of Stereotypes through an Interdisciplinary Lens*.

In *Riling Up the Base*, Kurylo and Reifowitz teach us how and why stereotypes worked on Trump's audiences. Drawing from research in psychology, communication, media and persuasion, sociology, and critical-cultural studies, the authors offer a compelling and insightful theory of how Trump's followers understand and process his messages. The overarching argument of the book is that Trump used stereotypes as a very effective strategy and that Trump's stereotype strategy was particularly effective in this historical moment and with his particular audience. In other words, this strategy was uniquely successful both because of how all of our brains process information and because of how Trump's followers process information in this political and media environment.

From *Riling Up the Base* we learn exactly why Trump's stereotype strategy worked: we're all so busy and our feeds and our scrolls move so fast that we don't have time to absorb and critically examine information. Kurylo and Reifowitz show that this creates vulnerabilities: we rely on heuristics and shortcuts and feelings instead of deliberately and carefully examining messages. When we are overwhelmed with information, we are easily led and manipulated by political figures like Trump.

But Trump's stereotype strategy did not just work because we are overwhelmed with information and distracted. Kurylo and Reifowitz show that it also worked because it activated "us versus them" polarization and framed Trump supporters as "heroes" fighting against their shared "enemies." Trump used stereotypes and fear appeals to scare his audience into submission while promising them that he was the only one who could or would protect them. His

---

6 Mercieca, Jennifer. *Demagogue for President: The Rhetorical Genius of Donald Trump.* (2020). Texas A&M University Press.

stereotype strategy is a form of war propaganda, attacking the minds of his followers with fear appeals and attacking his opposition by framing them as hate-objects.

All is not hopeless, however. We live in an age of catastrophe, but within any crisis there is opportunity—the opportunity to restructure, to rebuild, to reinvigorate our public sphere and strengthen our democracy. To rebuild we have to recognize that how governments, media, and citizens communicate matters for creating a trusting and stable political community. What kind of communication practices will encourage trust? Certainly not stereotypes. When political leaders use stereotypes against us, they violate our trust by taking advantage of our vulnerabilities, attacking our minds.[7]

Politics is not war, and political communication does not have to be warfare. Persuasion and propaganda are opposite ends of a continuum of verbal and nonverbal "influence strategies." Persuasion is a dialogic meeting of minds in which one person asks another person to think like they do, to value the same values, to remember or forget history in the same way. It does not force. It affirms human dignity by inviting. A person who seeks to persuade gives good reasons and formulates arguments in the best way they know how, always affirming that the recipient of the persuasive message has a mind, values, and experiences of their own and may not change their mind. Persuasion is difficult and time consuming. Propaganda is a much easier, much faster, and much simpler strategy for changing minds. Propaganda treats people as tools to be manipulated, it denies human dignity or immanent value (the value that each of us have just because we are people). Propaganda is *influence without consent*. Because persuasion does not exploit our vulnerabilities, it relies upon and builds trust; propaganda exploits trust.

Ultimately Kurylo and Reifowitz help us to understand the success of a political candidate like Donald Trump in a world awash in communication and democratic erosion. As we learn from *Riling Up the Base*, the propaganda tactics of name-calling and outrage weaken our democracy. Trump did not create this crisis, but he has taken advantage of its rhetorical possibilities to gain power.

Dr. Jennifer R. Mercieca
Professor, Department of Communication & Journalism

---

7 According to political philosopher Barbara A. Misztal, "Social trust is seen as a lubricant for cooperation because it mutually reinforces expectations about reciprocity." Misztal, Barbara A. "Trust and Cooperation: The Democratic Public Sphere." *Journal of Sociology* 37, no. 4 (December 2001): 371–86. https://doi.org/10.1177/144078301128756409 (accessed April 21, 2025).

Contents

Chapter 4
Social Identity Theory and Group Vitality Theory: The fight against the "angry left-wing mob" —— 64

Chapter 5
Psychodynamic approach: "Lock [her/him/they/them] up" —— 85

Chapter 6
Muted Group Theory and Critical Race Theory: Weaponizing snowflakes —— 104

Introduction

A great many books have been published on President Donald Trump and his political rhetoric, as well as the role the media played (and continues to play) in his meteoric rise to power. Some have argued Trump first reached the White House because of white racial anxiety, his conservative base, white women, social conservatives, or pushback against a politically correct ethos. These theories share a focus on who voted for him and why. Although each has value, and draws on documented data and demographic information, these claims nonetheless leave a theoretical gap. This book argues that above all stereotypes propelled Trump's victories. Various theories help reveal the reality that, regardless of who his competitors were, his uncanny ability to wield stereotypes enabled him to secure a strong base and win the presidency, twice.

Taking an interdisciplinary approach, we analyze how the voting populace, politicians across all political perspectives, the media, and various constituent groups—participating actively in some cases and inadvertently in others—ultimately contributed to the outcomes set in motion by Trump's use of stereotypes. *Riling up the Base* provides a full aggregate explanation of the seemingly mesmerizing attachment and adoration his core supporters feel by explaining the way seemingly disparate theories work both alone and together to expose the mechanisms at play. We build our overarching argument by examining Trump's language through numerous theoretical lenses that reflect varied disciplines, all of which highlight distinct but integrally related insights to his stereotype use. Although scholars have applied some theories—psychology theories in particular—to the relationship between Trump and his base, they have done so in isolation from other theories of stereotypes (e. g., MacWilliams, 2020) rather than comprehensively. When explored, applied, and combined to address Trump's rhetoric and communication of stereotypes, these theories are particularly illuminating.

While other texts have delved deeply into the twice-elected president's use of specific stereotypes (e. g., gender) or focused on the role of the media in enhancing his success with his base, this book provides a holistic view of his communication, regardless of media, and his stereotypes in total. We approach the stereotypes incorporated into his rhetoric and displayed in media portrayals of Trump without inherent presumption of animus. Rather, this book addresses a number of relevant theories throughout the chapters in the context of their own assumptions about the relevance of emotion inherent in each in order to build the book's dispassionate argument. In some cases, animus will be relevant to the theoretical underpinning of the chapter. In others, the theory will require a different stance on Trump's stereotype use. Using theories of stereotype processes, we demonstrate that his

https://doi.org/10.1515/9783111426327-003

electoral achievements and the continued support he enjoys from his base occurred not despite his use of stereotypes, but precisely because of it.

We provide an alternate understanding of Trump's political success that focuses not on *his* psychology or the media's intervention but on the manipulability of his base that resulted from his seemingly instinctual mastery of stereotypes as a communication tool. Several scholarly areas help unpack how his employment of stereotypes motivates his base. Theories from psychology, communication, media and persuasion, sociology, and critical cultural studies each provide insight into how Trump did this despite stereotyping being perceived largely as an "unsavory practice to be avoided or concealed" (Bodenhausen and Macrae, 1996, p. 232). Through applying these theories individually and collectively to modern political history in the United States, we make transparent the theoretical mechanisms underpinning how the twice-elected president engineered his political rise and continued relevance precisely through stereotypes—language that also significantly aggravated already existing divisiveness in American society.

The majority of theories discussed in the book pull from the fields of psychology and communication. Additionally, Media and Persuasion theories help illustrate how his mode of communication (e.g., Twitter/X, Truth Social, television) uniquely contributes to his ability to motivate his base. Specifically, *Riling up the Base* explores classic media and persuasion theories such as Elaboration Likelihood Model, Social Exchange Theory, and Agenda Setting Theory. The critical cultural approach stemming from sociology contributes several theories that elucidate how Trump activated his base, including Muted Group Theory and Critical Race Theory.

We examine stereotypes across a broad spectrum, rather than any one stereotyped group. Trump invoked stereotypes of many groups in divisive ways. This book demonstrates that the stereotypes he used accomplished similar goals regardless of the specific group targeted in each instance. Each chapter addresses one or two related prominent theories relevant to stereotyping processes and engages the reader in a persuasive unfolding of the role each theory played in his public communications. We bring these theories into conversation with one another as we connect them to the primary questions and themes of the book.

Chapter 1 expands upon the commonly (but not universally) held belief that people should not communicate stereotypes to explore the assertion by Kurylo (2013) that doing so creates an interactional dilemma. This dilemma results from the tension between a political correctness (PC) movement that condemns stereotype use—because it increases bias, prejudice, and discrimination—and the benefits (e.g., humor, scapegoating) communicating them provides. Rather than being a cause for admonishment, communicated stereotypes result in the appearance of consensus about the legitimacy of a stereotype, further perpetuating it. This chapter introduces and applies this concept to Trump's conversational use of stereotypes, which frees the members of his base from the constraints of political correctness. The first four chapters address the usefulness of stereotypes for those who use them.

In Chapter 2, we address the most fundamental belief held by Trump's base about stereotypes—that they stand as reasonable descriptions of group members (i.e., they are accurate) and, thus, perfectly appropriate to communicate. The twice-elected president reinforces this perspective through his employment of stereotypes and his insistence on their representing fact. This chapter explores his invocation of base rates—regardless of the absence of factual evidence to support them—as a hallmark of his political rhetoric.

There is no evidence supporting the accuracy of stereotypes, yet Trump employs them to trigger stereotypical assumptions among his followers. Chapter 3 addresses the mechanism through which he does so. Information Processing Theory explains how communicating stereotypes universally provides benefits of cognitive efficiency and inference. The twice-elected president validates for his constituency the value of stereotypes for unconscious processing, regardless of any negative consequences resulting from unconscious bias. Even Trump's campaign slogan 'Make America Great Again' (MAGA) invokes stereotypes to convince his base that America is not currently 'great' for them.

Chapter 4 exposes how Trump uses stereotypes to foment divisiveness by invoking a technique of group differentiation between 'us' and 'them'. Doing so leads to more polarized behavior, as predicted by Social Identity Theory. As the twice-elected president invokes dichotomies of Democrats/Republicans, Immigrants/Americans, and Us/Them to bolster ingroup identity for his base, he simultaneously attacks the credibility, authority, and even humanity of targeted group members in ways that provide succor to MAGA Republicans and bolster his brand in order to facilitate political ends. Extended from Social Identity Theory, Group Vitality Theory enumerates the mechanisms that people employ to create the perception of a strong ingroup identity: demographics, institutional support, and status. The chapter explores the application of this theory to Trump's communications to demonstrate how he nurtured the perception of a powerful and cohesive MAGA base.

In Chapter 5, we address how Trump's rhetoric exacerbates bias and prejudice as well as divides Americans by weaponizing his base's need to find an outlet for their anxieties and resentments. The Psychodynamic Approach to stereotypes provides two theories to explain how this occurs: Authoritarian Personality and Scapegoat Theory. Through understanding the concept of Authoritarian Personality, we see how communicating stereotypes, as rigid descriptors, encourages the blind dedication of some of his strongest supporters to a view of Trump as a hero for his political movement. Scapegoat Theory offers insight on the twice-elected president's use of stereotypes to target and bully opponents including, among others, his 2016 general election opponent, Secretary of State Hillary Clinton, and, later, his 2024 opponent, Vice President Kamala Harris. This chapter demonstrates the techniques that Trump utilizes to successfully appeal to the prejudices, insecurities, and fears of his followers.

Chapter 6 integrates the concept of power into the discussion of Trump's stereotype use. One of the earliest theories addressing dynamics related to power and communication is Muted Group Theory. More recently, terms like power, invisibility, privilege, and voice commonly appear in discussions that draw on Critical Race Theory. These theories help to explain how the twice-elected president (and others) hurl terms like "snowflake" to further silence those who would fight for the rights of the disenfranchised, as well as minority groups who seek a voice in the political sphere. This chapter analyzes how Trump's use of stereotypes changed the dominant narrative from political correctness to a new one attacking so-called woke snowflakes—people so fragile that words can hurt them. This process peaked with the ironic crescendo of characterizing Critical Race Theory as psychological abuse.

The expansion of Trump's reach and the amplification of his messaging by the media—even as he simultaneously undermines the credibility of mainstream outlets—is the topic of Chapter 7. The chapter draws on Elaboration Likelihood Model's discussion of how media content can reach people through central and peripheral routes. Trump's use of stereotypes was a key factor driving the unprecedented level of coverage he received even before becoming his party's nominee for president—something that benefited the media as well as the candidate. This chapter addresses how the twice-elected president expertly used the media to get his message out.

In Chapter 8, we analyze how Trump's base comes to treat his misinformation and disinformation (i.e., lies) as truth—even in the face of contradictory, documented facts. Drawing on semiotics, we address how Trump redefines language (e.g., war hero in the case of former Arizona Sen. John McCain) and asserts 'truth', 'facts', and claims about 'reality' in the absence of objectively verifiable evidence. Social construction articulates that we construct meaning through our messages. This theory rejects the assumption and expectation that objective reality or truth exists and, instead, views truth as a collaboration achieved through communication.

Our final chapter offers concluding thoughts and reviews how Trump's stereotype-laden messaging and political rhetoric reflects the theories we have discussed. We identify TrumpWorld as a space where his supporters search for a familiar home of an America that they can feel comfortable with, one that can be made great again.

Key terminology and assumptions

Most fundamentally for this book, a stereotype is an association between a group and a characteristic attributed to that group (e. g., Ashmore and Del Boca, 1981; Hilton and Von Hippel, 1996; Hinton, 2000; Katz and Braly, 1933; 1935; Leyens et al., 1994; McGarty, 2002; Oakes et al., 1994; Ottati and Lee, 1995; Stroebe and Insko, 1989). When a person communicates stereotypes, it affects everyone involved in the interaction, including both members of the targeted group and the stereotyper. The stereotype may either target a specific person or a group in general. We can also contrast stereotypes with generalizations. Generalizations permit exceptions because they include qualifiers such as: most, many, some, a few, and so forth that make clear that the association being made between the group and characteristic is not universal to all members of the target group. Instead, stereotypes claim to represent all people in a group and act as probabilistic associations between the group and the characteristic that are absolute, fixed, and rigid (i. e., without exception). For example, one generalization is that women are usually shorter than men. Stereotypical versions of this would state that women are short or that women are always shorter than men.

Kurylo (2013) coined the concept of communicated stereotypes. This focus on communication is an appropriate and necessary extension of stereotype research in psychology because "socially shared beliefs [i. e., stereotypes] are communicated between people" (Schaller and Conway, 1999, p. 820; Fiske and Taylor, 1984; Dovidio et al., 1996; Lyons and Kashima, 2001; Schaller, Conway, and Tanchuk, 2002). Schaller and Latané (1996) argue that the perpetuation of stereotypes and their resistance to change results from their evolution through communication processes. Kurylo (2013) explores the functions of interpersonally communicated stereotypes specifically, an observable and consequential phenomenon (Mokros, 2003), and posits that the interactional dilemma makes countering stereotypes in real time interaction difficult. This difficulty allows stereotypic knowledge to be maintained and perpetuated in the cultural knowledge base over time. In exploring stereotypes Trump has communicated, we do not seek to determine his intent, but rather we accept them at face value—regardless of whether they were initially said publicly or privately—in order to understand their impact. With many options to choose from, the stereotypes we address in the book span his career.

Lastly, the word "base" is very important here—it is in our title after all. Certainly, not everyone who cast a ballot for Trump falls into this category. Rather, we define his base as those voters who support him unreservedly, who share his "Make America Great Again" worldview and consider themselves part of the MAGA/Trump movement. The twice-elected president claimed on August 8, 2024: "I think the base is 75% of the country, far beyond the Republican Party" (Mehrara, 2024). More realistically, a 2023 survey found that 24% of Americans had a positive view of MAGA (Bowman, 2023). For this book's purposes, when we talk about how Trump uses stereotypes to rile up his base, we refer to this latter group, which, to be generous, likely covers somewhere between a quarter and a third of all Americans.

Our book does not explain how Trump got enough votes in the general election to win the presidency in 2016 and again in 2024. But we do argue that without stereotypes and other related rhetoric that prey on people's fears and anxieties, he would never have won the Republican nomination in 2016 and become the leader of the Republican Party—a position he has maintained since then, and without which he could never have become President of the United States that year, and again eight years later. Without a riled-up MAGA base, there is no President Trump.

Chapter 1
Grab them by the stereotype and exposing the interactional dilemma

On June 16, 2015, in New York City, America hammered the last nail into the coffin of political correctness—a concept centering on the rejection of stereotypes. After descending a Trump Tower escalator, Donald Trump launched his run for the White House with free-flowing remarks that in many respects mirrored the content coming from right-wing talk radio (Sherman, 2016, Reifowitz, 2019). Out of 6,364 words, 233 focused on America's border policy with Mexico, but one point caught the public's attention. These specific lines, delivered within the first couple of minutes, did not appear in the prepared remarks sent to reporters beforehand (Trump Campaign, 2015)—which merely mentioned that Mexico was "sending people that they don't want." The candidate expanded on that planned phrase with a typically Trumpian flourish. What he actually said proved to be the stereotype heard around the world (Washington Post Staff, 2015a):

> When Mexico sends its people, they're not sending their best. They're not sending you. They're not sending you. They're sending people that have lots of problems, and they're bringing those problems to us. They're bringing drugs. They're bringing crime. They're rapists. And some, I assume, are good people.

Riding stereotypes to the top of the polls

Stereotypes are "culturally shared mental representations of a social group" (Kurylo, 2004, p. 74). Lippmann (1922/1965) has generally been credited with introducing the concept of stereotypes as "pictures in the mind" that are, "rigid, oversimplified and selective" (Oakes et al., 1994, p. 9). Stereotypes are often associated with a stigma, or mark of "disgrace" (Goffman, 1963b, p. 2) causing people to avoid them (Bodenhausen and Macrae, 1996, Borisoff and Victor, 1989; Jussim, McCauley, and Lee, 1995). Despite—or, as we argue, because of—communicating this explicit and extensive stereotype of Mexican immigrants, Trump shot up in the polls for the Republican nomination. For example, in the Monmouth University Polling Institute's tracking survey, he went from 2% in mid-June, a few days before the announcement, to 13% in mid-July (Monmouth, 2015). His favorability ratings in this poll of Republican voters improved from 20% favorable/55% unfavorable in June to 40% favorable/41% unfavorable in July (Monmouth, 2015). Among self-identified

https://doi.org/10.1515/9783111426327-004

Tea Party[8] Republicans the numbers went from 20% favorable/55% unfavorable all the way up to 56% favorable/26% unfavorable over that same one-month span—a truly spectacular increase that indicates he had begun building a solid base of supporters riled up by his use of stereotypes (Monmouth, 2015). On a related note, in 2019 the Pew Research Center found that Tea Partiers supported Trump far more strongly than Republicans and Republican-leaning respondents who either opposed the Tea Party or offered no opinion on it (Pew Research Center, 2019).

Within a month of announcing his candidacy, and prior to any primary debates, polling showed Trump had become the front-runner, a status he continued to hold virtually every day from that point right up through his official nomination (Real Clear Polling, n.d.). On August 6, 2015, the first Republican debate of that election season took place, with Megyn Kelly as host. Kelly pushed him on the stereotypes he had communicated previously about women, reminding him, "You've called women you don't like 'fat pigs, dogs, slobs and disgusting animals,'" and adding: "Your Twitter account has several disparaging comments about women's looks. You once told a contestant on Celebrity Apprentice it would be a pretty picture to see her on her knees." After initially making a joke about his feud with television personality and well-known liberal Rosie O'Donnell, Trump responded by dismissing the concern over his use of slurs as a distraction from what he considered more important issues (Washington Post Staff, 2015b):

> This country is in big trouble. We don't win anymore. We lose to China. We lose to Mexico both in trade and at the border. We lose to everybody. And frankly, what I say, and oftentimes it's fun, it's kidding. We have a good time. What I say is what I say.

> And honestly Megyn, if you don't like it, I'm sorry. I've been very nice to you, although I could probably maybe not be, based on the way you have treated me. But I wouldn't do that. [Applause] But you know what, we – we need strength, we need energy, we need quickness and we need brain in this country to turn it around. That, I can tell you right now.

After this debate, a Fox News poll showed that Trump's polling numbers, at 25%, stood at double those of his nearest competitors, with former neurosurgeon Ben Carson and Sen. Ted Cruz of Texas at 12% and 10% respectively (Shutt, 2015). This occurred despite survey respondents declaring that Trump had "the worst debate performance" and was the "least likable Republican candidate" (Shutt, 2015). Apparently, potential voters either loved Trump or hated him. Either way, enough —in particular the growing share of Republicans who served as his nascent base—

---

8 The Tea Party was a movement of hard-right conservatives that emerged in the early months of the Obama presidency. For more, see Theda Skocpol and Vanessa Williamson, *The Tea Party and the Remaking of Republican Conservatism*, (Oxford University Press, 2013).

loved him to put him in the lead among a field then consisting of 17 major candidates. In an interview with Trump in 2023 on her Sirius XM program, Kelly noted that his answers to her questions at the debate—which doubled down on his misogynistic stereotypes—were to be credited at least in part for the increase in polling numbers saying, "You handled it well. Your poll numbers went up" (Johnson, 2023).

Using stereotypes was a deliberate strategy

The use of stereotypes in these key, early moments of Trump's campaign was no accident. It was in fact intentional and based on extensive research. Sam Nunberg had been working for Trump as a political aide since 2011 (Costa, 2018). Though Trump ultimately hired and fired Nunberg multiple times—and eventually sued him in 2016 (Cortellessa, 2017)—the crafty aide managed to meet his charge to find the common denominator that would motivate his boss's potential followers and catapult him to the presidency.

Relying on talk radio—which Nunberg said he spent "thousands of hours" listening to—Trump's advisers developed a sense of what was riling up the right-wing base, namely using stereotypes to stoke fear about people coming across the border illegally (Sherman, 2016). In 2014, Trump had told the audience at the annual Conservative Political Action Conference (CPAC) "we either have borders or we don't," and had already begun contemplating building a wall at the Mexican border (Sherman, 2016)—an idea Nunberg reportedly originated and convinced Trump to make central to his political brand (Cortellessa, 2017).

Whereas his primary rival in the summer of 2015, former Florida Gov. Jeb Bush, had characterized undocumented immigrants from Mexico as committing an "act of love" when they crossed the Rio Grande, Trump took the opposite approach (Sherman, 2016). In August 2015 his campaign attacked this Bush remark in a devastating ad that provided names and photos of dark-skinned, undocumented immigrants charged with or convicted of murder (Rucker, 2015b). The strategy was simple. By communicating outrageous stereotypes as persuasive points in his political rhetoric, Trump's behavior would capture attention that could secure media coverage and raise his public profile without having to pay for it. He continued to insult Mexico and its people throughout the rest of the campaign (Reilly, 2016a), and the approach he took in attacking Bush has remained a Trump staple in every campaign since. As Gabriel Sherman put it, "Trump openly stoked racial tensions and appealed to the latent misogyny of a base that thinks of Hillary [Clinton] as the world's most horrible ballbuster" (Sherman, 2016).

Donald Trump's comfort with shocking people during the 2016 campaign with hateful words was not new (Lopez, 2020). He had contributed outrageous and divisive political commentary throughout Barack Obama's presidency (Caldwell, 2016; Tatum and Acosta, 2017). It was that kind of race-baiting rhetoric about Obama himself that helped give Trump the credibility among right-wing Republicans necessary for him to make a serious run for the White House (Moody, 2016).

Trump was one of the most prominent "birthers." Drawing on racist tropes about non-white people being somehow less American, birthers baselessly questioned whether Obama was born in the U.S. and, thus, was qualified to serve as president. Trump engaged in birtherism on multiple occasions throughout early 2011:

> "I want him to show his birth certificate. There is something on that birth certificate that he doesn't like," he said in an appearance on ABC's "The View." On "Fox and Friends," Trump insisted Obama spent "millions of dollars in legal fees trying to get away from this issue," and floated the idea on Bill O'Reilly's show that the certificate could say the president is a Muslim. (ABC News, 2016a).

As Slotkin noted: "Trump's promotion of birtherism concealed an essentially racist message behind the screen of xenophobia" (Slotkin, 2024, p. 305). Trump often employed another hateful method of othering his predecessor when he suggested Obama is somehow hiding that he is Muslim and just pretending to be Christian (Moody and Holmes, 2015). More broadly, the election of our first black president provoked heightened white fear and anxiety on the right. A 2009 Department of Homeland Security report documented that: "the historical election of an African American president and the prospect of policy changes are proving to be a driving force for right-wing extremist recruitment and radicalization" (U.S. Department of Homeland Security, 2009). Trump was playing with fire.

In 2008, President Obama released the official certificate the state of Hawaii issued his family when he was born. On April 27, 2011, he released his long-form birth certificate. Nevertheless, Trump continued to raise questions, tweeting on August 6, 2012: "An 'extremely credible source' has called my office and told me that Barack Obama's birth certificate is a fraud" (ABC News, 2016a). As late as September 15, 2016, Trump still refused to state flatly that he accepted the documented facts on this matter (ABC News, 2016a). He also hyped a similar birther lie on multiple occasions in 2020 about another politician of color, Kamala Harris, then the Democratic nominee for vice president (Rogers, 2020). Harris, who was born in the U.S., had two immigrant parents, a fact Trump used to question—without merit—her qualification to serve as vice president or president.

Trump had been spewing stereotypes and bigotry long before stepping into the political arena, as dozens of examples make clear (Lopez, 2020). Regarding business dealings, there is his 1993 testimony to Congress, where he complained that certain Native American reservations should not be permitted to run casinos because "they don't look like Indians to me" (Brockell, 2016; Lopez 2020). As relates to more personal matters, it does not get much more casually sexist than what Trump told *Esquire* in 1991: "You know, it really doesn't matter what they write as long as you've got a young and beautiful piece of ass" (Kruse, 2015). As for less casual sexism, consider one of Trump's most notorious statements, the one that surfaced only a month before the 2016 election, which captured his conversation with Access Hollywood's Billy Bush: "You know, I'm automatically attracted to beautiful—I just start kissing them. It's like a magnet. Just kiss. I don't even wait. And when you're a star, they let you do it. You can do anything." After a reply from Bush, Trump added: "Grab 'em by the pussy. You can do anything" (Bullock, 2016).

Also in 1991, the former head of the Trump Plaza casino published a book quoting Trump as having offered the following:

> Black guys counting my money! I hate it. The only kind of people I want counting my money are short guys that wear yarmulkes every day. ... I think that the guy is lazy. And it's probably not his fault, because laziness is a trait in Blacks. It really is, I believe that. It's not anything they can control (Lopez, 2020).

Six years later Trump admitted he had "probably" made that statement (Lopez, 2020). He has a long, documented history of using language about African Americans that draws on racist tropes. As American University Professor Bev-Freda Jackson told the Associated Press, Trump has been "taking that historical racialized language that was offensive and insulting, and...subordinating of black persons, [and] applying it in a contemporary space" (Swenson and Alexander, 2023).

In addition to the aforementioned remark about Jews being good with money, Trump has made similar statements, namely that Jews are "the best negotiators" (Slotkin, 2024, p. 303), or when he said in a speech to Jewish Republicans: "I'm a negotiator like you folks...This room negotiates perhaps more than any room I've spoken to, maybe more" (Kelly, 2015). Such stereotypes reflect long-standing antisemitic tropes (Anti-Defamation League, (n.d.). Another slur is the notion that Jews are particularly clannish—which he echoed in private remarks he made as president to his aides, namely that Jews "are only in it for themselves" and that they "stick together" (Miller, 2020).

Trump also made a series of comments attacking Jewish Americans—whose votes he certainly wanted—for not supporting him in greater numbers. He suggested that they should vote for him not out of American patriotism but out of loyalty to *Israel*, adding on September 19, 2024, that if he did lose: "the Jewish people would have a lot to do with a loss" (Cameron and Gold, 2024). He also stated that Harris—whose husband and two stepchildren are Jewish, and who has staunchly backed Israel as vice president—"hates Israel" (Cameron and Gold, 2024). In a July 30, 2024 interview, when the host said that Harris's husband, Second Gentleman Doug Emhoff, was "a crappy Jew," Trump replied, "Yeah" (Alfonseca, 2024). On August 20, 2019, he criticized Democrats on Israel specifically, and opined: "I think any Jewish people that vote for a Democrat, I think it shows either a total lack of knowledge or great disloyalty" (Davis, 2019). The head of the Anti-Defamation League, Jonathan Greenblatt, condemned Trump's remarks, noting: "It's unclear who [President Trump] is claiming Jews would be 'disloyal' to, but charges of disloyalty have long been used to attack Jews" (Davis, 2019).

In an interview published on March 18, 2024, Trump went further: "Any Jewish person that votes for Democrats hates their religion. They hate everything about Israel, and they should be ashamed of themselves because Israel will be destroyed." (Cameron, 2024). On a call with a group of leading Jewish Americans, the twice-elected president even referred to Israel as "your country" (Hoffman, 2020). One of the more prominent antisemitic tropes is the accusation that Jews living in the Diaspora are loyal above all to some kind of nefarious world Jewish cabal—as well as, since 1948, the State of Israel. The first of these charges appeared in the infamous Protocols of the Elders of Zion, perhaps the most dangerously influential antisemitic publication ever crafted (United States Holocaust Memorial Museum, 2024).

In his role on the television show *The Apprentice*, Trump made a proposal in 2005 that demonstrated his willingness to ruthlessly exploit racial tension for his own personal gain. After relating that he "wasn't particularly happy" with the show's most recent season, he proposed "an idea that is fairly controversial—creating a team of successful African Americans versus a team of successful whites. Whether people like that idea or not, it is somewhat reflective of our very vicious world" (López, 2020). Additionally, after Randall Pinkett defeated a white woman in the final round (a fund-raising contest) and won the 2005 season, Trump asked him on air if he would share the prize with her. Pinkett was the only black contestant ever to win a season, and the only one ever asked to share the prize (Burke and Kinnard, 2024).

Stereotypes were primary features of Trump's toolkit. Incorporating them into his campaign strategy was a natural extension of his personality and, presumably, reflected his opinions on various issues. Many in his base viewed these opinions as inherently having value because of his supposed and much publicized prowess in business.

Trump appeals to the 'Everyman'

Long before he announced his run for the presidency, Trump had gained the reputation of being a successful businessman in part due to the popularity of his co-authored book, written earlier in his rise to fame, titled *The Art of the Deal* (Trump and Schwartz, 1987; Thomas, 2016). The media also played a role in building up his billionaire persona, even when the facts pointed in a different direction. For example, after the stock market crashed on October 19, 1987, Trump told a *Wall Street Journal* reporter that he had presciently sold his stocks just prior to 'Black Monday,' when the Dow Jones Industrial Average fell by 22.6%—the biggest percentage drop on any day in Wall Street's history. The story, which made Trump look like a financial whiz kid, was not true—he actually lost millions of dollars. But the reporter had been on a deadline, and never bothered to check the claim (Buettner and Craig, 2024). Such are the stories upon which public perception is built.

According to *Washington Post* fact-checker Glenn Kessler (2016):

> Trump consistently lowballs the help he got from his father. Trump has suggested he got his start when he obtained a $1 million loan from his father. "My father gave me a small loan of a million dollars," he told NBC in October, which he claimed he had to pay back with interest. "A million dollars isn't very much compared to what I built."

Consequently, many assumed Trump rose to the top through sheer talent, when in reality he was born into wealth and his father, Fred Trump, funded many of his projects (Kessler, 2016; Thomas, 2016; Mancini, 2023). The most recent analysis found that his father had given him $413 million over the years to keep his businesses afloat (Buettner and Craig, 2024).

Drawing on the playbook developed by the trailblazing Rush Limbaugh and other right-wing media figures (Reifowitz, 2019)—an approach Trump and his advisers had studied in depth (Sherman, 2016)—the campaign developed tactics and an overall strategy that would enable this wealthy, well-connected, businessman who had always lived a highly privileged life to transform into the 'everyman', or at least someone the everyman (primarily, albeit not exclusively, white men) could identify with.[9] Nunberg's research along with Trump's own instincts produced an understanding that defined his White House run—namely, that the everyman, as a character to be portrayed, involves two components: an indiscriminate use of stereotypes and a lack of concern for whether one is perceived to be abiding by social niceties.

---

9 Trump had emerged as a hip-hop icon in the 1990s as well, but his right-wing politics quickly turned overall opinion highly negative among black Americans after 2015 (Zaru, 2018).

As a presidential candidate, Americans saw this figure at the center of our national stage declaring without apology or qualification that political correctness was something of no consequence. Trump's communication of stereotypes right from the start gave oxygen to his campaign while simultaneously sealing PC's fate. His stereotype-laden rhetoric aided his efforts to define the groups of people his supporters should consider their enemies and strengthened the visceral bond that connected the leader to his followers. For stereotypes to allow a person to blend in may seem contradictory because they are a stigmatized form of communication. Trump's strategy proved otherwise.

Stigma

A stigma "involves the recognition of some distinguishing characteristic" (Dovidio, Major, and Crocker, 2000) that is considered "an attribute that is deeply discrediting" (Goffman, 1963b, p. 3). Stereotypes have been considered stigmatized (Goffman, 1963b) when communicated because of their association with prejudice and discrimination (Allport, 1954/1979; Bar-Tal et al., 1989; Fiske, 1998; Fiske and Taylor, 1984; Zanna and Olson, 1994). The stigma of stereotypes typically results in people avoiding their use and, to some extent, avoiding stereotypers themselves. Pryor et al. (2004) note that "a defining immediate response to stigma seems to be avoidance" (p. 436). The stigma associated with stereotypes may have helped decrease their use, especially when political correctness exercised greater influence than it does today. Nonetheless, people continue to communicate stereotypes, even though they are at best a poor communication choice (Kurylo, 2013).

See, for example, the June 27, 2024, debate with President Joe Biden when Trump claimed that migrants were taking away "Black jobs"—a stereotype that opened him up to the charge that he was pigeonholing black Americans as holding only the kind of low-wage jobs migrants might be able to get. National Association for the Advancement of Colored People (NAACP) President and CEO Derrick Johnson rebuked the comment, countering: "A 'Black job' is an American job. It is concerning that a presidential candidate would seek to make a non-existent distinction. But the divisive nature of this comment is not surprising for Donald Trump" (Brown, 2024). The twice-elected president has repeatedly stoked anti-immigrant sentiment among black Americans in this way. For example, in his interview at the National Association of black Journalists (NABJ) forum on July 31, 2024, he said, pointing at the overwhelmingly black audience: "these people coming in are taking your jobs" (Rupar, 2024). Black Conservative Federation President Diante Johnson defended Trump against the charge of divisiveness in talking about

"Black jobs," (Brown, 2024) but clearly this was a prime example of poor communication.

Managing impressions

Although political correctness seeks to stigmatize stereotypes and calls for avoiding them, people may still communicate them in certain interactions out of a desire to fit in. Stereotypes may be used like other forms of "communication [as] an impression-management tool" (Schaller and Conway, 1999, p. 827). For example, Crandall et al. (2002) found that "public expression of prejudice...was very highly correlated with social approval of that expression" (p. 359). These researchers argue that people were more likely to communicate their prejudice when doing so received social approval. The boys' camp studies (Sherif et al., 1961) provided foundational research that according to Crandall et al. (2002) "describes the development of prejudice-related norms within social groups and the pressures placed on individuals to conform to group norms" (p. 360). Similarly, Crandall et al. (2002) found that the normative appropriateness of a joke involving a stereotype helped determine whether listeners found the joke funny or offensive. Thus, communicated stereotypes can make positive impressions.

For Trump, wielding stereotypes enhanced his ability to fit in with those who rejected political correctness. He understood this and, when called out on his use of stereotypes, simply doubled down because he knew it benefited him, as it had at the aforementioned August 16, 2015 debate (Washington Post Staff, 2015b): "I think the big problem this country has is being politically correct. [Applause] I've been challenged by so many people, and I don't frankly have time for total political correctness. And to be honest with you, this country doesn't have time either." It should be no surprise that at a Dallas rally during this first campaign, one supporter showed up with a large banner reading: "FUCK POLITICAL CORRECTNESS!" Connecting multiple Trump campaign themes, the man holding the banner also verbally expressed the following sentiment to journalist Mark Leibovich: "and fuck Megyn Kelly" (Leibovich, 2022).

The concept of political correctness

Prior to Trump's twin assaults on political correctness—the remarks announcing his candidacy in June 2015, and his direct declaration of PC's insignificance two months later—that concept had attained significant cultural authority in the United States. The communication of stereotypes—at least in overt ways where the targeted group and characteristics associated with it were made explicit—had been increasingly discouraged in public and professional settings in particular, even for politicians (Mendelberg, 2001).

This aversion to communicating stereotypes, dubbed political correctness, occurred as stereotypes were increasingly viewed as a stigmatized and undesirable behavior. The concept of political correctness inherently views stereotypes as "bad and inaccurate" (Jussim et al., 1995, p. 3). Furthermore, PC condemns stereotypes because they perpetuate prejudice and discrimination (Allport, 1954/1979; Bar-Tal et al., 1989; Kurylo, 2013; Zanna and Olson, 1994)—harms that were antithetical to growing support for diversity, equity, and inclusivity (Golden, 2024). The building blocks of the politically correct cultural ethos began to form in the 1960s during the Civil Rights Movement. As Liberman et al., (1998) note: "the civil rights movement and feminism fostered work in how stereotypes, prejudice, and discrimination could be reduced" (p. 156).

The political correctness movement took more solid form in the 1970's and served to heighten awareness and encourage sensitivity to the disproportionate roadblocks faced by marginalized groups (Williams, 1995) with special attention paid to race, gender, and other aspects of identity (Stangor, 1995). Acting politically correct is to be: "sensitive (perhaps overly so) to the use of stereotypes in everyday life" (Stangor, 1995, p. 276). As a PC mindset became more widespread in society, a backlash followed closely against what critics considered unnecessary, even stifling levels of hypersensitivity (e.g., Thibodaux, 1994). Both the late-night talk show Politically Incorrect (which debuted in 1993) and the movie PCU (1994) reflected the general anti-PC zeitgeist. One of the biggest hit songs of the era—Shania Twain's 1997 country-pop anthem "Man! I Feel Like A Woman"—demonstrated just how mainstream the backlash had become:

> No inhibitions, make no conditions
> Get a little outta line
> I ain't gonna act politically correct
> I only wanna have a good time

Nonetheless, the stigma associated with stereotypes decreased the frequency with which explicit ones might otherwise have been communicated, for a while at least. Mendelberg (2001) terms this development the "norm of equality" (a phrase included in her book's title).

Celebrity vilification

Over time and as political correctness became more mainstream, one way people learned to be cautious about their own stereotype use was seeing celebrities face vilification for communicating stereotypes (Kurylo, 2013). Examples of celebrities — and, occasionally, non-celebrities—who were punished, publicly shamed, lost their jobs, or were otherwise eviscerated by the media and popular opinion—by today's terminology canceled—abound. Kurylo (2013) highlights several examples:

- December 23, 1999: John Rocker, who pitched for the Atlanta Braves, was suspended without pay after he offered a stereotype-filled rant in a *Sports Illustrated* interview about foreigners in New York City (Pearlman, 2014).
- January 14, 2005: Lawrence Summers, the Harvard University President, whose seeming endorsement of stereotypes around gender and mathematical ability, along with other controversies, led to his resignation (Dillon, 2005; Ebbert and Fernandes, 2024), and also likely prevented him from becoming U.S. Treasury Secretary under President Obama (a job he had held under President Bill Clinton) (Usborne, 2008).
- September 7, 2012: Paris Hilton, reality show celebrity, socialite, and businesswoman, was recorded uttering homophobic stereotypes, prompting outrage when they were released in the media. Ten years later, she apparently still felt compelled to show remorse, as discussed in her book *Paris: The Memoir* (Duke, 2012; Hilton, 2023; Wratten, 2023).

As political correctness gained momentum, political advertising that wanted to incorporate stereotypes yet also wanted to simultaneously stay politically correct would only *imply* them, employing dog whistles instead. For example, in 1988, an independent group produced an advertisement to support George H.W. Bush's presidential campaign that highlighted (and showed a photograph of) Willie Horton, a black man who committed murder while out of prison on a weekend furlough during the governorship of Bush's opponent, Massachusetts Governor Michael Dukakis, who had backed the furlough program (Baker, 2018). The ad did not mention race specifically, but white voters got the message. Political science professor Claire Jean Kim told PBS: "the insinuation is, if you elect Gov. Dukakis as president, we're going to have black rapists running amok in the country" (Withers, 2018). Michael Nelson, a scholar of the Bush presidency, noted: "In some ways, the Willie Horton ad is the 1.0 version of Trump's relentless tweets and comments about African Americans" (Baker, 2018). Two additional examples involving politicians deserve particular attention.

In August 2006, while campaigning for the U.S. Senate in Virginia, incumbent Republican George Allen referred to a member of his audience at an event with the racial slur 'Macaca' (Urban Dictionary, n.d.): "This fellow here, over here with the yellow shirt. Macaca or whatever his name is. He's with my opponent, he's following us around everywhere." Allen continued: "So welcome, let's give a welcome to Macaca here. Welcome to America, and the real world of Virginia." Allen quickly found himself in the difficult position of defending himself as not being racist rather than talking about policy issues (ABC News, 2006). After leading by a sizable margin throughout the months leading up to the Macaca incident, the race tightened considerably and Allen ultimately lost by less than one-half percent of the vote. He had been considered a leading contender for the Republican presidential nomination in 2008, ambitions dashed by his upset defeat.

In another notable and contrasting example, on October 10, 2008, then-Republican presidential nominee John McCain corrected an audience member who incorporated a stereotype about Barack Obama into a question she asked during a Q and A (Clemens, 2018).

> "I can't trust Obama. I have read about him, and he's not, um, he's an Arab," a woman said to McCain at a town hall meeting in Lakeville, Minnesota. McCain grabbed the microphone from her, cutting her off. "No, ma'am," he said. "He's a decent family man [and] citizen that I just happen to have disagreements with on fundamental issues, and that's what the campaign's all about. He's not [an Arab]."

McCain earned praise in the media for diplomacy and sensitivity in being able to "disagree without demonizing" (Clemens, 2018; Stewart, 2018) and for having the political courage to tackle such a seemingly difficult situation even at the cost of being booed by his own audience. McCain's behavior here is notable for being the opposite of Trump's birtherism and overall othering of Obama.[10]

Through these various examples, and many others, the vilification of celebrities made clear that communicating stereotypes would garner negative attention and consequences. For celebrities to avoid this scenario required:
- Stereotypes must be implicitly, not explicitly, communicated.
- Stereotypes must not be a substantive part of a political argument or content related to the profession of the celebrity.
- Stereotypes, if made known publicly, must be followed by an apology, the sooner the better.

---

[10] Some criticized McCain for not going even further, and explicitly rejecting the notion that there was anything wrong with being "an Arab" in the first place (Kim, 2008).

Watching politicians and other celebrities lose their cachet, credibility, campaigns, and their fanbase for communicating stereotypes (Kurylo, 2013) produced two outcomes. First, it reminded people that their own stereotype use must not be so easily identifiable. If they should choose to communicate a stereotype, they should deliver it in such a way as to be under the radar—for example by using an implied target group and/or implied characteristic. Second, these celebrity vilifications provided people an outlet to demonstrate their own sincere or feigned disdain toward those who communicate stereotypes—an act known as virtue signaling—even as many continued to use them, albeit in more subtle ways.

Interactional dilemma

Stereotypes are salient, and thus often hard to ignore when they come up in conversation precisely because of their associated stigma (Goffman, 1963b). This presents a difficult situation. Stereotypes communicated overtly present those in a conversation with an unenviable interactional dilemma (Kurylo, 2013). On the one hand, political correctness prescribes not only that people should avoid stereotypes, but also that a person should call out the offender upon hearing one. On the other hand, people generally shy away from conflict and prefer conversation to proceed smoothly according to conversational norms (Goffman, 1963a).

In this scenario, stereotypers risk being reprimanded—potentially in public, in front of constituents, customers, colleagues, friends, or family. Using overt stereotypes increases the risk even further. Subtlety, therefore, became a strategy during the political correctness era. Implicit stereotypes in which the target group and/or associated characteristics are implied provide a potential way to skirt this interactional dilemma. By communicating a stereotype implicitly, the others in the conversation may truly overlook it. However, even if a subtle stereotype gets noticed, Kurylo (2013) argues that using it as the basis for a reprimand might fail because the stereotyper could easily retort: "That's not what I said," "What do you mean?" or "I didn't *say* anything."

In part because of this interactional dilemma, people found various ways to respond to someone's communication of a stereotype that avoids disrupting the conversation (Kurylo and Robles, 2015). Their work shows that communicators have 12 possible ways to respond to stereotypes that leave the impression that they are appropriate to think, communicate, or both. Combined with the use of implicit stereotypes, "these responses ... construct stereotypes as tolerable" (Kurylo and Robles, 2015, p. 75). Only one response type—referred to by those authors as active disapproval—demonstrates condemnation of both thinking and communicating stereotypes. This thirteenth response type frames stereotypes as inappropriate (to think and communicate) in keeping with the concept of political correctness. Thus, as long as stereotypes are communicated implicitly, others in a conversation have tools to ignore their use, not reprimand the stereotyper, and keep the conversation flowing. This implicit form allowed political correctness to operate unencumbered while also providing a loophole through which people could continue to communicate stereotypes.

To recap, during the political correctness era three factors pushed people to avoid communicating stereotypes (Kurylo, 2013). First, a political correctness ethos told people to avoid stereotypes; the damage they caused in terms of prejudice and discrimination stigmatized their use. Second, celebrity vilification provided role models and, by default, scapegoats, that showed people the negative consequences that could result from being caught employing stereotypes. Third, the interactional dilemma created when people communicated stereotypes in a conversation was uncomfortable and needed to be managed. Despite these three deterrents, people continued to use stereotypes even as they relied on more subtle forms thereof.

Maas and Arcuri (1996) note that "language is probably the dominant means by which [stereotypes] are defined, communicated, and assessed" (p. 193; Brewer, 1996). This begs the question as to why people continue to communicate stereotypes (Maas and Arcuri, 1996). Kurylo (2013) explains that stereotypes function for people; that is, stereotypes help people to do things. This study articulates nine functions of interpersonally communicated stereotypes: altruism, control, efficiency, escape, inclusion, pleasure, reducing uncertainty, relaxation, and the aforementioned impression management. These functions include all six motives predicted by the broader Interpersonal Communication Motives Scale (Rubin et al., 1988), demonstrating that stereotypes function for people similarly to other types of non-stigmatized communication. Stereotypes, then, are just another tool for communication.

Throughout the political correctness era, people continued to benefit from subtly communicating stereotypes that functioned for them. However, as celebrity vilification showed, those who stereotyped were at constant risk of confrontation, reprimand, or other repercussions—social and material—for doing so. The result was a tension fermenting in American culture.

The death of political correctness

As political correctness gained momentum, an objection to subtle stereotypes also began to take shape as the word "microaggressions" entered the mainstream. It was named Word of the Year in 2015 by Global Language Monitor (Haslam,

2017) and, ultimately, added to the *Merriam-Webster Dictionary* in February 2017 (Merriam-Webster, n.d.). At the same time that the focus on subtle stereotypes was increasing in certain segments of American society, Trump's unprecedented electoral success after employing explicit stereotypes brought an end to the era during which political correctness appeared to wield authority across the political spectrum.

A fundamental shift occurred when Trump announced he was running for president and incorporated the stereotypes of Mexican people into his speech. His communication of stereotypes did not garner the same vilification experienced by those who had used similar kinds of naked stereotypes in the recent past. He was not completely shunned or otherwise punished at all. The media did not attack him mercilessly and hound Trump out of politics. In conversations, the overall American populace was not universally disgusted by what he said—those who would have perhaps approved quietly during the PC era now felt emboldened to publicly proclaim that they were on board with this way of speaking. We might have expected celebrity vilification to follow the established pattern; yet, it did not ensue.

Rather than cratering, Trump's popularity among Republican primary voters exploded, and he vaulted to the top of the pack. His overall favorability ratings remained low throughout the entire 2016 campaign—according to Gallup tracking polls, the low point was 28% and they hovered in the low- to mid-30s right up until he won the election (Jones, 2016). However, the fact that the former reality TV host had so many other rivals for the GOP nomination allowed him to claim that prize because he maintained solid support from enough Republican primary voters—namely, his base—while his rivals dropped out one at a time.

This was not only a unique political moment, it was a social inflection point in which vitriol against a group suddenly and seemingly single-handedly became permissible. Moreover, in hindsight, this was also the start of a social movement rising out of the ashes of political correctness. People could now talk about what Trump said without having to denounce its inappropriateness. Moreover, they could repeat in conversation the overt stereotypes he uttered and not necessarily face sanction for doing so as the tenets of political correctness had prescribed not long before. By the first Republican primary debate (Reston, 2015), people felt freer than previously to not only talk about Trump's stereotypes but also to communicate others themselves, without shame, stigma, or reprimand. Megyn Kelly made this clear in her preface to a question she asked Trump about the public's reaction to his 'Mexican rapists' slander as well other insulting language he had used in the past (Washington Post Staff, 2015b): "One of the things people love about you is you speak your mind and you don't use a politician's filter."

That lack of filter became even more evident the day after that debate, when he slandered Kelly to CNN as follows: "She gets out and she starts asking me all sorts of ridiculous questions. You could see there was blood coming out of her eyes, blood coming out of her wherever" (Rucker, 2015a). Although Trump later claimed that by "wherever" he meant her nose, the remark drew on the deeply sexist trope that women having their period act in "ridiculous" ways, and, thus, should be dismissed summarily.

Trump's eminently public communication of stereotypes gave people tacit permission to do the same thing, and—counter to the prescriptions of political correctness (Kurylo, 2013)—to do so explicitly rather than merely indirectly or implicitly (Mendelberg, 2001). Heidi Serrano, an immigrant from Guatemala who has lived for decades in Greenville, North Carolina, observed that: "Trump has allowed people to say what's in their hearts," and added: "There was a filter, and now the filter has been broken" (Witte, 2019). Fast forward to the twice-elected president's second victory and it becomes undeniable that a new era began when he launched his first White House bid by using stereotypes to rile up his base.

The day after Trump won the 2024 election, African Americans in Washington, DC and around 15 states received text messages informing them they would soon be forcibly re-enslaved and sent into the fields to pick cotton. In some cases, the sender either identified themselves as a Trump backer, or wrote that the message came from "the Trump administration" itself (Wu and Menn, 2024). Latinos and LGBTQ people received similarly threatening post-election messages. According to the FBI, "some recipients reported being told they were selected for deportation or to report to a reeducation camp" (Bellware and Menn, 2024). Nick Fuentes, a hard-right white Christian nationalist, posted: "Your body, my choice. Forever." The post garnered 90 million views and over 35,000 reposts in the first week after Election Day (Duffy, 2024). The Institute for Strategic Dialogue found that the posting on social media of misogynistic phrases such as "your body, my choice" and "get back to the kitchen" increased significantly in the days after Trump's second victory (Frances-Wright and Ayad, 2024).

Through the constant and repeated use of stereotypes as well as the explicit denunciation of political correctness starting early in his 2016 campaign, the twice-elected president showed that people no longer need pay heed to PC. He offered himself as a role model who, unlike his stereotyping predecessors, was able to get away with explicitly stereotyping without facing similar consequences. Trump demonstrated to the public that communicating stereotypes could be viewed as not universally wrong or problematic. He showed those who resented the yoke of political correctness that they were not alone, that they need not be silent. In this way, Trump made them feel seen and heard, gave voice to them, and served as their representative. He took the collective weight of PC guilt off the shoulders of those who never fully understood why they were being made to feel guilty in the first place. As conservative anti-Trumper Bret Stephens wrote in the wake of the 2024 election, Trump successfully hung the yoke of excessive political correctness around the neck of his political opponents, in particular Kamala Harris. Stephens (2024) argued:

> The politics of today's left . . . increasingly stands for the forcible imposition of bizarre cultural norms on hundreds of millions of Americans who want to live and let live but don't like being told how to speak or what to think. Too many liberals forgot this, which explains how a figure like Trump, with his boisterous and transgressive disdain for liberal pieties, could be re-elected to the presidency.

Trump emerged from each instance that he dealt in stereotypes even more popular than before, at least among his base. As one voter put it in September 2024: "He just knows where we're coming from." Another stated simply: "He gets us" (McCreesh, 2024d). The 45th and now 47th president found his base. In turn, his base helped put him in the White House not once, but twice, making him the first American since Grover Cleveland to win two non-consecutive terms as president.

Chapter 2
Some are good people: The persuasiveness of stereotype accuracy

A general frustration with political correctness in early 21st century-America should have been no surprise. Despite the PC movement having been brewing for years, many people remained unconvinced of its argument that stereotypes are inherently problematic, and they continued to use them. People using subtle stereotypes often avoided retribution from political correctness. Additionally, PC provided a reason for stereotyping to go essentially underground. Consistent with selective exposure theory (Hart et al., 2009), people found their own preferred locations or situations, including right-wing media and online communities, in which overt stereotyping was acceptable—somewhat reminiscent of secret speakeasies that popped up during Prohibition. Participants reveled in what they perceived to be the air of outlaw coolness that accompanied such rebellion. Placing oneself in environments that not only permitted but encouraged overtly stereotyping others provided an escape from the metaphorical PC police. Moreover, political correctness and the vilification of celebrities who violated the rules enabled people to overlook their own subtle, inadvertent, or, in any case, implied stereotyping. Instead they could just criticize celebrities who engaged in overt stereotyping (Kurylo, 2013)—an early form of virtue signaling—in order to mask their own transgressions. Stereotyping in public was acceptable as long as one executed it implicitly, with the target group unstated and/or the stereotyped characteristic omitted. Subtlety and deniability were key.

Then, came microaggressions.

Many people were not conscious of their own specific frustration with political correctness and remained unaware that so many others shared it. The frustration was latent. It was through Donald Trump's ability to overtly, intentionally, and strategically draw attention to political correctness in his campaign that this latent frustration gained a much wider public outlet. On behalf of a segment of the population already riled up by political correctness, Trump harnessed their frustration in powerful ways. The rise in discourse about microaggressions, which can be termed the second wave of political correctness, may have fueled this frustration.

https://doi.org/10.1515/9783111426327-005

Microaggressions

Chester Pierce coined the term microaggressions, and, more recently, in 2007 Derald Wing Sue brought it to the fore (Williams et al, 2021). Williams defined this subtle form of stereotyping as: "a form of oppression that reinforces unjust power differentials between groups, whether or not this was the conscious intention of the offender" (p. 992). More often than not, identification of the presence of a microaggression derives from the recipient's interpretation of a message. To a large extent, then, determining whether a microaggression has occurred can be out of the purview and, more importantly, control of the message's sender. We can communicate microaggressions verbally (e. g., asking someone who 'looks' Asian where they are from; complimenting a black woman on having 'good' hair) or nonverbally (e. g., crossing the street at night when a dark-skinned young male in a hooded sweatshirt is walking toward you). As such, because people who communicate a microaggression may not be aware of having done so, they are unable to predict the outcome of that interaction. It is important to note there is no consensus around the actual frequency with which microaggressions occur. As *The New York Times* noted:

> The notion that microaggressions are not only real but ubiquitous in interracial encounters is widespread in DEI [Diversity, Equity, and Inclusion] programs; a 2021 review of the microaggressions literature, however, judged it "without adequate scientific basis" (Confessore, 2024).

While microaggressions certainly take place, because they are both subtle and in the eye of the beholder, their ubiquity is harder to empirically confirm.

Microaggressions inherently and necessarily—because of the subtlety of these stereotypes—put the burden on the speaker to predict what *could* potentially be *interpreted* as offensive to another person *regardless* of intent. This was a step too far for many. Avoiding microaggressions requires a type of awareness that goes beyond merely not saying things that could be reasonably, reliably, and consistently interpreted as offensive by most people of any identity group—which political correctness had already trained many people to do. Living up to the prescription to avoid microaggressions also requires a person to place themselves into the positionality of the recipient and/or target of the stereotype. To do this, a person needs to be proactively *anti*-racist by understanding how each person's identity or identities relate to and delimit their relationship to others in American society. The inherent problem with this is that doing so requires a knowledge of rules that most people outside the target group do not know and, worse, may perceive as both subjective and constantly in flux. Not long after Trump's election in 2016, Ibram X. Kendi (2019) brought the idea of anti-racism into mainstream and common usage. He provoked people with his controversial assertion that each person is "either a racist or an anti-racist" (Taylor, 2023). The middle ground was disappearing fast.

To be anti-racist and avoid communicating microaggressions is a complex multi-step task that requires constant vigilance. One must have knowledge of and understand the viewpoint of the other person, internalize that viewpoint, translate it into language and behavioral choices, and then correct one's originally conceived communication choice accordingly—all before acting upon that choice by communicating it. In this way, the rules around microaggressions demand that the typical person absorb and commit to memory a far greater and more esoteric amount of cultural knowledge than ever before expected, in that they require a person to *know* in advance everything that could offend someone else—or, failing that, to engage in mind reading. This work is requisite regardless of the group membership of any of the people involved. In other words, even if a person speaking had never been in contact with a member of the group they were indirectly and unintentionally stereotyping and/or was not familiar with that group's culture, the speaker is nonetheless expected to predict that the stereotype, regardless of how subtly it was communicated, would offend that group member. To clarify, committing a microaggression might never produce the same level of consequences (i.e., vilification) as would violating PC norms by engaging in direct stereotyping. Nevertheless, the embarrassment of being called out for one's unconscious bias or even racism was something most people outside of the far right—who had long since disdained the notion of political correctness as a whole to begin with—wanted to avoid.

Those who proactively espouse an anti-racist stance—often those who also try not to communicate stereotypes as per the dictates of political correctness—could more easily avoid microaggressions. In 2016, however, few non-activists embraced a robust anti-racist stance. Indeed, microaggressions were only beginning, relatively speaking, to be discussed by academics, most typically those scholars who studied and published about critical theory. Separately, those who never sincerely espoused political correctness in the first place had rather something else in mind. Though some may have accommodated political correctness because it was the societal norm, many nonetheless continued to view stereotypes as something that made sense, were appropriate to communicate, and could be useful in decision-making (Kurylo, 2013). Because stereotypes offer a description of how people behave, many maintained the presumption that they were accurate even as they avoided communicating them broadly.

This mindset makes sense from the perspective that all stereotypes are base rates. In terms of stereotypes, Funder (1996) explains that base rates are: "pre-existing, probabilistic representations of what people (or things) are generally like"

(p. 143). If stereotypes are statistically accurate, then whether one uses them implicitly or explicitly is irrelevant. Thus, the belief that stereotypes are accurate fosters a belief in their appropriateness to think and communicate—whether by a neighbor or by the twice-elected president. Trump's assertion of a stereotype without any qualification—his typical modus operandi—leaves the audience with the understanding that he is stating it as fact, that he believes it and they should as well. On many occasions, Trump actually followed up a fact-free assertion with some variation of "it's true"—just for emphasis (Owen, 2018).

Filling our knowledge gap

The question as to whether stereotypes are accurate is *not* a straight-forward one to answer. To make matters worse, the answer has tremendous implications for how people think, communicate, and interpret stereotypes. In the absence of a definitive answer to this question, people inevitably rely on their own resources and resourcefulness to fill gaps in their knowledge. One explanation for why stereotypes should be considered accurate representations is the presumption that stereotypes exist because they contain a basis of truth. The Kernel-of-Truth hypothesis studied in early stereotype research (e.g., Katz and Braly, 1933; LaPiere, 1936; Vinacke, 1956) encapsulated the idea that stereotypes had some basis, even if only small, in objective scientific measurement (Gordon, 2009). Trump's stereotypes of immigrants provide a useful case to consider the question of whether stereotypes are accurate.

Let us dive deeply into one set of stereotypes, namely those relating to Muslims supposedly hating America and/or being terrorists. On September 30, 2015, Trump told rallygoers that he would forcibly expel all Syrian refugees from our country because: "they could be ISIS, I don't know. This could be one of the great tactical ploys of all time. A 200,000-man army, maybe" (Johnson and Hauslohner, 2017). On November 16 of that year, on MSNBC, he stated he would: "seriously consider" shuttering mosques because "some of the ideas and some of the hatred—the absolute hatred—is coming from these areas" (Johnson and Hauslohner, 2017). On November 30, Trump related: "We are not loved by many Muslims" (Johnson and Hauslohner, 2017). On December 7, at a campaign rally, he called for: "a total and complete shutdown of Muslims entering the United States until our country's representatives can figure out what is going on" (Taylor, 2015).

During a March 9, 2016 appearance on CNN, Trump opined: "I think Islam hates us. There's something there that—there's a tremendous hatred there. There's a tremendous hatred. We have to get to the bottom of it. There's an unbelievable hatred of us" (Johnson and Hauslohner, 2017). On March 22, he stated on Fox Business: "We're having problems with the Muslims, and we're having problems with Muslims coming into the country," and added: "You have to deal with the mosques, whether we like it or not, I mean, you know, these attacks aren't coming out of— they're not done by Swedish people." (Johnson and Hauslohner, 2017). That same day, Trump said of Muslims: "there's no assimilation. They are not assimilating . . . They want to go by sharia law. They want sharia law. They don't want the laws that we have. They want sharia law" (Johnson and Hauslohner, 2017). His mention of sharia law refers to the notion that Islamic religious teachings would form the basis for all laws in a country, making it a Muslim theocracy. There are many other examples (Johnson and Hauslohner, 2017).

President Trump signed Executive Order 13769, titled Protecting the Nation from Foreign Terrorist Entry into the United States (known colloquially as the Muslim Travel Ban), which prevented people from seven majority-Muslim countries— Iraq, Syria, Iran, Sudan, Libya, Somalia and Yemen—from entering the U.S. He acted consistent with the stereotypes he used, affecting tens of thousands of lives. During the 2024 campaign Trump promised to expand the ban to other Muslim-majority lands as well (Associated Press, 2023). Nevertheless, available data refutes his stereotypes about Muslims broadly hating Americans or Westerners, and supporting terrorist violence against them (Chambers, 2021).

The New York Times reported that in meetings with White House aides Trump spoke in graphic, violent terms about how to respond to immigrants coming across the Mexican border:

> Privately, the president had often talked about fortifying a border wall with a water-filled trench, stocked with snakes or alligators, prompting aides to seek a cost estimate. He wanted the wall electrified, with spikes on top that could pierce human flesh. After publicly suggesting that soldiers shoot migrants if they threw rocks, the president backed off when his staff told him that was illegal. But later in a meeting, aides recalled, he suggested that they shoot migrants in the legs to slow them down (Shear and Davis, 2019).

In October 2018 the twice-elected president had also urged the use of a "heat ray" on unarmed undocumented immigrants trying to enter the U.S. (Shear, 2020).

Trump's anti-immigration rhetoric continued into the 2024 campaign. For example, on December 16, 2023, at a campaign rally in New Hampshire, Trump— echoing Hitlerian rhetoric about Jews in Germany—claimed immigrants: "are poisoning the blood of our country" (Gibson, 2023). He made similar remarks on multiple occasions. By a margin of 42% to 28%, likely Iowa Republican caucus attendees responded that that statement made them more rather than less likely to support him, with the rest saying it would not matter, according to a December 2023 poll (Trautmann, 2023). A CBS poll found that about 80% of Republicans— compared to less than a quarter of Democrats—agreed that "immigrants entering the U.S. illegally are poisoning the blood of the country." This number rose by an additional ten percentage points when Republican respondents were told Trump had made the statement compared to when no name was attached (Bump, 2024a).

On March 4, 2024, Trump described undocumented immigrants thusly: "They're rough people, in many cases from jails, prisons, from mental institutions, insane asylums. You know, insane asylums, that's 'Silence of the Lambs' stuff... Hannibal Lecter, anybody know Hannibal Lecter?" (Terkel and Leibowitz, 2024). On April 2, 2024, in Michigan, the twice-elected president declared that undocumented immigrants are, in fact, not human, but are instead "animals," and that their arrival is: "country-changing, it's country-threatening, and it's country-wrecking. They have wrecked our country." (Terkel and Leibowitz, 2024). On July 19, 2024, he contended that the U.S. was experiencing an: "illegal immigration crisis. It's a massive invasion at our southern border that has spread misery, crime, poverty, disease and destruction to communities all across our land" (Terkel and Leibowitz, 2024).

Returning to his obsession with America's collective gene pool, on October 7, Trump opined:

> How about allowing people to come to an open border, 13,000 of which were murderers, many of them murdered far more than one person, and they're now happily living in the United States. You know now a murder, I believe this, it's in their genes. And we got a lot of bad genes in our country right now (Martin, 2024).

By contrast, four years earlier he had told an overwhelmingly white Minnesota crowd: "You have good genes. A lot of it is about the genes, isn't it, don't you believe? The racehorse theory. You think we're so different?" (Gold, 2024d). On October 11, the twice-elected president described undocumented immigrants using his typical hyperbole: "These are the worst criminals in the world . . . These people are the most violent people on Earth" (Hubbard et al., 2024). On October 24, 2024, Trump explored a new metaphor, declaring that undocumented immigrants had turned America into: "a garbage can for the world" (Kornfield and Iati, 2024). In other words, immigrants are trash.

Then Trump repeated a lie he had told many times: "Every job in this country produced over the last two and a half years has gone to illegal aliens—every job" (Bender, 2024a). Likewise, his running mate, former Ohio Senator and now vice president, JD Vance, also attacked undocumented immigrants as:

> People who shouldn't be here, people who are competing against you and your children to buy the homes that ought to be going to American citizens. Our message to Kamala Harris is: Stop giving American homes to foreigners who shouldn't be in this country. Start giving them to American citizens who deserve to be here" (Bender, 2024a).

One Trump voter, interviewed on September 23, 2024, by the right-wing outlet Newsmax, said that: "illegal immigration" was his most important issue. Not because it was hurting him directly, he acknowledged, but because "It's just the principle of everybody coming in and getting free stuff and taking stuff away from hard-working Americans" (Rupar, 2024). This clearly echoed Trump's campaign rhetoric.

On October 13, 2024, Trump brought together many of these false claims in a single statement: "The mass migration invasion has crushed wages, crashed school systems—your systems are a disaster—wrecked the standard of living and brought crime, drugs, misery and death" (Qiu, 2024a). Trump and Vance blamed undocumented immigrants coming across the Mexican border, and thus Kamala Harris, for a number of other real or imagined problems, including: increased hospital and emergency room wait times; a (non-existent) increase in the inflow of illegal guns; the weakening of Social Security and Medicare's finances—on this, the opposite is the truth because undocumented immigrants pay taxes into those systems yet cannot receive benefits; unaffordable home prices; and fentanyl overdoses. As *New York Times* fact-checker Linda Qiu (2024) noted: "Seldom is unauthorized immigration the actual cause of the problems [Trump and Vance] say plague the country." Qiu (2024a) debunked each of these claims.

These are a few of many, many recent examples of Trump stereotyping and fearmongering about immigrants, along with others going back to the day he began running for president in 2015 (Terkel and Leibowitz, 2024). As immigration historian Tyler Anbinder noted, Trump has made each of the following stereotypes about immigrants:

> They bring crime; they import poverty; they spread disease; they don't assimilate; they corrupt our politics; they steal our jobs; they cause our taxes to increase; they're a security risk; their religion is incompatible with American values; they can never be 'true Americans' (Anbinder, 2019).

Immigrants, as per Trump, thus threaten Americans' physical, financial, and cultural well-being —all this despite the country's historical embrace of its status as: 'the land of immigrants,' with 12,000,000 immigrants having traveled through Ellis Island from its opening in 1892 through 1954 (The Statue of Liberty—Ellis Island Foundation, 2022). Fact-checkers have thoroughly debunked the Trump stereotypes about immigrants that one can check against hard economic data and crime statistics (Boak, 2019; Valencia and Lillich, 2024). Nonetheless, the widespread assumption of stereotypes as factual provides an all too irresistible rationale for using them.

Benefits gained from assuming accuracy

Considering the negativity of the stereotypes the twice-elected president associates with immigrants, it would be incumbent on Americans to believe them if they were indeed true because not doing so would exacerbate the associated risks (e.g., fewer jobs for American citizens, more crime). Trump's presumption that his stereotypes are true, along with any potential statistical evidence (i.e., base rates) that seem to support them could justify not only perpetuating the stereotypes but also relying on them to make policy decisions. Indeed, during his first presidency, arrests and deportations increased significantly within three government bodies: Customs and Border Protection (CBP), Immigration and Customs Enforcement (ICE), and the Department of Homeland Security (DHS) (Gramlich, 2020).

Even the terminology of 'illegal immigrants'—a phrase the twice-elected president and others on the right-wing use all the time—itself presumes the accuracy of the stereotype in the absence of any data. The first crime of which an undocumented immigrant is presumed guilty is supposedly being 'illegal.' Making decisions on the presumption that stereotypes are true does make things easier, as there is no need to investigate the stereotype's accuracy—the stereotyper can instead simply take action based on the presumption thereof. No doubt many of those who helped Trump get elected in 2016 were grateful for his follow-through in carrying out at least some of his campaign promises related to immigration. However, even on his signature issue—the "big, beautiful wall" he promised to build with Mexico's money—he fell woefully short on completion, not to mention failed completely on getting Mexico to pay for it. Note that this did not stop him from falsely declaring the wall to be a "promise made, promise kept" (Rodriguez, 2021). More broadly, Trump's policies on immigration provoked huge protests nationwide (Ingber, 2018). Many of them were ultimately blocked by the courts (Naishadham, 2021) and his successor, President Biden, reversed most of the rest (Bredemeier, 2021). Only time will tell what will happen in the second Trump term. Nevertheless, his political aspirations and his agenda continue to benefit from the belief that stereotypes of immigrants are accurate and that there is nothing wrong with communicating them or basing decisions upon them.

Anecdotal evidence for stereotype accuracy

Regardless of the supposed benefits gained from assuming that stereotypes are accurate, it is difficult to deny that they appear to have an inherent accuracy—some at least 'feel right.' Our own experience with other people often provides ample evidence of the accuracy of stereotypes. This is because stereotypes can be "formed through the observations of behaviors performed by members of the stereotyped group" (Leyens et al., 1994, p. 41). Anecdotes and testimonials abound that attest to the supposed accuracy of any particular stereotype. Most people could easily explain to another person how someone they know—or themselves—fit into a stereotype.

In 2015, Trump incorporated a particularly persuasive immigration-related testimonial into his rallies to demonstrate the presumed accuracy of the stereotypes he uses. The father of Jamiel Shaw essentially became a spokesperson for the campaign. In 2008, his 17-year-old son had been killed near his home by an undocumented immigrant (Pamer et al., 2015). In 2024, Trump repeated this strategy after the murder of Laken Riley, committed by an undocumented immigrant from Venezuela. The twice-elected president brought Riley's family on stage for a March 9 rally in Georgia. He slammed the Biden-Harris administration's policy on the border, calling it: "a crime against humanity and the people of this nation for which [Biden] will never be forgiven," and contended that Riley "would be alive today if Joe Biden had not willfully and maliciously eviscerated the borders of the United States and set loose thousands and thousands of dangerous criminals into our country" (Boak et al., 2024). Likewise, on September 27 of the same year, Trump held a press call with the family of Rachel Morin, raped and murdered by an undocumented immigrant from El Salvador. The campaign presented her mother, who blamed Harris, and stated: "This is not a safe time for Americans" (Bradner, 2024). Then, on October 1, speaking of both Riley and Morin, Trump proclaimed: "Kamala murdered them just like she had a gun in her hand." By contrast, he claimed: "We're crime fighters. We'll restore light and hope, and I'll make America safe again. On day one of my administration, the invasion ends and the deportation begins" (Wisconsin Politics, 2024).

These are powerful testimonials of real tragedies that the Trump campaign knew would have an impact on voters. And for some of the twice-elected president's supporters, this anecdotal evidence was all that they needed to be convinced of the accuracy of the stereotype that undocumented immigrants are criminals, a theme that Trump has hammered more than any other individual stereotype since he began running for president. The facts, however, show something very different, namely that undocumented immigrants commit crimes at a lower rate than native-born Americans, meaning that, when factored into the national average, their presence reduces the crime rate in the U.S., thus making Americans safer on the whole (Garsd, 2024).

Some may object to the use of anecdotes or testimonials as evidence of stereotype accuracy. After all, anecdotes and testimonials need only rely on a single person to fit the description of any particular stereotype in order for someone to apply it to the target population at large. Lippmann (1922), who is often treated as the father of research on stereotypes, noted that: "we must avoid substituting the goal [of accuracy] for the starting point" (p. 98). In other words, Lippman warns that if the goal is for something to be true, then we will inevitably find examples that demonstrate its truth. He argued: "if we believe a certain thing ought to be true, we can almost always find either an instance where it is true, or someone who believes it ought to be true" (p. 98). The problem with anecdotal evidence is that it ultimately offers only a few or even one person's example—which could be accounted for by random coincidence or numerous confounding variables—as proof positive that a mass of people engage in a certain behavior.

There are two reasons why stereotypers may provide an anecdote or testimonial in support of their claim, as Trump has done. First, the stereotyper may sincerely not be aware of the problem of using these potential statistical outliers or exceptions, and may genuinely seek to provide evidence that contributes to understanding their decision-making process. Second, the stereotyper may be aware of the statistical fallacy and is, nonetheless, providing an anecdote or testimonial to distort reality in order to promote prejudice against a target group. The distinction between these two explanations (i.e., intent) of stereotype use is consequential (e.g., Mokros, 2003) but, regardless of the reason, anecdotes and testimonials are objectively not strong evidence for accuracy because they do not result from careful research. Put simply, anecdotes and testimonials are not real data that support a claim of a stereotype's accuracy. Instead, people treat them as intuitively true because they reinforce their existing stereotypic beliefs and are, therefore, memorable.

Trump supporters who view him as a credible source of information may not seriously question the insufficiently researched information he provides. Indeed, members of Trump's base may —even after seeing evidence that contradicts his claims—continue to view the twice-elected president as trustworthy in an overall sense, making them more susceptible to believing anecdotal and testimonial evidence rather than seeking out statistical data themselves. For example, after the 2020 election Trump repeatedly lied that there had been more votes cast than registered voters in cities like Detroit and Philadelphia that have heavily black populations. Checking publicly available data quickly and easily disproves this, yet 51% of Republicans and 58% of strong Trump supporters continued to believe this misinformation according to a 2024 *Washington Post*-George Mason University survey (Kessler et al., 2024).

For Trumpers who hear statements from him they know—or should know—are untrue, it may be easier for them to rationalize away the untruths as jokes or just deny the facts than it would be to acknowledge that he has repeatedly lied to them. Doing the latter would require accepting that significant parts of their right-wing, Trump-centric worldview—with all its carefully aimed grievances—center on falsehoods. Believing a lie is easier than shifting the foundation of one's identity. Although strong Trump supporters are significantly more likely to believe his lies than are other Americans (Kessler and Clement, 2018), even when some of them acknowledge that Trump has made false statements or flat-out lied about facts, their support for him does not waver (Resnick, 2017).

Base rates

A statement is accurate in scientific terms when there exists a correspondence between its content and criteria that people largely agree represents factual reality (Funder, 1995, 1996; Leyens et al., 1994). Base rates are frequencies (e. g., 70 % of people do x) measured as "the percentage of true cases over the total number of similar cases in the past" (Funder, 1996, p. 147). Generally, people assume that this straight-forward statistic provides the basis to claim that a stereotype is accurate. The phrase 'kernel-of-truth' refers to the idea that stereotypes exist thanks to some "realistic basis" which makes it reasonable to conclude that they are accurate (Ottati and Lee, 1995, p. 32). Fundamentally, if stereotypes are accurate then their use seems justifiable.

Supporters of Donald Trump may feel the presence of a real economic threat when they hear from a reliable source that 17.4 % of the current labor force is foreign-born (Bureau of Labor Statistics, 2022). Coupled with anecdotal evidence, the incorporation of a base rate provides seemingly strong backing to Trump's claim that immigrants are taking jobs away from those who were born in the United States. Echoing Lippman (1922), Vrugt (1987) argues that "the way in which everyday observations take place permits them to be directed by the assumptions of the perceiver... [you] may start with [an] expectation..., and then select events that confirm the initial expectations" (p. 374).

Many researchers have tried to determine whether stereotypes are accurate by studying the frequency of the stereotyped behavior in the target group, such as LaPiere's 1936 study of stereotypes of Armenians; Judd, Ryan, and Park's 1991 study of business and engineering student stereotypes; and Swim's 1994 meta-analytic study of the accuracy of gender stereotypes. The problem with base rates, however, is that they are context-based and dependent on the quality of the research study conducted. Judd and Park (1993) note that "differences in question wording, question context, and response formats" can affect research results (p. 113). We could and, truly, should ask questions about a research study that serves as the source of a base rate statistic:

- Where do these statistics come from? (i. e., operationalization and instrumentation?)

- How were these studies conducted and who participated? (i.e., research design and sample selection?)
- Are there other items that could have affected the study? (i.e., moderating or confounding variables?)
- Is it possible that these studies and those that promote their findings misrepresent the data, whether intentionally or not? (i.e., bias?)

The problem with base rate statistics is that each is a single data point, a snapshot of a moment in time and in some specific context. Once we remove the base rate from its context, we risk using it inaccurately in order to support our preconceptions. An important distinction to make, then, is between a generalization and a stereotype (see Introduction). A generalization involves a base rate applied to a portion of the target group. When people generalize, they typically use words like "some" or "many," which, notably, avoid casting aspersions on the entirety of the target group. In contrast, when people stereotype they typically exaggerate the base rate as if it applies to all members of the target group. Trump's communication style and political rhetoric consistently employs stereotypes rather than generalizations either explicitly—when he uses a word like "all"—or, as he does in most cases, by not clearly stating that he is only referring to some target group members.

For example, in 2015 then-candidate Trump said that undocumented immigrants were "taking our jobs, they're taking our manufacturing jobs, they're taking our money, they're killing us" (Boak, 2019). On August 19, 2016, he said of African Americans: "You're living in poverty, your schools are no good, you have no jobs"—this was part of a pitch to convince them to vote for him that ended with "what the hell do you have to lose?" (LoBianco and Killough, 2016). On July 26, 2024, the twice-elected president described immigrants coming from Mexico with an unqualified broad brush as "murderers, child predators and bloodthirsty rapists and drug dealers" (Gold, 2024a). Pomerantz (1986) introduced the idea of extreme case formulations in which absolutes expressed with words like always and never are used to talk about a topic. Even in cases when absolutes are not explicitly stated, but neither are qualifiers (e.g., some or many), the stereotype is expressed as an all or nothing assertion. Stereotypes can imply the absolute even when communicated with a 'silent' yet assumed extreme case formulation. There is no confusion for the listener. Every group member is assigned the characteristic.

Judd and Park (1994) describe three ways base rates can be misused in stereotypes. First, exaggeration accuracy, an "overestimation of stereotypicality" (p. 111) can occur when we apply base rates to individuals and misunderstand the claim that something occurring in a group (this will occur in X group 70 % of the time) to mean that this will occur with the same frequency for each individual group member (Sam is 70 % likely to do this). The exaggeration hypothesis suggests that "even when a stereotype is not altogether false [i.e., a kernel-of-truth], it is likely to be an exaggeration of the prevalence of stereotyped characteristics in the targeted group" (McCauley, 1995, p. 216).

Second, dispersion inaccuracy is an "underestimation of dispersion" (Judd and Park, 1994, p. 111). This occurs when the variability within the target group is flattened so everyone in the group is perceived to be the same with neither subtle nor strong varieties. Base rates can render invisible the individual distinctions that make each person unique by oversimplifying the complexity of a person and producing the appearance of homogeneity within the group. Thus, the characteristics of group members are an exaggerated one-dimensional and flattened version of the group. For example, people are not illegal, even if they do commit a crime. Yet Trump and others use terms like "illegal immigrants" or "illegal aliens"—he did both during his acceptance speech at the 2024 Republican National Convention (*New York Times*, 2024). Furthermore, the idea that immigrants can be called 'illegal' is both dehumanizing and inaccurate. Someone crossing the border when they are undocumented violates, generally speaking, a civil rather than criminal offense (ACLU, 2010). A more accurate term, then, is undocumented rather than illegal.

Third, in valence inaccuracy (Judd and Park, 1993) a particular group's traits are negatively or positively valued compared to individuals or groups with the same traits. This is particularly problematic because inevitably a one-dimensional group stereotype is contrasted with another group's stereotype to polarize intergroup differences. As a result, if one stereotype is viewed negatively, the commonly identified contrasting group may be viewed positively (e.g., black/white, men/women, old/young). Though base rates are often taken on their face as seemingly neutral statistical evidence, a negative bias can, nonetheless, result from treating base rates as evidence that a stereotype is accurate (Kurylo, 2013). For example, refugees that come to the United States seeking asylum, following a legal path to entry, are often vilified by those on the right and beyond as illegal immigrants, and some are sent to sanctuary cities through deceptive practices initiated by Republican-run governments in states like Texas. Trumpist rhetoric surrounding immigration rarely mentions that many seeking asylum have followed a legal path to entry. Compare this to how Trump appears to have moved mountains to enable his wife, Melania, to quickly gain a legal status she could likely not have gained without his help (Gunter, 2018). The difference between how the twice-elected president has treated asylum seekers as 'illegal immigrants' and a model he wanted to marry demonstrates a dichotomy between legal and supposed illegal immigrants as identified in valence inaccuracy. What we determine to be accurate and how we judge it is all too malleable when stereotypes are involved.

Cultural differences are proof of stereotype accuracy

Trump does not typically incorporate statistics as evidence when speaking to the media or in his speeches. Nonetheless, his assertion that groups have broadly shared characteristics—whether supported by base rates or anecdotal evidence —often goes unquestioned by acolytes. This makes sense to many Trump supporters because the existence of cultural differences among groups is a widely accepted belief. When we travel to another country, for example, we might read a travel book that tells us about the culture(s) of its citizens. Travel books represent a $124 million dollar industry (Stoller, 2018). Thus, the presumption that members of different groups collectively differ from one another is commonplace and, as a result, possesses a certain face validity regardless of whether it is true in each case.

A Cultural Stereotype Accuracy-Meaning Model (Lee and Duenas, 1996) suggests that cultural norms may offer a valid basis for a stereotype. Moreover, it can result in stereotype distortion as well. The CSAM Model acknowledges and appreciates the differences among cultures, and views these differences as distorted by the meanings imposed on them as part of perceptual and group categorization processes. This perspective stresses that difference is not value-laden (i. e., good or bad) but rather that through understanding cultural differences we can put stereotypic knowledge into perspective and foster understanding among groups. However, expectations about cultural groups that differ from our own can cause us to distort otherwise seemingly valid and neutral generalizations, resulting in a negative interpretation and stereotyping of that cultural group (Judd and Park, 1993).

Early stereotype research argued about whether stereotypes were accurate representations of social groups because it seemed that at face value groups must be inherently different. So, researchers sought to determine whether stereotypes constituted facts about the apparently obvious differences among groups. Many studies were conducted on different groups to determine if stereotypes accurately reflected their characteristics. Some researchers, like Katz and Braly, saw stereotypes as inaccurate, although others saw them as possessing some accuracy, though perhaps exaggerated. Vinacke (1956), for example, saw nothing inherently wrong with stereotyping because it reflects the presumed reality that groups are different. Katz and Braly (1933) conducted one of the first empirical studies of stereotypes, particularly stereotype content, when they studied the traits commonly associated with some ethnic groups.

Klineberg (1954) suggests that every stereotype should be studied to determine its accuracy. This, of course, presents an impossible task as there are hundreds if not thousands of stereotypes, with new ones emerging constantly while older ones can become outdated. As a result, Klineberg further surmised that without studying each stereotype, the Kernel-of-Truth hypothesis remains unproven. Moreover, research results suggest the endeavor is not necessarily worthwhile. For example, in their research on gender differences, Canary, Emmers-Sommer, and Faulkner (1997) found that only about 1% "of people's communication behavior is [directly related to] gender" (p. 93). We cannot base an assumption that a stereotype—in this case about gender—is true on such meager results and, so, the effort to study all stereotypes could be in vain. Nonetheless, assumptions about stereotypical differences, regardless of whether they are true, can be consequential.

Rather than pursue the impossible, other scholars have suggested that stereotypes are inherently inaccurate because the person who uses them is doing so based on assumptions rather than evidence (Katz and Braly, 1933). Research also found that regardless of whether people had any experience interacting with group members, they would nonetheless stereotype members of that group. Trump's rhetoric relies on this willingness of people to assume 'knowledge' about a targeted group because 'everyone knows it's true'—even without understanding the context of a base rate and without having ever interacted with the stereotyped group.

Individuating information

As mentioned, a base rate may be used as evidence of the accuracy of a stereotype; however, that statistic is not particularly useful when you are talking about one person from that group. Let us say the base rate is, for example, that in 2008, 67% of Latino voters selected Barack Obama for president. That does not mean that a particular 2008 Latino voter has a 67% chance of having done so. That person only either did or did not vote for Obama; the base rate does not tell us how that individual voted in 2008, and certainly does not predict their future vote in any way. This is because in a specific moment a person, with the benefit of free will, can engage in innumerable activities, any of which might not fit the confines of stereotype expectancies. People can never be reduced to base rates because base rates only have meaning on the large scale, and the past behavior of group members does not predict one member's future behavior. Instead, individuating information about a person is that which is unique to that person and does not reflect or may even contradict a stereotype related to their perceived group. Unfortunately, people often dismiss such information as an outlier or exception to the stereotype, rather than as evidence that disproves it.

There are many reasons why an individual person may not act stereotypically. Conversely, just because people *may* act stereotypically does not mean that the stereotype is an inherently accurate representation of the group. People who do, in a given interaction, act stereotypically, may do so for many reasons, including their willingness to accommodate or diverge from a stereotype, or based on what they presume about another person's stereotype of them (i. e., meta-stereotypes). Kurylo (2013) and Kurylo and Hu (2024) have explored stereotype use in the interpersonal and organizational contexts in which they are communicated. Some researchers have suggested that we should take the context of interactions in which stereotypes are communicated into account when trying to understand them (Hamilton and Sherman, 1994; Ryan et al., 1996). These contexts are important because: "conversation as it takes place in face-to-face interaction occurs within real time constraints . . . [and] it is a production with a social end, which requires synchronization with another's comprehension" (Semin, 2000, p. 597; see also Haslam et al., 2002; Jussim et al., 1995; Ottati and Lee, 1996). In other words, a person may gain some benefit from communicating in a stereotypical way in a particular interaction.

Moreover, people's individuality could affect the data that is collected in a research study as well. Self-report instruments may lead to biased responses. Judd and Park (1993) note that: "Self-presentational issues may also have large effects on self-reports (e. g., responses designed to maximize social acceptance or social desirability)" (p. 113). If asked for self-reporting on issues for which stereotypes exist, stereotypes may influence the answer. In such cases, because of self-report bias the answer may be exaggerated and the instrument may actually be measuring stereotypes rather than delivering accurate information. For example, in one study of gender and behavior the researchers were forced to conclude that their participants were more likely to have reinforced stereotypes in their answers than to have answered honestly (Kirtley and Weaver, 1999).

In self-report studies, other factors can play a role. Self-fulfilling prophecies can play out in an interaction in ways that reinforce stereotyping of group members (Hamilton, Sherman, and Ruvolo, 1990), regardless of any individuating information that might otherwise counter a stereotype. Moreover, individuals are better able to recall information that confirms a stereotype compared to that which contradicts one (Judd and Park, 1993)—a tendency that reflects confirmation bias. Individuals or events that do not fit the group stereotype may be considered an exception and disregarded, leading to the overestimation of consistency within a group (Judd and Park, 1993).

Additionally, individuals may have shifting standards (Biernat and Manis, 1994) that can impact the result of their self-report. Biernat (1995) defines the Shifting Standards Model as referring to: "when perceivers make judgments about members of social categories on stereotype-relevant dimensions, they do so by calling to mind a within-group standard of comparison" (p. 87). For example, considering whether a person whose height measures 5' 9" is tall depends very much on which group that person is being compared to—if we are talking about a man, one would generally compare him to other men and say that he is not especially tall, whereas a woman of that height would be compared to other women, and thus be considered tall. While the previous example is based on statistical tendencies (base rates), the standards by which people assess something can also depend on their preferences (Judd and Park, 1993).

For example, throughout his political career, Trump has been able to lie with impunity to a degree that has been afforded no other major politician because the media as well as his supporters apply a different standard to him and, seemingly, only him when it comes to telling the truth (McAdams, 2020; Carlson et al., 2021). As for his supporters specifically, a Harvard study on misinformation found that fact-checking his false claims only made them more likely to believe the claims even when they were lies: "Trump voters with high political knowledge judged election misinformation as more truthful when Trump's claims included Twitter's disputed tags compared to a control condition" (Blanchar and Norris, 2024). The implications of this shifting standards model are, therefore, important for stereotype accuracy research. These shifting standards act as a rubber band in which we can stretch standards/yardsticks on which we base judgments in various ways depending on the individual's frame of reference. In sum, there are numerous ways that research can display the appearance of accuracy and, yet, merely serve to perpetuate stereotypes. We simply lack sufficient evidence to suggest that stereotypes are inherently accurate when applied at the group level or to a particular person.

Making racism cool again

During the political correctness era, the idea of microaggressions represented a step too far for many who remain convinced stereotypes offer value as accurate representations of groups. The twice-elected president's brazen stereotyping treats stereotypes as accurate despite either the absence of evidence or, in some cases, the presence of evidence proving them false. Nonetheless, members of his base view these stereotypes as credible and factual because they fit with prejudices and general impressions they and their leader already hold; they confirm existing biases. As a result, Trump became the first major celebrity and political figure to get away with publicly communicating such explicit stereotypes without being vilified to the degree his peers had been. In addition, he benefited in the polls from doing so (see, for example, the Monmouth poll results discussed in Chapter 1).

Trump gave his supporters a fun way to be rebellious by enabling and, indeed, encouraging them to thumb their noses at the oppressiveness of political correctness. Rush Limbaugh and other right-wing shock jocks—and even other hosts like Howard Stern, on whose show Trump appeared dozens of times through 2015 before falling out over the latter's hard-right politics (Bushard, 2023)—provided Trump with a blueprint on this. Their audience, which is disproportionately white and male (Wicks et al., 2014; Agence France-Presse, 2023), has long reveled in the transgressive nature of entertainment built around insults and slurs—few things are more exciting than breaking the rules, in particular by taking a dig at one's perceived opponents or enemies. Listeners found it both thrilling and cathartic. In the Trump era, Republicans across the board have aimed to 'own the libs' every time they communicate with the public (Robertston, 2021). Trump is an expert at trolling his opponents to get under their skin. The twice-elected president, more than anyone else, made stereotyping members of minoritized groups fair game in an overt and unapologetic way. This is far from the anti-racist stance required to live up to the standards around microaggressions and, more broadly, political correctness.

The second wave of political correctness was short-lived. The introduction of microaggressions into a politically correct ethos reset the discussion. The general feeling among those who resented this shift was: *If we are going to get blamed for stereotypes anyway, even if that is not what we intended or actually communicated, then why would we not just go ahead and stereotype freely? We never had a problem with it anyway. We were just trying to be polite. We never understood why we couldn't stereotype under the PC regime in the first place!* Trump uses stereotypes to tell people: "I'm on your side"—people who would feel comfortable hearing or communicating the same stereotypes, that is. By talking the same way they do, he makes his supporters feel seen by their leader, bonding them more strongly to him and one another.

In a sense, what Trump does actually parallels the use of inclusive language by and for those on the left. Functionally, using the term Latinx as opposed to Latinos is a form of virtue signaling, something one does to show that they stand on the side of the people who also talk that way, i.e. progressives, not Latinos themselves, very few of whom would use such ivory tower terminology (Newport, 2022; Falcon, 2023).[11] If you use the right code—Trump uses stereotypes, those on the left use 'inclusive' language often developed and/or promulgated by academics—you are a member of the team. Although the right-wing stereotypes come from a place of wanting to stigmatize and harm those they target, whereas the left-wing language comes from a more positive (if misguided) place of inclusivity, both functionally play the same role—signifying membership in the group. The left virtue signals, while the Trumpist right signals their shared vices.

---

11 Only 4% of Latinos said they use the term in a November 2023 survey (Noe-Bustamante et al., 2024), consistent with previous results.

Prior to his emergence, Trump's supporters lacked a leader who effectively gave voice to all this. Starting in mid-2015, they began flocking to someone who, in a world of confusing rules and changing norms, reached out a hand to pull them out of the quagmire of trying to keep up with political correctness—the latest trend was microaggressions. Trump's base followed a leader who provided a way to channel the frustrations they felt. With Trump speaking their truth, the floodgates of resentment opened.

Chapter 3
Making stereotypes great again: Information Processing Theory as a validation of the usefulness of stereotypes

Sight is our most valued sense (Enoch et al., 2019). This is why we remember, for example, visual cues such as memes about Donald Trump's orange-hued skin. Still, everything we see, if we could process it in all of its intricacy, is only a minute portion of what exists to be seen. Someone standing in the same spot as you but turned to the left or right has access to significantly different visual information. As an example, in one college class assignment students watched the same commercial and were asked to identify all the visual details that contribute to the messaging. More than half the ads were a mere 30 seconds (Insights, 2014). Yet each student contributed a unique detail to the discussion. Students were able to report twice and three times each because there were so many details to see in just 30 seconds. Think of all the information that exists at our disposal through the *additional* senses of sound, touch, smell, and taste. Our five senses experience information overload each moment (Fiske and Taylor, 1984) as they are confronted with seemingly infinite amounts of data (i. e., information).

This data that we personally experience provides only a portion of the available data to which we might be exposed. The information that is available where we are *not* present to experience it is unfathomable in its enormity. As of December 19, 2023, the Internet Archive, for example, contained: "735 billion web pages, 41 million books and texts, 14.7 million audio recordings (including 240,000 live concerts), 8.4 million videos (including 2.4 million Television News programs), 4.4 million images, and 890,000 software programs" (Insights, 2014). In sharp contrast to the seeming infiniteness of information, humans have a limited capacity to receive and process it, even with spending an average of 400 minutes on the internet every day (Leake, 2024).

Perception: The limitations of humans

A person would be rendered incapable of carrying out the most basic of everyday activities if they *needed* to experience anew every piece of information with which they come into contact. Imagine having to attempt to process every individual data point you see right now (e. g., the black on white printed letters, what the page numbers are, how many lines of text appear per page, what is farther in your

https://doi.org/10.1515/9783111426327-006

field of vision beyond this book), in other words, everything you are ignoring right now that is not in your direct line of vision—until, that is, you turn your head even slightly left, right, up, or down. Instead, to get through the day, people must reduce the amount of information they take in, culling it down to what is *relevant* to process in order to function in the world. For example, you are unlikely to spend a lot of time on the color of the text on a page or the size of the font relative to the page length because you take this information for granted, along with the current noises, smells, and tastes that you are currently experiencing, as well as the feel of the book (digital or hard copy) in your hand. These fade into the background while you focus on the words on the page to the exclusion of other stimuli. At least we hope so.

This explains why a lot of misunderstanding and arguing takes place—whether over politics, what to have for breakfast, or where to send your child to school. Limited by our human abilities, we can only process a small amount of the information we experience at a given time. Because of this necessary reduction in information, there is no environment that people experience fully, in all of its totality. Rather, people interact with the world and experience information only and always through their individual perception of it. The complex and personalized perception process involves three stages: selecting, organizing, and interpreting.

Selection: Insults and stereotypes shape what we focus on

Selecting is the process of choosing the information we attend to out of everything we come into contact with. A stimulus stands out to us when it is salient. There are many reasons one piece of data might stand out over another, such as when it reminds us of the past or a personal association, seems contradictory, does not meet expectations, disappoints or frustrates us, has specific types of contact (e.g., longer, more intimate, physically nearby, causes discomfort), is isolated, is likable, desirable, or fun, is the first (i.e., primacy) or most recent (i.e., recency) time we come into contact with something, reminds of a future task, is familiar, has ambiguity or is confusing, or is unusual (e.g., stronger, louder, tastier), seems particularly important or mundane, or is of particular interest for other less predictable reasons. These rationales do not occur at all times for all people, but rather for each person at a given moment one or more of these may explain why a particular stimulus stands out.

As we discussed in Chapter 2, people assume that those from other cultural groups—or other types of groups—are different. Because of our perceptual processes, we will more likely notice those who look, sound, or act differently from us than those who do not. For example, here is an incident with which one of us has personal experience: An American student was encouraged to take Mandarin—the only Asian language offered at the school—for no apparent reason other than because he looked Asian. When the student did not do well in the course, the teacher called and asked the parents to help their son with learning the language. The parents had to explain that they did not know Mandarin either, and made the point clearer by saying, "Imagine that we are blonde-haired and blue-eyed." Despite similarities among people, we select and pay attention to differences, and make assumptions that follow therefrom. The student was never asked if he was familiar with Mandarin before being enrolled in the course. Rather, because he looked different from the predominantly white administrators at the school, this selectivity governed their decision on something as important as what course he should take.

Selectivity (Wu and Kurylo, 2010), a general term for all types of this phenomenon, affects decoding and encoding of information with which we come into contact, regardless of whether we are aware of what we are doing. There are several specific types of selectivity that further describe what types of data we allow through our perceptual lenses (i.e., selective exposure, selective attention, and selective recall). *Selective exposure* occurs when we limit the type of data we allow ourselves to come into contact with. This can occur when we avoid certain content, situations, or conversations and, instead, place ourselves in the position to be exposed to others. When we choose to watch predominantly Fox News or MSNBC, for example, we are selectively exposing ourselves to some information over others.

Selective attention occurs when we limit what we pay attention to in a given moment. Trump certainly seems to understand this, as he tends to pick on a random aspect of an opponent's appearance or demeanor in order to focus voters' attention there rather than on matters of greater substance. For example, on multiple occasions during the 2024 campaign he mocked Vice President Harris's boisterous style of laughing. Trump even tried building one of his trademark monikers around it. "I call her 'laughing Kamala'," he told rally goers in Michigan on July 24, 2024, adding: "Have you ever watched her laugh? She is crazy. You can tell a lot by a laugh . . . She is nuts" (Gilbert, 2024). A Trump campaign ad also mocked Hillary Clinton's laughter during the 2016 campaign (LoBianco, 2015).

This stereotype of labeling people as crazy is one of Trump's most common insults. He has slandered perhaps his longest-standing and most formidable female opponent, former Speaker of the House Nancy Pelosi, as "Crazy Nancy" countless times (Montanaro, 2024), and also referred to Secretary Clinton and Democratic Vermont Senator Bernie Sanders as "crazy" (Seitz-Wald, 2020). Additionally, after an August 2024 incident in which Trump brazenly violated the law about producing campaign propaganda at Arlington National Cemetery, his spokesperson attacked the employee who attempted to enforce that law (and who was assaulted by campaign staff in the process) as a person "clearly suffering from a mental health episode" (McLeary and O'Brien, 2024). There is no content to these kinds of attacks, nor do they use humor to make a larger criticism about a political rival's ideas, character, or governing style. Instead, these seem like nothing more than childish insults. Nonetheless, Trump has found them effective and used them in every campaign. These insults (Allsop, 2019) work on a cognitive level to shape selective attention:

> In the 2016 primary, for example, Trump took several opponents who had decent name recognition in the general population and redefined them in an instant. What's less cognitively demanding: reading about Jeb(!) Bush's policy platform in granular detail, or dismissing him because he's "Low Energy Jeb"? The same held true for "Liddle Marco" Rubio and "Lyin' Ted" Cruz . . . Trump's insults provided voters with a new framework for processing information, but it also affected which information they paid attention to in the first place.

> What Trump did was devastating even to candidates who were well known among political activists. But schemas can be much more fluid during first impressions, when there is no existing intellectual scaffolding to dismantle or rearrange. When someone is a blank slate, fresh schemas can destroy political careers in a matter of minutes (Klaas, 2023).

Perhaps the most familiar selectivity is *selective recall,* which refers to the process by which individuals, with limited capacity to recall all the possible details of any event, will recall only some aspects of an event over time. Selective recall is particularly noteworthy because it warns us that our memory is often faulty and inherently biased. A person chooses specific information because that content may be meaningful for that individual (Coffey and Atkinson, 1996; Nisbett and Wilson, 1977). Tracy (2002) notes that: "people are notoriously bad at remembering" (p. 156). Recall is limited by the delay in time between an event's occurrence and when an account is made. This delay moderates the account's quality. Over time, we are more likely to recall impressions than specific details of events (Stafford, Burggraf, and Sharkey, 1987). Stafford and Daly (1984) found that when prompted individuals recall an average of at most 10 % of the content of a past interaction.

Researchers have found that certain content included in stereotypes people hear is more likely to be stored, recalled, and communicated and, thus, more likely to be reproduced over time (Kenrick et al., 2002). Abstraction-based stereotype content is more communicable than instance-based stereotype content (e. g., Klein et al., 2003; Thompson, Judd, and Park, 2000). Stereotype-consistent information is more communicable than stereotype-inconsistent information unless the inconsistent information is especially salient or provides individuating information about the target (e. g., Brauer et al., 2001; Kashima, 2000; Klein et al., 2003; Lyons and Kashima, 2001, 2003). Research has also found a negativity bias according to which we are more likely to recall and, thereafter, communicate information that echoes negative stereotypes (Ford et al., 2001; Schaler and Conway, 1999; Schneider, 1996).[12] Understanding why stereotype content is communicable is particularly important for examining the implications for the members of the target group, who often face prejudice and discrimination fueled by stereotypes (Allport, 1954/1979; Fiske, 1998; Fiske and Taylor, 1984).

Once recalled, the specific information may be more consistent with expectations about that event type or stereotypes than the details of the original specific event itself (Coffey and Atkinson, 1996; Nisbett and Wilson, 1977). For example, Kessler et al. (2024) report: "Six years ago, just about 1 in 4 Republicans (26%) agreed that millions of fraudulent votes were cast in the 2016 election. Now, 38% of Republicans—and 47% of strong Trump supporters—believe that is the case."[13] In contrast, behaviors that violate social conventions (e.g., something impolite) or that are unique to the individual (i.e., individuating information) are more memorable than other behaviors and may prompt individuals to recall specific event details more reliably (Kemper and Thissen, 1981).

Consider engaging in a brief activity for a moment. Write down what you know about politics today. Make a list of three to five items. Then, try to remember from where you gained that knowledge. Lastly, consider which of the types of selectivity enabled you to know that information. Now please recall that selectivity is only the first stage of perception.

Organization

After we select certain information, our minds organize it. Organizing is the process of categorizing this selected information into compartmentalized and familiar groupings. These groupings are typically based on categories that we are familiar with due to some pre-existing reasons. As a result, the way we organize information has a face validity to it, that is, the organization seems to make inherent sense to us and so we use it to make decisions. For example, Trump's March 6, 2017 executive order regarding the aforementioned ban (see Chapter 2) on entry to the U.S. from seven Muslim countries stated: "These are countries that had already been identified as presenting heightened concerns about terrorism and travel to the United States." The Trump White House put these countries in an easily under-

---

12 Other types of content have also been studied (e.g., Crandall et al., 2002; Klein et al., 2003; Schaller et al., 2002).

13 There is no evidence to support this belief (Kessler et al, 2024).

stood category of threat that drew on what many Americans already stereotypically believed about them.

Kurylo (2013) explored how stereotypic content is clustered together in ways that reinforce the impressions people have about different races. This research found that minority, majority, and so-called model minority categories were based on specific stereotypical associations that distinguished between these. This research showed there were numerous kinds of stereotypes of minorities (e. g., dark-skinned Americans). These involved interconnectedness among the stereotypes, they were comprehensive and covered many aspects of a person's life, and these stereotypes were generally either neutral or negative in terms of desirability. By comparison, stereotypes of majority groups (e. g., white Americans) were fewer in quantity, were less interconnected and comprehensive, and were more neutral or positive. Model minority stereotypes involved large numbers of undesirable characteristics that were interconnected. However, as with majority groups, model minorities such as Asian and Jewish Americans were not stereotyped with characteristics in a comprehensive way. Kurylo (2013) defines comprehensive as relating to a vast array of aspects of a person's life. The inductive finding that Asians and Jews were aligned with minority groups along three characteristics but aligned with majority groups along the fourth allowed model minority to stand out as its own category distinct from either minority or majority groups. From a cognitive perspective, the lack of comprehensiveness means stereotypes of the model minority groups would be less likely to come to mind during recall because they are more narrowly focused and not as universally relevant.

One way people organize information is to rely on punctuation, a metaphor for how to organize a sequence of behaviors. Punctuation "organizes behavioral events and is therefore vital to ongoing interaction" (Watzlawick et al., 1967, p. 56). The way in which we punctuate a "stream of events" (Bateson, 1972, p. 166) brings meaning to those events because of how it frames that interaction (Bateson, 1972). Considering political rhetoric as a long conversation in which interactions build on one another, we can apply this term to Trump's communication around Biden and inflation.

For example, Trump repeatedly criticized the Biden Administration on inflation as measured year-over-year by the Consumer Price Index (CPI). The CPI rose significantly after Biden took office in January 2021 and peaked at 9.1% in June 2022, before falling significantly and dropping to 2.4% by September 2024, and rising to 2.6% in the final reading before Election Day (Bureau of Labor Statistics, n.d.). Trump's criticisms, however, ignore the role of COVID in creating the very low inflation during 2020—a year that included the single largest quarterly contraction in Gross Domestic Product in U.S. history after businesses shut down and consumer spending contracted—and the role that the resulting snapback to economic recovery had in spurring inflation (Krugman, 2024b). Additionally, the entire developed world followed a very similar pattern to that of the U.S., and in fact by July 2023 the U.S. had the lowest inflation rate among the G-7 countries, and one of the lowest among the largest 30 economies (Jacobson, 2023). This fact demonstrates that Biden's policies had little to do with the spike in inflation. Trump's criticisms, and the extent to which people believe them, rely on a particular way of punctuating this economic information and crafting it into a political message.

When we punctuate a stream of events, we isolate particular information from other information about events that also took place. This leads us, for example, to dismiss another perspective or ignore what might be a legitimate argument by viewing that other information as irrelevant, simultaneously treating the information we have isolated as reasonable and important. Trump and his most avid supporters used punctuation to their advantage when it came to Biden and inflation, along with many other issues. The differences in people's general knowledge of politics and history leads to differences in how we interpret new information. Because we 'don't know what we don't know,' we rely on what is fed to us, which enables partisan media or politicians to (mis)shape an audience's understanding of the truth—especially for those who rely solely on partisan sources for their information.

A fundamental part of our perception is that when we process information, we use our cognitive resources economically. For example, as mentioned previously, in the 2024 campaign Trump focused on Harris's laugh. In doing so, he sought to prime voters to do the same, to pay attention to the laughter instead of the substance of what she said. Additionally, there is a clear element of sexism and racism in Trump's attack on Harris's laughter and his related and repeated slurs of her as: "stupid," "mentally unfit," "slow," an "extremely low IQ person" (Parker, 2024b), "incompetent" (Woodall, 2024), "crazy," "nuts" (Coster et al., 2024), "lazy"—which has racist connotations when hurled at black people (PBS, 2024)—"dumb as a rock," a "wack job"; "real garbage"; "a bum"; and—to mention a slur he has hurled against many women—"nasty," (Bensinger et al., 2024) as well as in his seemingly innocuous focus on her looks, such as when he called her "a beautiful woman" (Sentner, 2024). On October 22, 2024, the twice-elected president called his opponent "lazy as hell," "low IQ," "slow," and "a stupid person" before throwing out baseless charges by asking "Does she drink? Is she on drugs?" (Beaumont and Colvin, 2024). More broadly, Trump has long employed hate-filled language against female opponents other than those mentioned here, including Democrats like Massachusetts Senator Elizabeth Warren and New York Representative Alexandria Ocasio-Cortez, along with many others (Vazquez and Carvajal, 2020).

After the September 10, 2024 debate in which Harris, by all accounts, soundly defeated Trump, he baselessly claimed she had cheated by receiving answers fed through her earpiece. The implication was that she could never be smart enough to beat him on her own (Balz, 2024). On September 28, 2024, in what he himself admitted was a "dark speech," Trump called his opponent "mentally impaired," and added "she was born that way." Additionally, he mispronounced her first name multiple times, something he did constantly, and which her supporters have argued is a racist attempt to 'other' her even further (Vazquez and Rodriguez, 2024, Kornfield, 2024).[14] Trump made similar remarks about the vice president's mental impairment the next day and on occasions thereafter such as in remarks at a private dinner with megadonors where he referred to her as "retarded" (Swan et al., 2024).

Othering Harris as a deliberate strategy

At the aforementioned July 31, 2024 NABJ forum, in a bald attempt to both other Harris and insinuate that all her stands on matters of race are somehow tainted by her basic insincerity and opportunism on the matter, Trump accused his opponent of having been "Indian all the way," before she "all of a sudden she made a turn" and "became a Black person." He continued: "I didn't know she was Black until a number of years ago when she happened to turn Black, and now she wants to be known as Black. So I don't know, is she Indian or is she Black?" (Tucker and Knowles, 2024). Through this fabrication—which of course ignores the reality that Harris could be both black and Indian—Trump cast an overall sense of doubt on his opponent. Moreover, making such an absurd charge in an interview with the National Association of Black Journalists guaranteed that the media would amplify his accusations. The twice-elected president continued to push this sleight of hand; at a Pennsylvania rally his audience saw a huge image projected on a screen above the podium of a headline about Harris that referred to her as the "first Indian American U.S. Senator" (Lerer and King, 2024). By contrast, four days before the election he offered this aside about his own skin color just after criticizing his opponent: "That white, beautiful white skin that I have would be nice and tan. I got the whitest skin 'cause I never have time to go out in the sun. But I have that beautiful white, and you know what? It could've been beautiful, tanned, beautiful" (Luciano, 2024).

---

14 Just about half of the people who spoke at the 2024 Republican National Convention and said Harris's first name mispronounced it (Recht et al., 2024).

Trump's attempts to other Harris included referring to her policy proposals as a "regulatory jihad"—an attempt to connect her to Islam and terrorism—along with the questions he posed about her background: "I wonder if they knew where she comes from, where she came from, what her ideology is" (LeVine et al., 2024) As *The Washington Post* noted:

> In his comments, Trump echoed his 2019 barb against several Democratic congresswomen of color—Reps. Alexandria Ocasio-Cortez (N.Y.), Ilhan Omar (Minn.), Rashida Tlaib (Mich.) and Ayanna Pressley (Mass.)—telling them to "go back" to where they came from. That comment was widely condemned at the time as racist and xenophobic" (LeVine et al., 2024).

In a *New York Times* interview, presidential historian Adam Naftali put Trump's remarks in context: "Whenever the United States is poised to break a political glass ceiling, we see an intensification of othering in our politics. What makes Trump a singularly poisonous political player is that the top of the ticket is overtly engaging in othering against his political opponent" (Nagourney, 2024).

Trump's sexist stereotypes

Well before Harris first became a candidate for national office in 2019, the twice-elected president had built an extensive track record of going after women by "demeaning their looks, mocking their bodily functions or comparing them to animals" (Shear and Sullivan, 2018). Additionally, *The New York Times* reported that: "In private, he uses misogynistic language to describe [Harris]" (Swan et al., 2024). Gonzalez, 2024) explained how Trump's rhetoric connects all these stereotypes:

> [He suggests] that because a woman is beautiful, she must be dumb, and if she's successful nonetheless, that's only because she slept her way to the top. He's used this strategy before too. He called Megyn Kelly a bimbo and Representative Alexandria Ocasio-Cortez "not even a smart person." He said Mika Brzezinski had a "low IQ" and implied that she had made it to *Morning Joe* only because she was dating her co-host. He told a female reporter once, "You wouldn't have this job if you weren't beautiful," and wrote that "early victories by the women on *The Apprentice* were, to a very large extent, dependent on their sex appeal."

The previous quotation cites the single most vile stereotype in the long, sordid history of sexism, namely that a woman in leadership gained her position by having sex with a powerful superior. Trump invoked this stereotype with a post on his Truth Social account that included a photo of Vice President Harris and Hillary Clinton with the following text beneath it: "Funny how blowjobs impacted their careers differently" . . . (Gold, 2024b; Rashid, 2024a). This was not the first time he had slandered Harris in this way on Truth Social, as he had also posted a video that included the following: "She spent her whole damn life down on her knees to be commander in chief" (Gold, 2024a; Wolf, 2024). Both posts referenced a relationship she had in 1994–95 with Willie Brown, then Speaker of the California State Assembly. Trump got even more specific on August 3, 2024, at a rally in Atlanta, Georgia: "She had a very good friend named Willie Brown . . . He knows more about her than anybody's ever known . . . Could tell you stories that you're not gonna wanna hear" (Forbes Breaking News, 2024). As Nikole Hannah-Jones explained, these kinds of slurs evoke "tropes of Harris as an incompetent, lazy, "low IQ" diversity hire who, in the tradition of the Black Jezebel, had slept her way to the top" (Hannah-Jones, 2024).

All of these sexist slurs—each one delivered in just the first few weeks after Harris became the presumptive Democratic nominee—allow Trump to draw on stereotypes of women as not possessing the gravitas, brains, temperament, or other (presumably 'male') qualities required to be a leader. The twice-elected president's implied message is that someone—who always just happens to be a woman —with a crazy laugh cannot be trusted with the nuclear codes. The message, and the sexism underlying it, comes through clearly—even without him saying that last part out loud.

Heuristics, lenses, and schema

To help us organize information that we have selected, we rely on shortcuts such as heuristics, lenses, and schema (Fiske and Taylor, 1984). Heuristics are guidelines or tools that aid the processing of information by allowing certain information (data) in the world to stick out to us because of how it relates to other information. The availability heuristic refers to our prediction that something is more likely to occur frequently in the population at large because it comes more easily to our own mind. Accordingly, as we organize data, we are more likely to use stereotypes that are constructed in a way that keeps them cognitively active. In her study of people's reports about the content of stereotypes they communicated in conversation, Kurylo (2013) found that a large number of minority stereotypes were interconnected, comprehensive, and negative. Kurylo argues that, as a result, it is not surprising that we may find stereotypes of minorities quick to come to our mind when we need to organize information. In a media landscape in which 'if it bleeds it leads' remains the guiding mantra, this can result in belief perseverance, the resistance we have—consciously or unconsciously—to changing our beliefs about differences among racial and other groups. Even in the presence of contrary information, we often weigh most heavily the information that our minds can most easily access.

Another way that we organize information is through our use of lenses (e.g., Bem, 1993). This kind of lens is the perspective a person has, and is guided by the environment, norms, and values of a culture with which they identify (Kurylo, 2013). Our identities (e.g., gender, racial, ethnic, religion, education level, age, political view, etc., as well as combinations thereof) necessarily create lenses that affect how we view information, just as prescription glasses affect how our eyes see. A lens provides benefits by enabling members of the same culture to view certain things similarly. This helps those with similar interests to process information quickly. However, a lens can be detrimental if it causes information to be misinterpreted. Unfortunately, we are often unaware of how our lenses affect our perception because our cognitive processes are automatic and instantaneous.

The twice-elected president's supporters are disproportionately white, male, straight, and Christian. A full 80 % of white evangelicals voted for him in 2016, 2020, and 2024 (Gjelten, 2020; Smith, 2024b). In January 2016, Trump promised: "Christianity will have power. If I'm there, you're going to have plenty of power, you don't need anybody else. You're going to have somebody representing you very, very well. Remember that" (Dias, 2020). *The New York Times* reported: "The idea that American government should be grounded in a Christian worldview found a place in Mr. Trump's administration, as well as at the Supreme Court, state legislatures and school boards" (Dias, 2024). As Robert P. Jones, founder and head of the Public Religion Research Institute, explained to the Associated Press, Trump's slogan "Make America Great Again" evokes a mythical past, an "ethno-religious vision of a white Christian America, just barely underneath the surface" (Smith, 2024a). Eric Taylor Woods and Robert Schertzer likewise noted that their research found:

> Trump's support stems from his ability to tap into an "ethno-nationalist" tradition of American identity in his campaign rhetoric . . . Trump uses this vision of American identity to garner support from white Americans by campaigning on the idea that he will defend them from the threat posed by people who are not perceived as real Americans—particularly the ostensible threat posed by undocumented migrants (Woods and Schertzer, 2024).[15]

The twice-elected president's hammering away at an invasion of immigrants that will transform our culture, traditions, and heritage appeals to those longing to preserve those things—along with the status that comes with membership in the here-

---

15 See also Schertzer and Woods, 2019; Woods, Fortier-Chouinard, Closen, Ouellet and Schertzer, 2023.

tofore dominant group in a changing country, not to mention world. This is white Christian identity politics. Trump appeals to their identity, which provides a lens through which they organize a good bit of the information they encounter.

One more way we organize information is through what is called a schema. Schemata are "mental structures containing information defining concepts' characteristics as well as those characteristics' interrelationships" (Macrae and Bodenhausen, 2001, p. 84). Schemata provide a presumed pattern or representation of information. Stereotypes are a type of schema that organize characteristics by attributing them to specific groups. Sacks (1992) introduced the concept of membership categorization devices (MCD's) to describe how language is used to name categories of people and their associated characteristics. Slightly broader than our understanding of stereotypes, MCD's include categories with associations we presume to be true, such as that doctors treat patients and mothers take care of babies (though not all doctors or all mothers do). Sacks (1992) provides the example of "The baby cried. The mommy picked it up" to explain how we presume characteristics even without the availability of explicit information. The organizing of the word 'mommy' near 'baby' prompts us to presume the relationship between the two. Similarly, stereotypes juxtapose a category and a characteristic. Organizing information in this way plays a role in how information related to a target group is perceived.

Stereotypes have a sense of 'all-ness'—meaning that we perceive all group members covered by a given stereotype to be alike with little room for variation barring an exception that, by definition, proves the stereotype to be true. A non-black person saying to a black person, for example, that 'you speak so articulately' or 'you have good hair' invokes an inherent racial stereotype underpinning each supposed compliment. Bem (1993) offered the idea of polarization in order to understand gender stereotypes. Bem discusses how men/male and women/female are often treated as a binary set within the category of sex/gender. As a result, characteristics attributed to each are often polarized such that whatever men/males are said to be, women/females are said to be the opposite. This organization of men and women as polarized binary options in a set affects how we process stereotypes about men and women. Similar polarized binaries occur with other stereotypes, such as racial stereotypes of black people and white people. According to Fiske and Taylor (1991), "One can think of stereotypes as a particular kind of role schema that organizes people's expectations about other people who fall into certain social categories" (p. 119). How a target group and its stereotypically associated characteristics are situated vis-à-vis other groups and their stereotypes provides a way for people to organize information.

Interpretation

The final step in perception is interpretation, or the process of giving meaning to the selected and categorized information. This interpretation of information is a value-laden process. Furthermore, perception can change to allow people to interpret a particular piece of information differently over time. Put another way, there is no value-neutral information because data is necessarily interpreted immediately as we perceive it and is therefore always potentially biased, if not inherently so. Trump's stoking of increasing white anxiety provides an example. There exists a stark partisan divide on how people feel about a piece of information that is, on its face, value-neutral: the projection that the U.S. population will be "majority-minority" by 2050. A 2019 Pew Research Center survey found that 50 % of Democratic respondents believed such a development would prove very good or somewhat good for America, versus only 16 % of Republicans who felt the same (Parker et al., 2019). Likewise, 12 % of Democrats compared to 37 % of Republicans thought it would have a very bad or somewhat bad impact; the rest were neutral. The partisan gap was even wider than the gap between white and either black or Hispanic respondents. Interestingly, as a point of contrast, the Pew survey found no partisan gap on the broad question of how people feel about "the future of the U.S. over the next 30 years." Therefore, we can identify fear of demographic change rather than overall pessimism about the future as a defining feature of how conservative Americans think. Republicans interpret the information around demographic change differently than Democrats—and Republican politicians like Trump know it.

Interpretation bias, more often than not, is unconscious. Unconscious bias occurs in part because of the automaticity of perceptual processes which are outside of our awareness. When we process information, we gain two particular cognitive benefits. Cognitive efficiency and attribution (i.e., inference), respectively, allow a person to simultaneously limit and expand data (Hamilton and Sherman, 1994). Consider the following, albeit overused, examples. Read the sentence:

I love Paris in the the springtime.

It is likely that as you read the sentence you may not have recognized the redundant use of the word *the*. Outside of your awareness, your brain processed this automatically and made a proactive decision to limit the information it made accessible to you. Watzlavick, Beavin, and Jackson (1967) help us to understand redundancy and habit. Cognitive efficiency reduces the information in the sentence to just what we need to understand. We automatically eliminate the redundancy of information that is not needed or valued in a given situation.

In addition to cognitive efficiency, which decreases the information we have available, we also expand the information we have available through inference. Recall Sacks' example of: "The baby cried. The mommy picked it up" (1992), which helps us to understand indexicality. Indexicality occurs when we refer back to some knowledge that we are not communicating, but which is needed to understand the information. Consider the sentence:

> T e info ma ion lef ou of th s sent nce doe n t mak it impo ible to un ers and.

Although there are letters missing in the previous sentence, you nonetheless likely grasped its meaning without much difficulty. Inference allows you to automatically expand information. In this case, you were still able to understand the sentence even though it omitted letters. We use attribution similarly to give meaning to behavior. Inference and attribution add information beyond what is immediately present. Doing so is necessary because the information we perceive is always incomplete. This incompleteness is exacerbated by cognitive efficiency that limits what information we take in.

When we are young, we learn what type of information to add and what type to omit. This knowledge is reinforced throughout our lives. Socialization is the process through which we absorb our cultural knowledge base—what we view as important, true, valuable, and so forth within our culture. Socialization also provides us with a presumed basis for our biases (Kurylo, 2013). We gain our cultural knowledge base by listening to and watching those around us at home and in school (Lippmann, 1922) as well as in our social and religious institutions, and so forth. Although media can play a role in socialization and bears some responsibility for perpetuating stereotypes, interpersonal communication with friends and family may well play a larger role on this front (Mackie et al., 1996). New York City provides an example to consider. From the 1970s through the 1990s it was a relatively dangerous place to be, particularly locations like Times Square. Today, NYC ranks as the fifth safest city with a population over 300,000 in the United States (Bloom, 2024), and, on a per capita basis, is quite a bit safer than most suburban and rural areas (Fox, 2022). Despite this, New York City is still depicted in the media—in particular but not only in right-wing media—as unsafe, and parents still warn their children about traveling there.

More broadly, Trump has, in every presidential campaign and throughout his time as president, repeatedly painted cities as crime-infested hellscapes. He ignores the facts cited above as well as the data showing that the U.S. murder rate fell during Biden's presidency, including in 2023 when it dropped by 11.6% —the single biggest one-year decline ever recorded (Arango, 2024). Similarly, the violent crime rate hit a 50-year low in 2023—this despite the large increase in the number of migrants and the "deadly plague of migrant crime" Trump falsely claimed they instigated, and for which he blamed the Biden-Harris administration (C. Brennan, 2024; Bump, 2024b; Contreras, 2024; Krugman, 2024a; Nilsson et al., 2024). On August 20, 2024, in Detroit he also contended that the "Kamala crime wave" had brought about levels of crime "nobody has ever seen before" (Mauger, 2024), but which he would, of course, greatly reduce. These falsehoods are central to building his support. On September 28 and 29, 2024, he gave his audience a series of very specific numbers about immigrants and crime that were completely made up, as a CNN fact check explained:

> Trump falsely claimed Friday and Saturday that the statistics are specifically about criminal offenders who entered the U.S. during the Biden-Harris administration; in reality, the figures are about offenders who entered the U.S. over multiple decades, including during the Trump administration. And Trump falsely claimed that the statistics are specifically about people who are now living freely in the U.S.; the figures actually include people who are currently in jails and prisons serving criminal sentences (Dale, 2024c).

These lies have an impact on Americans' perceptions of reality, or at least those of some Americans. A CBS poll found that respondents who believed that immigrants "commit more crimes" support Trump over Harris 83% to 17% (Salvanto et al., 2024).

On a related note, there also exists a tremendous partisan gap on perceptions of crime levels. An October 2024 Gallup survey asked respondents: "Is there more crime in the U.S. than there was a year ago, or less?," 90% of Republicans but only 28% of Democrats said more (Brenan, 2024). Likewise, the survey asked if the problem of crime was either "extremely serious, very serious, moderately serious, not too serious or not serious at all?," 78% of Republicans but only 35% of Democrats responded that it was either extremely or very serious. Gallup conducts this survey annually, and during Trump's time in the White House the partisan gaps were much smaller and, in some years, non-existent. According to the same survey, the gap was larger during Obama's presidency than Trump's and then exploded to historic levels under Biden. Overall, this data from Gallup suggests that Republicans' perceptions of crime in the U.S. have recently grown more and more dependent on who is president, while Democrats' perceptions track the actual data far more closely. The Republican misperception flows from their significantly greater consumption of right-wing media, which has downplayed the drop in U.S. violent crime during the Biden presidency. In fact, Fox News presented falsehoods aimed at undermining the FBI data released on September 23, 2024, which shows the most recent decline (Passantino and Reilly, 2024). News anchor Bret Baier reported that "critics say the report is not accurate because it does not include big cities." (Passantino and Reilly, 2024). Right-wing social media spread this lie, but the FBI noted that "every city agency covering a population of 1,000,000 or more inhabitants contributed a full 12 months of data" (Passantino and Reilly, 2024). By reporting what "critics say," Baier can claim he did not lie. But he certainly played a part in spreading the lie and shaping his viewers' (mis)perceptions.

Furthermore, this kind of reporting complemented Trump's strategy on crime, which *New York Times* fact-checker Linda Qiu (2024b) explained: "has evolved this election cycle from false claims on crime rates to an attack on the credibility of any evidence that refutes him." Qiu continued: "This dark assessment of soaring violence and lawlessness under Mr. Biden and Ms. Harris has been central to Mr. Trump's re-election campaign—even though the facts show otherwise."

Returning to Trump's August 20th Detroit speech, the twice-elected president offered a picture one can perhaps charitably characterize as a wild exaggeration, or more accurately call a flat-out lie:

> The crime is so out of control in our country. I mean, you have cities—I will say this, the top 25, almost all are run by Democrats, and they have very similar policies. It's just insane. But you can't walk across the street to get a loaf of bread. You get shot. You get mugged. You get raped, you get whatever it may be. And you've seen it and I've seen it, and it's time for a change. We have to bring back our cities. We have these cities that are great cities where people are afraid to live in them, and they're fleeing the cities of our country. (Bump, 2024b).

On October 10, Trump again cited Detroit—an overwhelmingly black-populated city—as a model for what America would look like if he did not return to the White House: "Our whole country will end up being like Detroit if (Harris is) your president. You're going to have a mess on your hands" (Main, 2024).

Socialization and Trump's invoking of the familiar

It is through socialization that biases are introduced and reinforced. Once we are socialized to be familiar with a stereotype, it is available for use in our perceptual processes. There are many ways bias occurs in the interpretation stage, including the following:

- Fundamental attribution error is the tendency to attribute other people's behavior to internal causes rather than the social or environmental forces affecting them (Heider, 1958) such that we blame people for their mistakes rather than give them the benefit of the doubt.
- Actor-observer effect is the tendency for people to attribute their actions to external forces but the behavior of others to internal reasons such that we blame

our own mistakes on external factors that are presumably out of our control. (Fiske and Taylor, 1991).

- Self-serving bias is when people make an internal attribution that allows them to take credit for their success, regardless of whether they are the cause of that success (Fiske and Taylor, 1991) such that when things go well for us, we give credit to ourselves rather than to external factors out of our control.
- A positivity bias occurs when our gestalts—general global impressions of a person—are more likely to be positive than negative (Fiske and Taylor, 1984).
- The halo effect is the "tendency to positively interpret nearly anything someone says or does because we have a positive gestalt of them" (Nisbett and Wilson, 1977).
- The horn effect is the tendency to negatively interpret nearly anything someone says or does because we have a negative gestalt about them (Noor et al., 2023).

When it comes to how we interpret information, these are merely a selection of the many biases that cause us to "know what isn't so" (Gilovich, 1993).

As a result of our biases, Trump's stereotypes become more than assertions of the characteristics attributed to a group. Their implications stretch well beyond the moment in which he communicates them. They dig deeper into our past and our minds. They extend farther into the future to impact our beliefs, behavior, and interactions with the targeted groups. Trump's stereotypes do not just reflect the beliefs of his audience, they shape and sharpen the prejudices people hold about the members of targeted groups. As Enns and Jardina (2021) explained:

> The strong association between Trump support and whites' views on racial issues identified in previous studies . . . was not merely a result of Trump attracting racist whites by way of his own racist rhetoric, or as a reflection of partisan racial sorting that had already occurred; it was also a result of white Trump supporters changing their views to be more in line with Trump's over the course of his presidential campaign. In other words, Trump not only attracted whites with more conservative views on race; he also made his white supporters more likely to express more extreme views on issues related to immigration and on issues like the Black Lives Matter movement and police killings of African Americans (pp. 541–42).

On the long-term impact of Trumpist language on American society, Enns and Jardina noted:

> Our results also paint a potentially more pessimistic picture than much literature on race and the 2016 election. Rather than driving whites away with his racially charged rhetoric, or at least limiting his appeal to those whites who were already antagonistic to Black Americans and immigrants, we find that Trump may have pushed many whites to become more hostile toward these groups—an outcome that does not bode well for the future of race relations in

the United States, particularly if future political candidates attempt to adopt racialized strategies similar to Trump's. Even if they lose, our results show that when politicians race-bait white voters during political campaigns, they may not merely be making pre-existing racial hostilities more salient, they may also be contributing to greater levels of racial animus among their core supporters (p. 566).

When Trump, for example, tried in 2020 to scare "people living their Suburban Lifestyle Dream" about Democratic policies he claimed would lead to "low-income housing [being] built in your neighborhood," he evokes the same racist fears that led many whites to flee cities for the suburbs a half-century ago—a phenomenon known as white flight (Karni et al., 2020). White flight drew on both fears—however exaggerated—for family members' personal safety due to increased crime, and the economic fear of watching the family home—which made up the bulk of most middle-class families' net worth—lose its value, potentially sending the family tumbling out of the middle class itself (Pais et al., 2009).

The twice-elected president was referring to the Affirmatively Furthering Fair Housing rule—implemented under Obama—that aimed to promote greater housing integration in the suburbs. Trump rescinded the rule on July 23, 2020, then Biden reinstated it shortly after taking office, only for Trump to undo it again on March 11, 2025. Along the same lines, Trump—who himself has a documented history of racial discrimination when it comes to his own properties (NPR Staff, 2016)—noted in 2020: "People fight all of their lives to get into the suburbs and have a beautiful home," and then added that if he won re-election: "There will be no more low-income housing forced into the suburbs." However, if Biden were to win, he "will destroy your neighborhood and your American Dream" (Karni et al., 2020). Unsurprisingly, Trump returned to this theme in 2024, telling voters that a Harris victory would mean "the suburbs will be overrun with violent crime and savage foreign gangs" (Weissert and Price, 2024). Just three days before the election, his imagery grew even more lurid: "The suburbs are under attack right now. When you're home in your house alone and you have this monster that got out of prison, he's got six charges of murdering six different people, I think you'd rather have Trump" (Leary, 2024). Such rhetoric tracks with other statements of his, namely that black and Latino Americans are "poor" and reside in places that are "unfit for human beings" (Slotkin, 2024, p. 303). Trump warned that Democrats want 'scary' black and brown criminals to move into your nice, white, suburban communities—a stereotype-laden message that both draws on and exacerbates fear and hate learned through socialization.

As mentioned previously, we are more likely to retain and retransmit information that is consistent with existing stereotypes. Thus, Trump's language on crime, cities, and suburbs gets spread far beyond his original assertions. He communicates stereotypes about urban (read: black) crime, which invoke the past experience of his target audience—even an imagined or mythologized past their parents or grandparents experienced, e. g., mid-20th century white flight. In doing so, the twice-elected president motivates people today to vote for him on the basis of policies like his opposition to encouraging residential desegregation through government support for low-income housing.

Trump grew up in Jamaica Estates, a wealthy, overwhelmingly white enclave in the New York City borough of Queens that his father played a significant role in building, and which—like the suburbs—consisted then (and to a good degree now) largely of free standing, single-family homes (Horowitz, 2015). Equally importantly, the Trumps lived barely a mile from Jamaica, then a mostly black and poor area. He has a visceral, almost tribal connection to the fears he now peddles about race, place, and crime. African Americans moving into *his* neighborhood—something he and his father sought to prevent through illegal discrimination—almost certainly provides the foundation of his entire worldview on these matters (Garcia, 2016). As Garcia (2016) put it: "Trump and many of his supporters would likely prefer the Jamaica Estates of the 1950s—homogenous, prosperous, and white, still protected by gates—multiplied to fit all over the country."

Stereotypes to the rescue: Prediction

There are two metaphors that help explain how humans use stereotypes to process the vast amounts of information they receive in each moment. First, people are intuitive scientists. This means we are theory-driven and want to explain the world (Nisbett and Ross, 1980). We are motivated to observe and collect information, look for patterns, and find causal—not necessarily correlational—relationships so that we can make predictions. Often the problem with our attempts is that once we have an answer that confirms our prior expectations, regardless of its accuracy, we stop looking for or even reject hearing evidence that could prove contradictory. As mentioned in Chapter 2, this is called confirmation bias.

A second metaphor is that we are cognitive misers. According to the cognitive miser metaphor (Fiske and Taylor, 1984), people stingily conserve their mental capacities by processing data quickly and economically (Hamilton and Sherman, 1994). As cognitive misers, stereotypes function as our categorization "tools" (Gilbert and Hixon, 1991, p. 510) that preserve information processing resources and act as energy saving devices (Macrae et al., 1994). Ryan, Park, and Judd (1996) concisely explain how stereotypes function in cognitive processes: "According to the cognitive approach, human beings have a limited capacity for processing information. Stereotypes serve to organize and simplify a complex social world and they are often likely to take the form of overgeneralizations" (p. 123). Stereotypes work for people because they describe characteristics about groups (Kurylo, 2013) that enable us to infer information, regardless of its accuracy, when we think of, talk about, or come into contact with a member of a particular group, while also allowing us to ignore other information unrelated to stereotypes about that same group. Because of the utility of these tools and the limited resources that people have to process tremendous amounts of data, Baron (1995), more cynically, argues that "we are less cognitive misers than social realists trying to do what works in specific sociobehavioral settings" (p. 115).

As his base looks to test their predictions, Trump's stereotypes help with information processing. He serves as a 'truth bringer' who says out loud what everyone is already assuming to be the case due to stereotype-based expectancies. Political correctness and, in current terms, wokeness dissuade most people from stating these stereotypical predictions, but not Trump. When he violates a supposedly woke belief by offering stereotype-based predictions of doom relating to the 'invasion' of migrants or the 'browning of America', just to cite two of many examples, he presents himself as a truth bringer using his predictions to protect America from harm. For the sake of comprehensiveness, the would-be Nostradamus makes plenty of other predictions as well, namely that his opponent will destroy Social Security, Medicare, our economy, our democracy, and so on (Blake, 2024b).

A dog whistle is a sound that only dogs or, when it comes to politics, some people who are attuned to them can hear. The twice-elected president's stereotypes often act as something even more explicit than a typical dog whistle. Most people have a sense of what he means, and those who support him generally understand when they are being called upon to process information through a lens that reflects a MAGA worldview. His conservative white base certainly understands that Trump, when he talks about 'Making America Great Again,' is aiming to bring back the United States of the segregated 1950s, at least in terms of white, straight, Christian men exercising a predominant share of cultural as well as political power (Steinhorn, 2022).

The downside of stereotyping

Problems with information processing exist. Cognitive processes are value-laden, omit important details, and add in often unnecessary ones. Moreover, the bias inherent in perception serves as a mechanism for perpetuating hate and the high-stakes, harmful outcomes associated with it (Hamilton et al., 1990; Hinton, 2000; Kurylo, 2013; Lippmann, 1922). Stereotypes are inherently packed with emotional and social baggage that have consequences for the targets of the stereotype because they are not necessarily accurate. Stereotypes erroneously treated as factual can feed prejudice and discrimination that affect life-altering decisions, such as who is approved for a mortgage loan (Stempel, 2007; Press Release, 2022).

The history of redlining reflects exactly this process (Federal Reserve History, 2023). Bigotry toward black Americans and fear—based on stereotypes—that their moving into a given neighborhood would negatively impact the white residents drove a federal government policy that enshrined in law the deliberate, across the board denial of loans to African Americans looking to live anywhere outside a black neighborhood. The Federal Housing Administration's own 1938 manual stated that it sought to prevent the "infiltration of inharmonious racial groups" into white areas (Federal Reserve History, 2023). From 1934 until the practice was banned by the Fair Housing Act of 1968, racial discrimination was official U.S. government policy, and stereotypes stood at its foundation.

Stereotypes act as figurative noise—just like a horn honking loudly when you are trying to hear someone—that obscures the content of a message. Trump's stereotypes make it hard for his audience to assess the accuracy of what he is saying. Instead, many on the right have a positivity bias toward whatever he says, while many on the left have a knee-jerk negativity bias. And even if his record seems to justify the latter, such bias prevents people from absorbing any true or accurate statements he might make. Both prevent people from experiencing information beyond what their selectivities allow.

With regard to Trump and prejudices that his rhetoric stokes, forewarned is forearmed. We can begin to process the information shared by the twice-elected president—or indeed any politician or person—by having an increased awareness of our own perceptual processes. Of those affected by Trump's stereotypes, there is a giveaway or a tell that can serve as a signal, namely when he addresses a stereotyped group by using the word "they" as in, "well, you know how *they* are." Using the word "they" is particularly powerful as a rhetorical and stereotypical tool because it invokes a dichotomy between an "us" and a "them." Doing so is a highly effective way to set up factions and stoke division.

Chapter 4
Social Identity Theory and Group Vitality Theory: The fight against the "angry left-wing mob"

Absolute and irrevocable division does not occur in nature. Nature provides for variation, movement, and dynamism. For example, in places where there are four seasons, spring and fall assist in the transition to the harsher extremes of summer and winter. Even what we so often, too often, take for granted as a natural, inherent divide is not the case. Continents divided by water for millions of years were once connected in the form of the single supercontinent Pangaea. Long before there were terms in the mainstream like transgender, genderfluid, and nonbinary that counter the more traditional gender binary narrative, there have always been people who were born not distinctly or genetically fitting neatly within that binary—either physically (i.e., intersex), or who did not fully identify with either gender (Stockett, 2005). Despite this well-documented reality, Trump incorrectly claimed on February 1, 2023, that these ideas around gender represent: "a concept that was never heard of in all of human history... It was all when the radical left invented it just a few years ago" (Trump, 2023a). Exceptions are one of many types of possible variations that nature allows for. For every species that has seemingly immutable characteristics, there are mutations that allow for exceptions. Because of their rarity, many people may be unaware that such mutations exist or, as is sometimes the case, they may be close to non-existent. This, for example, is the case with the white or albino rhino, a mutated version of the rhinoceros, which has been reduced to only two left on Earth (Almond, 2024).

Political division

Although the idea of an inherently fixed, unrelenting, and enduring division is a myth, it indisputably remains a powerful one. The World Economic Forum has declared that: "societal polarization" is a top three immediate risk for humanity (World Economic Forum, 2024). However, make no mistake, the makeup of the 'divided' sides have repeatedly shifted over time. In the U.S., for example, the Republicans were the party of Abraham Lincoln, and by the mid-1860s strongly supported legal equality as well as varying degrees of civil rights for black Americans, while Democrats of the time were pro-slavery and pro-segregation. However, from the 1960s through today black Americans have overwhelmingly voted for Democrats over Republicans. Likewise, the socially accepted definition (separate from the

https://doi.org/10.1515/9783111426327-007

legal distinctions in Jim Crow America) of 'white' in the early 20th century did not necessarily include Jewish, Italian, or Slavic immigrants, a definition that evolved to include those groups more clearly after World War II (Kelkar, 2017).

Because free will allows for infinite varieties of emotional expression, knowledge, and experience, people are innately complex, rendering the idea of absolute division less credible. At no time can an individual be entirely divided from another individual. While two people may be divided on one social or political issue, it is unlikely that those two will be divided on every issue. Enter a third person and the likelihood is that whatever issue the first two *are* divided on, the third person will be divided from each of them on different issues. Sam and Tracey may be adamantly divided over Issue A, but Chris may be at odds with Sam on Issue B and at odds with Tracey on Issue C, whereas Sam and Tracey are both in agreement on Issues B and C. Though this example demonstrates the point with only three issues, it is worthy of note that the World Economic Forum identified over 30 substantive issues that can divide people (or not). Furthermore, they identify how these issues are not discrete but rather interconnected (World Economic Forum, 2024). The takeaway is that no two people can be completely and permanently divided from each other. Division occurs along some number of issues understood in a given social moment and historical context, and is not eternal or applicable across the board. Variability is normal in nature.

The suspension of disbelief

The concept of 'division' as an absolute, fixed, and immutable state of being only works if we suspend our disbelief. This suspension of disbelief can produce a great and awful impact. Apartheid states and genocides in countries around the world demonstrate the cost of viewing a people as absolutely divided. These commonly discussed Western examples demonstrate some tropes that have historically been the focal point of division around the world.

–   Religious belief versus scientific knowledge as an absolute division is a longstanding divide. For example, though in 1543 Copernicus proposed that the earth revolved around the sun in his heliocentric findings, nearly 100 years later Galileo was sentenced to house arrest for life as a heretic for endorsing the idea.

–   Fear of communism has been a repeated theme of division—in the U.S., all Americans must either be Communists or loyal patriots. The Red Scare of 1919–1920 and McCarthyism in the 1950s separated large numbers of families and destroyed many lives.

– A belief in racial division has haunted generations. In Nazi Germany, because of a belief in eugenics and the supposed racial superiority of the Aryan/Nordic 'race,' people who were Jewish or otherwise non-Aryan, had disabilities, or were viewed at the time as deviant were targeted for sterilization, forced migration, torture, or, ultimately, extermination.

Division and, at its core, difference have always existed. How we view, define, and treat these phenomena has a significant impact. For example, a belief that black people were inherently better suited for enslavement rather than freedom undergirded the race-based system of slavery in the post-Columbus era Americas. Similarly, the aforementioned Trump comments (see Chapter 1) defining black people as possessing a "trait" for "laziness" reflects this kind of division.

Difference

Division necessarily involves high levels of emotion because of the consequences that flow therefrom. This emotional element can cloud how we understand the meaning of various differences. Difference between groups is the fundamental mechanism underlying and undergirding division. To remove the emotion from an understanding of difference, one foundational study centered on the entirely unemotional act of differentiating between lengths of lines (Tajfel and Wilkes, 1963). Participants in a control group and a treatment group both received a set of six lines of varying lengths. Researchers colored the groupings of lines only for the treatment group; one set was black (for the three shorter lines) and the other red (for the three longer lines). Researchers found that those participants who viewed the colored groupings of lines identified their lengths differently than did those in the control group—even though the lines placed into each grouping were consistent for both sets of participants. Moreover, this categorizing of the groups of lines also affected future line groupings. The study showed that once people are given a way to categorize, they may be more likely to use those categories, even when presented implicitly, to polarize and exaggerate differences between the perceived groups.

This new understanding of the impact of naming, often a communicative act, represented a fundamental shift in the research on stereotypes at the time. Rather than stereotyping being an inherently mental process determined and controlled by individuals in their own mind, the social aspect was now brought to the forefront, helping to make scholars aware that there was "not enough research on how stereotypes function in our social lives" (Schneider, 1996, p. 421). Moreover, and more recently, it has become a commonplace assertion that stereotypes are tools through which, as Kitzinger (2000) discusses, the social order of power and oppression are "processes continually created and sustained... in interaction" (p. 167).

Some scholars have argued that stereotyping is inherently an interactional process and have stressed the need to study stereotyping in the interactional contexts in which they occur (Dovidio et al., 1996; Fiske and Taylor, 1984; Schneider, 1996). This is a logical extension of stereotype research because stereotyping is often triggered through visually salient characteristics of age, gender, and race made available in interactions (Fiske and Taylor, 1984; Schneider, 1996; Hamilton and Sherman, 1994). Division among human groups, whether visually triggered or otherwise, has at its core two simple words: 'us' and 'them'.

Us and them

The simple group differentiation between 'us' and 'them' is universally understood, comforting, appealing, persuasive, and motivating. Research from a cognitive approach (see Chapter 3) productively explored how cognitive schemata such as stereotypes reduce vast amounts of data into manageable pieces. However, the limitation of this research domain is that focusing solely on perceptual processes necessarily overlooks the social component of stereotypes. The importance of this social component is nowhere more self-evident than in the famous boys' camp studies (Sherif et al., 1961). This research took a behaviorist approach, arguing that division among people had, at its root, not pre-existing prejudice, but rather was the outcome of a relatively simple stimulus and response association. Social Identity Theory does not assume that a person's motive is to derogate groups (Stroebe and Insko, 1989). Instead this theory argues that the steps a person undergoes when acquiring prejudice mirror the processes involved in any other type of learning (Stroebe and Insko, 1989). In this way, Social Identity Theory distinguishes between division based on prejudice and that which occurs in the absence of or is independent from prejudicial thoughts and feelings.

The boys' camp studies (Sherif et al., 1961) demonstrated how manipulating interactions trigger stereotypes as a basic response. The boys in these studies had no preconceived divisions among them, no history or experiences that might be viewed as warranting the actions. None of them knew each other. Like what occurred in the study of lines mentioned earlier, the mere placement of individuals into groups and the assignment of specific names to those groups resulted in exaggeration and polarization. Through manipulating the environment to be competitive through games that awarded prizes and perks, the researchers were able to trigger the groups to communicate stereotypes. Boys in the study were from similar demographic backgrounds and were randomly assigned to groups. Despite this, their placement into these groups led to group members differentiating themselves from members of the other group. This categorization creates meaning for the individual (McGarty, 2002). Group members viewed and treated themselves as bonded to their named group and treated fellow group members as a part of their ingroup. Ingroup members then began communicating stereotypes targeting members of the other group, which is defined as their outgroup. Social Identity Theory explains that members of groups differentiate themselves in this way in order to meet self-esteem needs. (Hamilton and Sherman, 1994).

Social Identity Theory (e.g., Tajfal, 1969) posits that individuals "derive their social identities from group membership" (Oakes et al., 1994, p. 8). People have a basic human motivation for social comparison (McGarty et al., 2002). This theory predicts that dividing people into these two named groups allows ingroup members to view themselves in a positive light (McGarty, 2002) along with bolstering the individual member's self-esteem (Oakes et al., 1994) juxtaposed with outgroup members whom they viewed negatively by contrast. Based on a behavioral conditioning model and social learning (Bandura, 1963), this line of research exposed the transiency of division by showing that stereotypes can be triggered by "labels [that] are acquired through social learning and are maintained through social reinforcement" (Hamilton and Sherman, 1994, p. 48). These studies emphasize: "the importance of the social environment in the formation and maintenance of stereotypic belief systems" (Hamilton and Sherman, 1994, p. 48).

Certainly, stereotypes can be consistent over time. Karlins et al. (1969), replicating Katz and Braly (1933) and Gilbert (1951), found that after three generations of research on stereotypes in America: "the collections of traits selected to characterize specific groups are very much alike from one generation to the next" (p. 14). As such this information becomes part of the American cultural knowledge base that people absorb through socialization, much as they do other aspects of culture such as customs, norms, rituals, traditions, and values (Stangor and Schaller, 1996). Stereotype maintenance research explores the communication processes that facilitate this reproduction of stereotypes over time (Kenrick et al., 2002). However, what the boys' camp studies showed is that stereotypes need not be regularly communicated. Even the simplest designations of Group A and Group B could prime people to communicate stereotypes, for example Group A touting their dominance for simply (and arbitrarily) being in the "A" group. Divisions, therefore, are not natural or enduring. They are products of the messages we send and receive in our interactions with others.

Think of the word associations we have that trigger a polarized response: light or dark, top or bottom, old or young. Extend this discussion of polarized labels further to terms like men or women, gay or straight, black or white, Republican or

Democrat, conservative or liberal. These categories—widely perceived as binary even if they are not in reality—do not even require that both terms be uttered. Indeed, just saying one in the pair is enough to prompt someone to think of or state the other—a seemingly reflex-like response. Sacks' economy rule (1992) tells us: "a single category from any membership categorization device can be referentially adequate" (p. 333) to enable the recipient of the message to infer that the other category is also referenced, and in a contrasting way (Boss, 1979). For example, Trump has often characterized his opponent as "weak" and/or "not strong," in contrast to his own alleged strength—for one example among many, as he did multiple times at different rallies on a single day, August 5, 2016, in attacking Hillary Clinton (Diamond, 2016).

The twice-elected president ran an ad during the 2024 Republican primary contest that attacked another female opponent—in this case the one who ultimately got the second most votes and earned the second most delegates, former South Carolina Governor and UN Ambassador Nikki Haley. The ad bore the title "Weakness." He also ran an ad against Kamala Harris with the same title. Maureen Dowd (2024a) analyzed it thusly:

> The ad claims Harris is not tough enough to deal with China, Russia, Iran or Hamas. It features actors playing Vladimir Putin, Hamas fighters and a tea-sipping ayatollah watching videos of the candidate who wants to be the first woman president. It ends with four clips of Kamala dancing—a lot better than Trump does—and a clip of Trump walking on a tarmac with a military officer and a Secret Service agent. The tag line is: "America doesn't need another TikTok performer. We need the strength that will protect us."

Trump contends that strength—which he claims to possess in great quantities—is a prerequisite to be president, and that the weakness of his various opponents over the years has disqualified any of them from holding the office.

Furthermore, Trump repeatedly codes the strength he possesses as male, as seen in the "Weakness" ads described above, or in this 2019 statement where he cites traditionally male groups as being on his side: "I have the support of the police, the support of the military, the support of the Bikers for Trump – I have the tough people, but they don't play it tough – until they go to a certain point, and then it would be very bad, very bad" (Stracqualursi, 2019). Note that Trump also threatens that these "tough" groups might get violent if they do not get what they want, something he threatens more or less obliquely on a regular basis (Blake, 2024a). Poniewozik (2024) characterized the final night of the 2024 Republican National Convention as beginning with a "pageant of hypermasculinity, with musclemen and ripped garments" who offered "testimony to [Trump's] macho fighting spirit." Poniewozik added: "This is what male identity politics looks like." More broadly, Serwer (2024b) offered that "reactionary masculinity" is "emblematic of the Trump era, as if conservatives listened to feminist critiques of 'toxic masculinity' and decided to shear all virtue from their conception of traditional manhood and retain only those parts that involve dominance and exploitation of others."

These kinds of hypermasculine men, as well as the man they support, are "alpha" males—strong and dominant. Trump codes any man who opposes him and supports Democrats as a "beta male"—in other words, weak. He hurled this epithet at Howard Stern in October 2024, after the host endorsed Harris and broadcast an in-depth interview with the Democrat (Kellman, 2024). At a dinner that same month, Trump similarly offered the following: "There's a group called 'White Dudes for Harris,' but I'm not worried about them at all, because their wives and their wives' lovers are all voting for me" (Green, 2024). He is clearly coding male Harris supporters as being not real, masculine men, suggesting that they cannot even satisfy their wives sexually. They are instead cuckolds, a word that has —along with "beta"—become a particular obsession on the far right and among Trump supporters (Roy, 2016). JD Vance, for example, likewise highlighted research that "connect[s] testosterone levels in young men with conservative politics" (Cameron et al., 2024).

In 2024 Trump engaged in a media outreach strategy specifically aimed at reaching male voters by appearing numerous times on podcasts and with social media influencers who have disproportionately male audiences (Kurtzleben, 2024)—a group of platforms collectively dubbed the "manosphere" (Haskins, 2024), and which overall strongly backed the Republican nominee. Years of political correctness (see Chapter 1), which included widespread condemnation of 'toxic masculinity,' produced a profound cultural backlash. The election of Trump in 2016 and, perhaps, even more so in 2024 given his campaign's systematic weaponization of masculinity, represents that backlash's most lasting impact.

Ingroups and outgroups

Stereotypes aid the categorization of people into ingroups and outgroups often identifiable in communication using the words 'us' and 'them' (Kurylo, 2013). This is not surprising considering that the definition of stereotypes includes absolute presumptions about group identities. People consider members of ingroups to be complex, multi-dimensional, and necessarily as unique, distinct individuals. We typically avoid generalizing about ingroup members and, instead, we personalize and individuate when discussing or thinking about them. Therefore, we see significant heterogeneity within our ingroup. Nevertheless, perhaps even ironically, we simultaneously underestimate differences between ourselves and our fellow ingroup members (Hilton and Von Hippel, 1996). In this way, identifying one similarity with an ingroup member begets the assumption that more similarities exist within the group. When we identify a difference, we discount additional and otherwise potentially meaningful differences among members. Allport (1954/1979) explains that with ingroup members we assume a shared past that provides cohesion and enhances group bonding. As a result, this encourages us to believe that we have things in common.

Allport (1954/1979) notes that a "reflex preference for the familiar grips us all" (p. 44), in part, because "it requires less effort to deal with people who have similar suppositions" (p. 17). This preference for viewing our own ingroups positively results in bias, and can cause ethnocentrism. Ultimately, "the familiar is preferred. What is alien is regarded as somewhat inferior, less 'good', but there is not necessarily hostility against it" (Allport (1954/1979, p. 42). Of course, every cultural group has something of value to offer and no group is inherently superior. However, learning about other groups takes effort, uses resources, and can be frustrating. Hence, we have a preference for people who we view as like ourselves.

In sharp contrast to ingroup members, people consider the outgroup to exist as a single, collective entity where generalization (Allport, 1954/1979) and base rates apply as discussed in Chapter 2. Ingroup members view outgroup members as one-dimensional and homogeneous (Hamilton and Sherman, 1994; Hilton and Von Hippel, 1996). To ingroup members, outgroups "inevitably seem outlandish and, if not inferior, at least slightly absurd and unnecessary" (Allport, 1954/1979, p. 43).[16] Moreover, ingroup members will be inclined to interpret ostensibly nonnegative behavior by an outgroup member as negative. For example, white men may consider women of any race speaking with one another at the 'water cooler' to be gossiping, and consider black men doing the same to be goofing off. In contrast, white men may presume other members of their group to be talking about business.

Overall, ingroup members will assume differences exist between themselves and members of the outgroup, and overemphasize the importance of these differences. This includes an assumption of distinctly different pasts, upbringing, and experiences. Ingroup members may augment rather than discount the differences between the two groups such that even "a minor offense, overlooked in a member of our own group, seems intolerable when committed by a member of an outgroup" (Allport, 1954/1979, p. 139). Moreover, the presumption of difference may result in the ingroup members viewing the outgroup as so different that their needs are not the ingroup members' concern (i.e., not my problem). The ingroup/out-

---

16 See also Miner, 1956; Bohannan, 1966.

group distinction results in a familiar/unfamiliar prejudice such that we do not feel obligated to seek out more information about an outgroup member or the outgroup itself. After all, "even a citizen without prejudices of his own is likely to blind himself to injustices and tensions, which if acknowledged, could only upset the even tenor of his life" (Allport, 1954/1979, p. 503).

Donald Trump creates the enemy

Donald Trump's rhetorical bifurcation of the American populace into divided groups helped propel him to the presidency in 2016 (Major, Blodorn and Major Blascovich, 2018; Reifowitz, 2019). Trump—certainly with help from many of his fellow Republicans—promotes the idea that America is divided. If the mechanism for division—for creating 'us' and 'them'—is labeling a group, then Trump is the master mechanic. He did not invent this strategy, nor is he the only one to use it (Reifowitz, 2019). Rather, it is a relatively common process predicted by Social Identity Theory. First, one defines the ingroup. In doing so, the twice-elected president not only includes ideological conservatives and Republicans, but also adds everyone among the American people more broadly who want to "Make America Great Again"—his speech on July 4, 2020, at Mount Rushmore (The White House, 2020), which we discuss below, provides but one example among many. In doing this over and over again, he is able to make his ingroup appear rather large—and much larger than a single political party. These concentric circles grow from the same central point—Trump himself.

Second, name the ingroup. Trump does this along jingoistic or nationalistic lines through which patriotism is defined by association with the twice-elected president himself as well as the American greatness at the center of his political brand (The White House, 2020). He is the person who will lead the people to make America great, again. Trump, to his base, then becomes synonymous with patriotism, nationalism, and Americanism. The ingroup, as defined by his political rhetoric, are Americans, or at least staunchly 'pro-America' Americans. The Americans Trump refers to include his base of supporters but, in theory, the group could include all U.S. citizens (at least anyone willing to accept his vision of the country). The use of "again" in the slogan 'MAGA' proclaims that America had previously reached great heights but had since fallen, necessitating the need to be made great again.

Third, name and define the outgroup because, after all, "unless we can identify our enemy, we cannot attack him" (Allport, 1954/1979, p. 139). Trump's self-defined American base is decidedly anti-immigrant (at least anti-immigrants of color), as undocumented immigrants are one of the primary outgroups he targets.

Trump adviser Stephen Miller—noted for driving the twice-elected president's immigration policy—proclaimed at the October 27, 2024, Madison Square Garden campaign event that only his boss would fight for the principle that "America is for Americans and Americans only" (Goldmacher, Haberman and Gold, 2024). For Trump, the immigrants he targets are animals rather than human beings (see Chapter 2), they are taking American jobs (see Chapters 1 and 2), poisoning America's bloodline (see Chapter 2), and some—he was specifically referring here to black immigrants from Haiti or Africa—come from "shithole countries" (Fram and Lemire, 2018). Trump likewise stated that Haitian immigrants "all have AIDS," and offered that if the U.S. permitted Nigerians to enter the country, it would be impossible to get them to "go back to their huts" (Bump, 2021).

In his February 5, 2019, State of the Union address, Trump offered a rapid-fire list of ways undocumented immigrants harm society, detailing how "working-class Americans are left to pay the price for mass illegal immigration, reduced jobs, lower wages, over-burdened schools, hospitals that are so crowded you can't get in, increased crime, and a depleted social safety net" (NPR Staff, 2019). Although Trump's message often plays on white racial anxiety, here and elsewhere he made a non-racial, economic argument in order to appeal to the fears of non-white Americans about the impact these immigrants might have on their own lives (Medina, 2024). On a related note, the twice-elected president often asserted without evidence that: "illegal immigrants are treated better in America than many of our vets," and claimed that liberal politicians like Barack Obama and Hillary Clinton prioritized the undocumented over U.S. veterans (cited in Sides et al., 2018, p. 176). Other similar Trump lies included: "illegal immigrant households receive far more in welfare benefits" (cited in Sides et al., 2018, p. 176).

As Slotkin (2024) pointed out, "Trump weaponized popular anxieties over immigration by framing the issue as a form of 'savage war,' identifying the enemy as non-White and primitive," and added that Trump's rhetoric on immigration is defined by: "fear of intrusion by cultural aliens" (p. 305). Slotkin further noted that Trump connected together:

> The immigrant onslaught to a supposed economic war being waged by the Mexican state: through its exploitation of NAFTA, that Brown nation was humiliating White America: "They're laughing at us, at our stupidity." He would characterize the arrival of economic migrants and refugees as an "invasion" riding in "caravans" supported by Mexico; by sinister liberal activists like the Jewish billionaire philanthropist George Soros, an iconic bogeyman of the Far Right; and of course by politically correct Democrats. In a tweet he echoed [Trump adviser] Stephen Miller's "replacement" theory: "Democrats . . . want illegal immigrants, no matter how bad they may be, to pour into and infest our Country, like MS-13. They can't win on their terrible policies, so they view them as potential voters!" (p. 305).

Trump has repeatedly made the baseless claim that Democrats have been enabling millions of "illegal immigrants" to vote (see Chapter 2), and that this continues to pose a threat to election integrity today. As elections expert Richard Hasen told *The New York Times*, in this rhetoric: "the immigrant becomes the boogeyman" (Bensinger and Fausset, 2024). Democrats are the people who bring the boogeyman inside your house, which is why the twice-elected president characterized the opposing party on Twitter as an "angry left-wing mob" who: "have become too EXTREME and DANGEROUS to govern" (Scott, 2018).

Trump's lies on this matter connect to the white nationalist/white supremacist "Great Replacement Theory" promulgated by Stephen Miller and Tucker Carlson among others, according to which liberals plan to: "replace" white Americans with dark-skinned immigrants—presumably to bring in enough of them to reduce whites to a relatively powerless minority in an increasingly diverse society (Swenson and Alexander, 2023). According to an AP-NORC (2022) poll conducted in December 2021, 47% of Republicans believe that: "a group of people in this country are trying to replace native-born Americans with immigrants who agree with their political views"—more than twice the percentage of independents and Democrats.

Tiki-torch carrying neo-Nazis voiced these sentiments at the infamous 2017 Charlottesville march, chanting alternatively "you will not replace us" and "Jews will not replace us"—this references the belief that Jewish liberals were predominantly driving the so-called Great Replacement (Rosenberg, 2017). On a related note, a number of white supremacists, including David Duke and Richard Spencer, praised Trump for saying—after the violence that left one anti-Nazi protester dead —that there were "very fine people on both sides" (Thrush and Haberman, 2017). *The New York Times* reported that, in these remarks, the twice-elected president: "buoyed the white nationalist movement on Tuesday as no president has done in generations, equating activists protesting racism with the neo-Nazis and white supremacists who rampaged in Charlottesville" (Thrush and Haberman, 2017). In 2022, he also hosted an intimate dinner for four people at his Mar-a-Lago home that included Kanye West—who had very recently faced widespread denunciation after making antisemitic remarks—and Nick Fuentes (see Chapter 1), who has an extensive public record of antisemitism and Holocaust denial (Haberman and Feuer, 2022). During the 2024 campaign, Trump brought Laura Loomer—who has, likewise, engaged in antisemitism as well as other right-wing bigotries— into his inner circle (Bensinger, 2024. Trump himself has employed antisemitic tropes in his own rhetoric (see Chapter 1).

To return to immigration, federal law bars non-citizens from voting in any federal election—conviction for which is punishable by a heavy fine, a jail sentence, and likely deportation—and no state currently permits them to vote in a state election (a handful of localities allow non-citizens to vote for local offices only) (Brown et al., 2024). Furthermore, there is no evidence of non-citizens voting illegally to any significant degree. Even the Heritage Foundation, a conservative group leading the effort to spread falsehoods on this issue, was able to substantiate only 68 instances of ineligible non-citizens voting—and only 10 instances of an undocumented immigrant doing so—going back four decades, during which many billions of votes were cast (Berzon, 2024). The libertarian CATO Institute—more often than not associated with Republicans, although they are not as ideological as Heritage —stated that "non-citizens don't illegally vote in detectable numbers" (Bensinger and Fausset, 2024). More broadly, Trump has threatened "long-term prison sentences" for the "Lawyers, Political Operatives, Donors, Illegal Voters, and Corrupt Election Officials" he might deem to have cheated in any way—cheating he falsely claims is rampant, and which supposedly cost him the 2020 election (Sullivan and Forrest, 2024).

Going beyond immigrants of color and their liberal allies in the U.S., Trump defines anyone he sees as not pro-American and/or pro-MAGA (his rhetoric defines America and MAGA as equivalent) as an enemy. This includes "the radical left thugs that live like vermin within the confines of our country," whom he pledged on Veterans Day 2023 to: "root out" (Gold, 2023), along with groups like Muslims— whom he cites as posing a physical threat to Americans in the form of their supposed propensity for terrorism (see Chapter 2). On September 7, 2024, Trump offered the following about Harris's allies and supporters: "It's the people that surround her. They're scum. They are scum, and they want to take down our country. They are absolute garbage" (Clark, 2024).

Going further, on October 13, 2024, the twice-elected president called for using military force on Election Day against unspecified opponents:

> I think the bigger problem is the people from within. We have some very bad people. We have some sick people. Radical left lunatics. I think it should be very easily handled by, if necessary, by National Guard, or if really necessary, by the military, because they can't let that happen (Vazquez, 2024).

He added that: "the enemy within . . . is more dangerous than China, Russia and all these countries," and named Democrat Adam Schiff, the then-presumptive favorite to become U.S. Senator from California (he eventually won that race), as one of those enemies who, presumably, the military should handle: "The thing that's tougher to handle are these lunatics that we have inside, like Adam Schiff" (Vazquez, 2024).

The next day, October 14, Trump offered the following about those who oppose him politically: "They are so bad and frankly, they're evil. They're evil. What they've done, they've weaponized, they've weaponized our elections. They've done things that nobody thought was even possible" (Lerer and Gold, 2024). In a Fox News interview that aired on October 16, he repeated these themes and this time added: "the Pelosis"—it was unclear if he meant to include any of Nancy Pelosi's relatives—as also being a "more difficult" threat than China or Russia (Bump, 2024d). Two days before the 2024 election, he called the Democratic Party "demonic" (Gold et al., 2024). At his final 2024 rally, the night before the election, Trump took one final shot at Pelosi: "She's an evil, sick, crazy bi- oh no. It starts with a 'b,' but I won't say it. I want to say it!" (Parker and Dawsey, 2024). He also proclaimed that he was: "running against an evil Democrat system" made up of "evil people" (Brennan, 2024).

All these elements work together in Trump's push to define the outgroup as the enemy of the ingroup, namely the people he defines as "real Americans." JD Vance neatly summed up the bifurcation of the American people around which MAGA centers: "I think our people hate the right people" (French, 2024). Research has found that this is how U.S. politics works under Trump. Julie Wronski told *The New York Times* that her work (Kane et al., 2021) indicates that: "people form their party attachments based upon their feelings toward the groups in each party, with people moving away from a party once it starts to contain people they do not like." She added that: "Trump activated his MAGA coalition based on hostility toward minority groups linked with the Democratic Party" (Edsall, 2024).

The fourth step as predicted by Social Identity Theory is the use of simple binary language choices to further cement the us versus them dichotomy. We see this in the aforementioned quotation from Slotkin (p. 305), where "they" (Mexico/immigrants) laugh at "us" (America). Trump talks about us and them constantly, on virtually every issue (Paquette, 2024). For another example, consider the juxtaposition of the Black Lives Matter movement and the counter-movement of Blue Lives Matter, which refers to police officers who typically wear blue uniforms (Bacon, Jr., 2016). This false dichotomy—inherent in the very ideas underlying the use of the term Blue Lives Matter—suggests that multiple groups of people's lives cannot simultaneously matter, that people have to choose, and that blue lives and black lives are discrete categories with no overlap. In this mindset, the two groups are competitors in a zero-sum game rather than fellow citizens working together toward a common goal of improving public safety for all Americans. This dualistic, Manichaean approach—which corresponds to what psychologists call "splitting" (Guralni, 2024)—requires seeing everything as black or white (or, in this case, blue), without gray.

The fifth step is to create talking points that foment the divide. These talking points must exaggerate ingroup and outgroup distinctions in ways that reflect bias in favor of the ingroup (Kurylo, 2013). Subsequently, polarization magnifies differences and makes them appear to be mutually exclusive and opposite. This, for example, occurs with the aforementioned Trump stereotypes of white Americans—law-abiding, productive—contrasted with black Americans—lazy, criminal-minded; as well as males—coded as strong, action-oriented, and smart (if they agree with Trump at least)—contrasted with females—weak, crazy, passive, dumb.

Sixth, this messaging requires consistency and collaboration with others who communicate in ways that demonstrate that they share the same beliefs so that the target audience is able to view the us/them division as absolute (Tracy and Robles, 2013). This consistency requires ignoring evidence to the contrary and stating what is unfalsifiable (i. e., cannot be objectively proven true or false), including numerous conspiracy theories on topics ranging from COVID-19, to who was actually calling the shots in the Biden White House, to who (i. e., Jewish billionaire George Soros—a long-standing bête noire for right-wingers) has been funding various left-wing protest movements (Dale, 2020).

Seeing Trump's bifurcation in action

Bifurcating Americans stands at the heart of Trump's rhetoric. Perhaps no remarks better encapsulate this than the aforementioned speech he delivered on Independence Day 2020 at Mount Rushmore, in the midst of his re-election campaign, and at perhaps the high point of the protests[17] inspired by the murder of unarmed African American George Floyd by a white police officer in Minneapolis six weeks earlier:

> Our nation is witnessing a merciless campaign to wipe out our history, defame our heroes, erase our values, and indoctrinate our children . . . Angry mobs are trying to tear down statues of our Founders, deface our most sacred memorials, and unleash a wave of violent crime in our cities. Many of these people have no idea why they are doing this, but some know exactly what they are doing. They think the American people are weak and soft and submissive. But no, the American people are strong and proud, and they will not allow our country, and all of its values, history, and culture, to be taken from them.

> One of their political weapons is "Cancel Culture"—driving people from their jobs, shaming dissenters, and demanding total submission from anyone who disagrees. This is the very definition of totalitarianism, and it is completely alien to our culture and our values, and it has absolutely no place in the United States of America. This attack on our liberty, our magnificent liberty, must be stopped, and it will be stopped very quickly. We will expose this danger-

---

17 After a few of these protests turned violent, Trump asked Gen. Mark Milley, the Chairman of the Joint Chiefs of Staff: "Can't you just shoot [the protestors]? Just shoot them in the legs or something?" (Martin and Ermyas, 2022).

ous movement, protect our nation's children, end this radical assault, and preserve our be-loved American way of life.

In our schools, our newsrooms, even our corporate boardrooms, there is a new far-left fas-cism that demands absolute allegiance. If you do not speak its language, perform its rituals, recite its mantras, and follow its commandments, then you will be censored, banished, black-listed, persecuted, and punished. It's not going to happen to us.

Make no mistake: this left-wing cultural revolution is designed to overthrow the American Revolution. In so doing, they would destroy the very civilization that rescued billions from poverty, disease, violence, and hunger, and that lifted humanity to new heights of achieve-ment, discovery, and progress. To make this possible, they are determined to tear down every statue, symbol, and memory of our national heritage.

[. . .] Against every law of society and nature, our children are taught in school to hate their own country, and to believe that the men and women who built it were not heroes, but that [sic] were villains. The radical view of American history is a web of lies—all perspective is removed, every virtue is obscured, every motive is twisted, every fact is distorted, and every flaw is magnified until the history is purged and the record is disfigured beyond all rec-ognition.

[. . .] No movement that seeks to dismantle these treasured American legacies can possibly have a love of America at its heart. Can't have it. No person who remains quiet at the destruc-tion of this resplendent heritage can possibly lead us to a better future.

[. . .] Those who seek to erase our heritage want Americans to forget our pride and our great dignity, so that we can no longer understand ourselves or America's destiny. In toppling the heroes of 1776, they seek to dissolve the bonds of love and loyalty that we feel for our country, and that we feel for each other. Their goal is not a better America, their goal is the end of America. In its place, they want power for themselves. But just as patriots did in centuries past, the American people will stand in their way—and we will win, and win quickly and with great dignity (The White House, 2020).

In these remarks, the twice-elected president employed all six of the aforemen-tioned steps described in Social Identity Theory. He thoroughly and repeatedly div-ided American society into two groups. On the one side are: "the American peo-ple"—with whom Trump identifies himself and his cause, calling them "we" and "us." This side is strong, patriotic, and possesses continuity with our country's founding, its accomplishments, and its liberty-centered values. The other side— the left wing, totalitarian ideologues and the angry mobs in the streets—hates America, is alien to it, opposes all for which it stands, and wants to destroy it. When it comes to bifurcation, no one does it better than Trump.

The ideas presented at Mount Rushmore remain at the core of what the twice-elected president stands for. He revisited these themes throughout the rest of the 2020 campaign and beyond. One day before the 2020 election, Trump officially cre-ated the 1776 Commission. Two days before he left office after losing that contest, this body issued a longer document mirroring the Mount Rushmore speech. This report aimed at completely remaking the discourse around American history—it also appears to have been plagiarized (Nguyen, 2021). Trump's commission—right down to the name—was an explicit rejection of The 1619 Project (New York Times, 2019), which to him embodied an anti-American approach, and which has stood at the center of right-wing attacks on Critical Race Theory since its publication. Academic historians have raised issues with some of The 1619 Project's content, and subsequent issues have included corrections (Lozada, 2021). With the 1776 Commission project, Trump helped further exacerbate the toxic battles over how American schools teach our history (Meckler, 2024).

Trump himself on September 17, 2020, connected the commission's purpose directly to the George Floyd protests and the ideology supposedly underlying them. He blamed the latter for how our schools teach American history:

> The left-wing rioting and mayhem are the direct result of decades of left-wing indoctrination in our schools. It's gone on far too long. Our children are instructed from propaganda tracts, like those of Howard Zinn, that try to make students ashamed of their own history.

> The left has warped, distorted, and defiled the American story with deceptions, falsehoods, and lies. There is no better example than The New York Times' totally discredited 1619 Project. This project rewrites American history to teach our children that we were founded on the principle of oppression, not freedom

> [. . .] Critical Race Theory, the 1619 Project, and the crusade against American history is toxic propaganda, ideological poison that, if not removed, will dissolve the civic bonds that tie us together. It will destroy our country. That is why I recently banned trainings in this prejudiced ideology from the Federal Government and banned it in the strongest manner possible (Peters and Woolley, 2020).

The 1776 Commission's report drew withering criticism from professional historians. For example, James Grossman, head of the American Historical Association, the leading organization of historians of the U.S., characterized its content as not resembling history at all, calling it instead "cynical politics." He added:

> This report skillfully weaves together myths, distortions, deliberate silences, and both blatant and subtle misreading of evidence to create a narrative and an argument that few respectable professional historians, even across a wide interpretive spectrum, would consider plausible, never mind convincing. They're using something they call history to stoke culture wars (Crowley and Schuessler, 2021).

Within days of taking office, President Biden dissolved Trump's history commission. However, on January 29, 2025, President Trump reestablished it (Pérez and Wilkes, 2025). He has since made clear that in his second term he aims to reshape to his own liking how schools teach American history (Sheffey, 2025).

Through these steps, the twice-elected president can provide a group identity to his followers and imbue it with a tremendous sense of MAGA pride, as well as animosity toward, if not hatred of, opponents he defines as not wanting America to be great. This process is self-reinforcing and self-perpetuating. Once Trump identifies the ingroups and outgroups, the group and individual identity continues to be bolstered as long as the related stereotypes are activated. The boys' camp studies (Sherif et al., 1961) showed that this is a temporary state, however. This kind of tactic does not necessarily create inherent, permanent prejudice. By changing the dialogue/rhetoric, a person can change the group alignment. This provides some hope for the future. In the end, the boys in this camp study became friends. Why? Because the researchers manipulated the context to provide a reason for the two groups to need to work together for mutual benefit. The research confirms that division can be a temporary situation. Given the state of the country and the perseverance of Trump's rhetoric, however, polarization and division are unlikely to abate anytime soon. This is not surprising. Making America Great Again is no less than a fight over the definition of Americanness, and who gets to be an American.

Group Vitality Theory

Group Vitality Theory extends Social Identity Theory further by arguing not only that group identity helps an individual bolster their self-esteem, but that a cultural group's survival depends on how successfully it negotiates group membership (Giles, 1978; Harwood et al., 1994). Group Vitality invokes the idea that a cultural group's ability to garner a larger amount of requisite demographics (i.e., members/supporters), greater levels of institutional support, and higher status within the larger cultural context than other groups determine its ability to survive and thrive over time. This theory has its roots in trying to understand why certain groups (e.g., pagans—who once dominated Europe, or Freemasons—whose numbers have plummeted in recent decades) or certain languages (e.g., Latin) go extinct or become endangered (Giles, 1978; Harwood et al., 1994).

In terms of the demographics of the United States, Trump's rhetoric, on the surface, communicates that he has a strong base. Projecting strength is one of his rhetoric's core intents—it suggests why he persistently talks about how he wins or is winning, as he did for example, on April 11, 2016:

> You are going to be so proud of your country. Because we're gonna turn it around, and we're gonna start winning again! We're gonna win so much! We're going to win at every level. We're going to win economically. We're going to win with the economy. We're gonna win

with military. We're gonna win with healthcare and for our veterans. We're gonna with every single facet.

We're gonna win so much, you may even get tired of winning. And you'll say, "Please, please. It's too much winning. We can't take it anymore. Mr. President, it's too much." And I'll say, "No, it isn't!" We have to keep winning. We have to win more! We're gonna win more. We're gonna win so much (Willingham et al., 2017).

Trump projects this strength about more than just the future. He defies objective reality about things that have already happened. For example, we have Trump's repeated denial that he lost the 2020 election, that it was rigged, and that it was stolen not only from him but, as he said in a video statement posted on December 2, 2020, that it was "stolen from the American people" (C-SPAN, 2020)—this despite the courts having debunked and rejected every specific charge of fraud brought before them by the Trump campaign and its allies (Yen et al., 2020). The twice-elected president's rhetoric defines his ingroup as, potentially at least, all Americans—even those who are presumably unaware of or unwilling to acknowledge that Trump is fighting on their behalf. This suggests a large demographic base. At least he would like people to see it that way, and he presented it as such at the aforementioned Mount Rushmore speech, among many other occasions.

In American culture, institutional support is often presumed to rest with the government. Trump, proudly acknowledging himself as a non-politician, a potential disadvantage, rhetorically maneuvers to discredit traditional politicians—even those in his own political party who oppose him. He did this quite powerfully on the way to winning the 2016 Republican nomination, when he ran against the GOP establishment, in particular the Bush family. Not only had they produced two presidents, but Jeb Bush was the early front-runner until Trump wrested that position from him (DelReal, 2015). Then-candidate Trump opposed the so-called warmongers in both parties (Vance, 2016), and rejected the neoliberal, bipartisan orthodoxy on free trade reflected in NAFTA and the Trans-Pacific Partnership (TPP). On opposing the latter, he (along with opponents on the left like Bernie Sanders) even brought Democrats like Hillary Clinton and later Joe Biden with him (Roberts and Felton, 2016).

Even while Trump was president—holding the most powerful position in the world—as well as while he was out of office, he opposed the establishment as he defines it. While running for re-election as an incumbent in 2020, he was still railing against the so-called "Deep State" that supposedly sought to constrain his powers, and continuing to pledge that he would drain the swamp, even though he had been in Washington, DC for four years (Dawsey et al., 2020; Parker, 2020).

Finally, upon winning re-election in 2024, Trump's announced picks for various cabinet positions included numerous people so far out of the institutional mainstream—separate from the matter of their qualifications (or lack thereof) and, in some cases, publicly documented crimes and transgressions—that they represented, according to a *New York Times* headline, a "seismic shift." As Baker (2024d) described the President-elect's initial chosen roster of people to lead major departments such as Defense, Justice,[18] National Intelligence, and Health and Human Services among others: "Somehow disruption doesn't begin to cover it. Upheaval might be closer. Revolution maybe." The reasons why these picks terrify the establishment are exactly why they thrill his core supporters. "I think it's so crazy, and I love it," one Trump voter from Montana told The *New York Times* (Corkery et al., 2024). And the craziness is the point. Through these picks, Trump demonstrates to his base that he rejects the norms of what a president is supposed to be and do, and seeks to achieve dominance over the existing institutions. In terms of how he presents himself to the American people, the twice-elected president is perhaps the single most anti-establishment figure ever to occupy the Oval Office.

Throughout his political career, right from the start, Trump has attacked as a whole the political system that he sought to lead, did lead for four years, and will be leading again presumably for another four. Such attacks undermine that system's credibility and validity, right down to its ability to produce election results that an overwhelming majority of the American people widely accept no matter who wins (Kim et al., 2024). Instead, Trump claims that his base of support comes from the very same American people—at least the good, pro-American ones—whom he views as truly imbued with the legitimate authority to affect change, by any means necessary. These include even the means we saw in the insurrection on January 6, 2021, when Trump supporters—incited by the twice-elected president himself—stormed the Capitol while Congress was performing its constitutional duty of certifying the results of the 2020 presidential election (Peñaloza, 2021).

Status, another core element of Group Vitality Theory (Giles, 1978; Harwood et al., 1994), can be attained in many ways. Trump has emphasized his status as a supposedly successful billionaire and businessman, a status burnished through decades of publicity—including a good bit of embellishment (Buettner and Craig, 2024)—that culminated in his fifteen-year run as the host of "The Apprentice" on NBC—during which tens of millions of Americans watched a (heavily edited) depiction of him presiding over a billion-dollar company. This conditioned Amer-

---

18 Florida congressman Matt Gaetz, Trump's first choice for Attorney General, bowed out due to multiple ongoing criminal investigations relating to scandalous behavior (Amiri, 2024).

icans to see him as both powerful and highly competent. Trump reminds his base of his supposed business acumen through his rhetoric with great consistency.

Race can also be (mis)used to establish, measure, and compare status. Trump uses white Americans' fears about losing status to gain support (Reifowitz, 2019). The country's changing racial demographics (i.e., the browning of America) contribute to Trump's support among white Americans whose race/ethnicity is central to their identity—with between 30 and 40% of them identifying strongly with their whiteness (Jardina, 2019). Furthermore, as Daniel J. Hopkins told *The New York Times*, Trump "activated" racially resentful white voters by employing inflammatory rhetoric to win more of their votes. He added:

> Anti-black prejudice has the strongest predictive power for the 2016 elections involving Trump. I certainly don't think that anti-black prejudice is the entire explanation for Trump's 2016 victory. But my evidence indicates that it was clearly an element in Trump's electoral support, and that its role in 2016 was notably different than in prior elections. (Edsall, 2019)

Other studies have confirmed this finding (Schaffner et al., 2018). Furthermore, a study carried out by Major, Blodorn, and Major Blascovich (2018) found:

> Reminding white Americans high in ethnic identification that non-White racial groups will outnumber Whites in the United States by 2042 caused them to become more concerned about the declining status and influence of white Americans as a group (i.e., experience group status threat), and caused them to report increased support for Trump and anti-immigrant policies, as well as greater opposition to political correctness.

Diana C. Mutz compared survey data from the 2012 and 2016 presidential elections and drew the following conclusion: "Those who felt that the hierarchy was being upended—with whites discriminated against more than Blacks, Christians discriminated against more than Muslims, and men discriminated against more than women—were most likely to support Trump" (Mutz, 2018).

A 2024 CNN poll asked: "Overall, do you think having an increasing number of people of many different races, ethnic groups, and nationalities in the U.S. is mostly threatening or mostly enriching American culture?" They asked the same question in 2019 and 2023. There was little change in the responses of Democrats and Democratic-leaning voters over time, and about nine in ten answered "enriching" in 2024. Republicans were another story. In 2019, about 21% answered "threatening," a level that jumped to 41% in 2023, and 55% in 2024 (Blake, 2024d). These nativist sentiments among Republicans are both driven by Trump and redound to his electoral benefit.

Trump hypes concerns about anti-white racism

Any rhetoric that heightens white Americans' fears that they have lost their status as the dominant group in society provides a clear, documented advantage to the twice-elected president. As one study explained: "Many whites now view themselves as an embattled and even disadvantaged group, and this has led to both strong ingroup identity and a greater tolerance for expressions of hostility toward outgroups" (Valentino et al., 2016). Addressing the matter of white status anxiety more directly, when asked about the notion that "anti-white racism now represents a greater problem in the country than anti-black racism," Trump criticized the Biden-Harris administration's policies on this front, claiming:

> They're sort of against anybody depending on certain views. They're against Catholics. They're against a lot of different people" and then added: "I think there is a definite anti-white feeling in this country and that can't be allowed either.... I think the laws are very unfair right now. And education is being very unfair... if you look right now, there's absolutely a bias against white and that's a problem (Time Staff, 2024).

This kind of rhetoric makes crystal clear whom racially anxious whites must support.

Chapter 5
Psychodynamic approach: "Lock [her/him/they/them] up"

Stereotypes are often viewed as inherently prejudicial in nature, prompting responses that condemn racism, sexism, xenophobia, homophobia, and so forth. A psychodynamic perspective views stereotypes as wedded to prejudice and assumes that an individual has a "propensity to prejudice" (Allport, 1954/1979, p. 27), "a strong need for a sense of personal status" (Allport, 1954/1979, p. 320), and is unaware "of the psychological function that prejudice serves in his life" (Allport, 1954/1979, p. 352). Two theories comprise the psychodynamic approach to stereotypes: Authoritarian Personality and Scapegoat Theory. Both apply to Trump's communication of stereotypes. The Authoritarian Personality helps explain how communicating stereotypes, as rigid descriptors, encourages his base to blindly view the twice-elected president as the heroic leader of a political movement. Scapegoat Theory sheds light on the vilification technique that he uses—one that relies heavily on bullying stereotypes—to target opponents like, among others, Hillary Clinton and Kamala Harris. This chapter demonstrates the techniques that Trump utilizes to successfully appeal to the prejudice, insecurity, and fears of his followers. As public intellectual and historian Heather Cox Richardson (2024d) put it: "Trump's behavior is Authoritarianism 101."

In almost every story, fiction or nonfiction, there is a hero and a villain. The story of how Trump motivates his base neatly fits this familiar trope. With the twice-elected president as the hero, there remains only the villain to determine. For Trump, there are many villains and, indeed, anyone who does not vocally support him almost certainly finds themselves outside of his ingroup and, often, lumped together with those on the presumed anti-American left. In each one of Trump's quests for the White House, he identified a primary target of his vitriol and rhetoric, namely the Democratic nominee. In 2024, that opponent was Kamala Harris—after Joe Biden, Trump's 2020 opponent, ended his run for re-election and she became her party's choice. In 2016, it was Hillary Clinton. That year, Trump portrayed her as the villain in order to rile up his base of supporters, convince them that they were victims, and spur them to view him as the hero—the knight in shining armor who would save them from her supposedly evil clutches.

https://doi.org/10.1515/9783111426327-008

The shift to victimhood

The coming demographic shift away from a white majority in the United States has created concern that has worked to Trump's advantage (see Chapter 4). Many white Americans—influenced in part by Trump's rhetoric—have begun to draw some conclusions about their changing status. White resentment derives in part from long-standing antipathy over government benefits for poor people (i.e., Temporary Assistance for Needy Families [aka 'welfare'], Supplemental Nutrition Assistance Program [aka 'food stamps'], Medicaid) going to Americans of color, in particular black Americans, who do receive a disproportionate share of these benefits (King, 2022). The legacy of slavery, Jim Crow, redlining and more, as well as present-day discrimination, certainly play a part in that disparity.

Conservative politicians have, for decades, hammered away at this point specifically to keep white Americans thinking that African Americans receiving means-tested benefits are somehow dependent, lazy, and cheating (white) taxpayers of their hard-earned money (Gilens, 1999; López, 2014). Ronald Reagan in his 1976 presidential campaign hurled stereotypes about "welfare queens" driving Cadillacs, and "strapping young bucks" using food stamps to buy T-bone steaks (López, 2014). Rush Limbaugh operated along similar race-baiting lines during the Obama presidency, as did former House Speaker Newt Gingrich during his 2012 run for the Republican presidential nomination (Reifowitz, 2019).

Trump has also employed rhetoric around welfare that evokes the same kinds of stereotypes (Ye Hee Lee, 2017; Covert, 2018). For example, on May 4, 2024, he characterized welfare recipients as people who "get welfare to vote" Democratic as part of some corrupt scheme, rather than people who deserve assistance (Granderson, 2024). Given that African Americans vote around 90 % Democratic, the racial implications of this corruption are clear. Additionally, as Reifowitz (2019) noted:

> President Trump's rhetoric and policy approach to welfare, food stamps, and other forms of government assistance have strongly paralleled that of Limbaugh and like-minded conservatives. In December 2018, an executive order proposed stricter work requirements for those seeking food stamps. The White House press release announcing the proposal spoke about "self-sufficiency" and railed against the existing "system" which, it claimed, promoted "lifelong dependency." As for his personal rhetoric, on November 29, 2017, Trump repeated some of the worst lies about supposedly rampant welfare abuse: "I know people that work three jobs and they live next to somebody who doesn't work at all. And the person who is not working at all and has no intention of working at all is making more money and doing better than the person that's working his and her ass off" (p. 96).

We see these stereotypes echoed in the words of racially resentful, right-wing white Trump supporters who oppose Americans of color getting help that they see as somehow coming at their expense. As per Sides et al. (2016): "racialized perceptions of economic deservingness were . . . strongly related to support for Donald Trump" (p. 176).

Beyond the resentment around means-tested government-provided benefits, which are by law racially-neutral, there is the resentment around policies that take race into account in ways that benefit racial minorities (as well as, in some cases, women)—or at least which right-wing rhetoric claims give them some kind of special treatment. Affirmative action is the best-known of these policies, and it has arguably stirred up the most race-based resentment over many decades—aided by right-wing political rhetoric aimed at inflaming it.

Perhaps the most notorious of countless examples is a 1990 ad North Carolina Republican Senator Jesse Helms's campaign ran against Harvey Gantt, his black Democratic opponent. Viewers see a pair of hands belonging to a white man holding a letter. The voice-over solemnly delivers the lines: "You needed that job. And you were the best qualified. But they had to give it to a minority because of a racial quota. Is that really fair? Harvey Gantt says it is" (James, 2012). One of the people who created the ad, Carter Wrenn, admitted to NPR years later: "That was absolutely a racial ad... We played racist politics . . . We played the race card and I'm not proud of it . . . It was wrong . . . There's no point in trying to say it wasn't because it was that" (James, 2012). Although race-based affirmative action for (mostly elite) colleges—which was struck down on June 29, 2023, by the U.S. Supreme Court—receives a great deal of attention, the Helms ad makes clear that resentment over affirmative action resonates far beyond the ivory tower. This resentment also fuels at least in part the battle over DEI policies, which reaches into not only academia but corporate America and virtually every workplace.

Another more recently developed policy also sparked discord. The American Rescue Plan passed by Congress (without a single Republican vote in either chamber) and signed into law by President Biden in 2021, included $4 billion of debt relief that would benefit all indebted farmers of color—most of whom are black. White farmers sued on the basis of racial discrimination—the program forgave loans, and defined eligibility strictly on the basis of race. Their suit was successful, and the program was blocked (Levenson, 2021). Congress subsequently amended the law, broadening eligibility and giving out funds targeted to compensating for specific instances of discrimination (Ballentine, 2024). What did racially resentful whites take away from this? It further cemented their belief that a Democratic president and Congress—focused on equity of outcomes rather than equal rights —stood on the side of minorities and stood opposed to white interests.

Perhaps more than ever before, white Americans now believe there are benefits to being non-white, or at least being seen as not white—something that heretofore had been viewed as a such a disadvantage that, not that long ago, some very light-skinned African Americans sought to "pass" as white (Hobbs, 2016). Whiteness brought clear social, economic, and legal advantages (not to mention the violence that white dominance imposed on African Americans in particular). In fact, there were many legal cases—at least 52 by one count—between 1878 and 1952 where a person went to court in order to be "declared white by law after being denied citizenship rights by immigration authorities on the grounds of racial ineligibility" (Tehranian, 2000).

More recently, we have examples of the opposite occurring, with white people trying to claim membership in a minority group, such as Rachel Dolezal (now officially named Nkechi Diallo), a white woman who falsely claimed to be black and became the head of the Spokane, Washington NAACP (Moyer, 2015). Beyond this somewhat sensational incident, there are other similar cases, for example, white professors like Jessica Krug, who posed as black, or others who posed as Native American (Tensley, 2021). Similarly, Americans with ancestry in the Middle East or North Africa—who have until now been instructed to identify as white on the U.S. census, have advocated for and won their own line on the census as a separate race/ethnicity (H.L. Wang, 2024). Whatever their motivations, these Americans of different backgrounds have no interest in identifying as white.

Trump himself has long expressed the belief that being white is in many instances a disadvantage. Back in 1989 he told NBC News: "A well-educated black has a tremendous advantage over a well-educated white in terms of the job market . . . [I]f I were starting off today, I would love to be a well-educated black, because I believe they do have an actual advantage" (Kruse, 2015). Republican voters—influenced by Republican rhetoric of the kind cited above—have come to agree. A December 2023 poll found that Republicans are far more likely than Democrats to say that white Americans face discrimination and that such discrimination is worse than what black Americans deal with (Economist/YouGov, 2023). A 2017 poll found similar results, and further noted: "Lower- and moderate-income white Americans were more likely to say that whites are discriminated against—and to say they have felt it, either when applying for a job, raise or promotion or in the college admissions process" (Gonyea, 2017). In all three of his White House runs, Trump has captured approximately two-thirds of white voters without a college degree. (Igielnik et al.,2021; NBC News, 2024). In 2024, there existed a significant educational voting gap among white voters, with Harris winning those who have a degree by seven points, and Trump winning those without a degree by a whopping 34 points (Alonso, 2024). This gap increased by a few points from 2016 to 2020, and a few more from 2020 to 2024 (Wolf et al.). All of these data points connect and redound to the twice-elected president's political benefit.

There is no doubt that Americans of color still confront disadvantages because of their race. However, this new phenomenon of whites passing as non-white makes clear that there are at least some areas of American society where white people believe that being non-white is a plus, in particular areas where progressive values or policies hold sway. These cases received wide media coverage, and only served to reinforce white racial resentment over the perceived benefits of being a member of a minority group—in particular being seen as black, Latino, or American Indian.

It is also true that many white Americans endure significant headwinds in their lives, even if these are not caused by racial discrimination. So-called deaths of despair—people dying from drug and alcohol overdoses and suicide—have shot up among white Americans during this century. In the past few years, however, black Americans erased the gap that had opened up, and in 2022 their rate of deaths of despair actually slightly exceeded that of whites, as both continued to climb (Johnson, 2024) through that year—although drug overdose deaths dropped 10 % from April 2023 to April 2024 (Weiland, 2024). Other recent data has shown that poor whites are doing materially worse, even as black Americans' prospects improved in absolute terms. As one study found:

> For white children in the U.S. born between 1978 and 1992, earnings increased for children from high-income families but decreased for children from low-income families, increasing earnings gaps by parental income ("class") by 30 %. Earnings increased for black children at all parental income levels, reducing white-black earnings gaps for children from low-income families by 30 %. Class gaps grew and race gaps shrank similarly for non-monetary outcomes such as educational attainment, standardized test scores, and mortality rates (Chetty et al., 2024).

Fears about the declining status of white people drive support for right-wing populism. In broad terms, Eric Kauffman's 2019 book about white identity addresses how these fears can center on a desire for group solidarity in a society, such as the U.S., that is transitioning away from being majority white (see Chapter 4), and not just on hatred or negative feelings toward other racial groups. In this sense, whites are like any cultural group who sees their influence waning—a percentage of them evinces a desire to preserve some cultural space and a way of life that looks like the America of their youth. Although the parallels, in particular as it relates to economic impact, are not identical, this white anxiety about demographic change does in many respects resemble, for example, how black residents of

Harlem fear that gentrification will change the character of their neighborhood.[19] The character of the society that older white Americans grew up in is changing in ways that are out of their control. Just like black Harlemites, these whites did not ask for this change, and, thus, feel like outsiders in their own country.

The twice-elected president, however, exploits those concerns about white interests and their nostalgia for an imagined lost past, and then fans the flames of hatred by presenting himself as willing to go outside the bounds of acceptable political discourse, as Kauffman explained in an interview with *The New Yorker:* "On the immigration front, for example, Donald Trump was the black marketeer who, because of the strictures on what is deemed acceptable to campaign on, because [being] anti-immigration was seen as kind of racist, had a marketplace that he could fill" (Chotiner, 2019). This allowed him to stake out otherwise unoccupied political ground as the most stalwart defender of white Americans.

Thus, in this argument, the support from Trump's base for anti-immigrant policies, or opposition to the Black Lives Matter movement and other related positions may not derive 100 % from racial hostility. A slower rate of change in the country's demographic shift might have lessened the growth of the 'us' and 'them' sentiment that smoothed the path for the acceptance of Trump's rhetorical manipulation. Whiteness, according to such thinking, could simply represent a cohesive group identity. After all, the preservation of one's cultural group heritage is not inherently problematic and, instead, is typically considered laudable. Kauffman (2019) has argued that the disparity in how the attempts by whites and various non-white groups to do this preservation work are judged by elements in mainstream culture lead to the expression of "more negative" forms of white identity (Chotiner, 2019).

Chapter 4 discussed how the ingroup often views members of the outgroup as homogeneous in terms of possessing a lower group vitality (as measured by status, number of members, and institutional support) even though ingroup members do recognize some limited differentiation among them. At the societal level we can still use the words "ingroup" and "outgroup," but with an important distinction. The term "ingroup" can similarly refer to the group with the most perceived or actual group vitality. In this usage, the ingroup member, however, is not a role just anyone can play. It is a role reserved for members of the dominant group. Others are part of a societal level outgroup, who are outside of the dominant group. This homogeneity is nonetheless not a blanket uniformity that exists objectively across all group members. Although the homogeneity that ingroup members perceive in the outgroup does not reflect objective reality, there does exist a level of cohesiveness that comes with outgroup members' shared experience of being treated as the

---

19 For more on gentrification in Harlem, see, for example, Hackman, 2015.

'other.' Among members of minority groups as a whole, the cohesiveness may in some cases extend beyond the cultural, racial, or geographic group and into their shared identity as people of color who experience being in a racial outgroup. As such, they also share a second-class status and reduced institutional support—compared to whites—despite their increasing share of the population. In sum, minorities still have less power in the United States than majority group members.

However, majority group members may not view their own ingroup members as homogeneous or cohesive. Indeed, whiteness has often not registered as a core part of a white Americans' identity to the same degree that their ethno-racial identity has long done for Americans of color (Jardina, 2019). One's whiteness, rather, is often invisible and unremarked on at least to those who share that attribute. The benefits or privilege that come with whiteness include that invisibility. Through Trump's rhetoric, however, white identity has become more visible and discussed and has taken form to a greater degree than before him.

A system that formally or informally advantages whites certainly provides benefits to members of that group—albeit more to some than others. However, such a system does not necessarily serve the overall material interests of all whites, in particular those at or below the median income level, who bundle their interests with those of very wealthy whites rather than darker-skinned Americans with whom they share similar economic straits (McGhee, 2021). President Lyndon B. Johnson was famously quoted saying: "If you can convince the lowest white man he's better than the best colored man, he won't notice you're picking his pocket. Hell, give him somebody to look down on, and he'll empty his pockets for you" (Moyers, 1988).

Affirmative action is a case in point, although it certainly predates Trump. This new, vocal, white would-be minority believes that affirmative action provides opportunities for minorities that whites cannot access. With a sense of grievance exacerbated by the twice-elected president, these whites aim to reclaim the power they had before affirmative action, when a preference for white people was the default in America. Such an effort turns a blind eye to systemic racism (as well as gender discrimination), and unconscious bias endemic in societal systems. It also ignores documented present-day discrimination, in the job market for example, where multiple studies showed that applicants with the same exact information on their resumes were more likely to be called for an interview if they had white-sounding names like Emily or Greg than if they had names that appear black like Jamal or Lakisha (Young and McMahon, 2021). Despite these facts, Trump continues to claim that whites are behind the eight ball and, thus, need to get together behind him.

Even though whites have long been the dominant group in American culture and society, Trump has helped convince his supporters to think of themselves for the first time as potentially a minority group, and helped give them a collective voice (see Chapter 4). As he tells the story, the supposed benefits available to minorities inherently mean fewer benefits for whites because there exists only a finite pool of resources. If that were true, then it really would be a zero-sum game. The browning of America will only make things worse for those who are white, according to Trump, that is.

The scapegoat

Whatever the differing benefits for his supporters might be, the benefits for Trump of riling up his base and creating a scapegoat whom they can blame for their problems are substantial. Creating a space whereby a large percentage of whites in the U.S.—who will remain the majority race in numerical terms for at least a couple more decades and may well wield disproportionate power in collective terms even beyond that point—could view themselves as a disenfranchised, victimized minority represents nothing short of a genius rhetorical strategy. This strategy mixes ethno-racial nationalism, racial resentment, hope, and pride into a cocktail of white identity politics that evokes strong emotions of loss and fear in particular among the middle- and lower-classes. These people's present-day situation falls short of both the past they imagine that their forebears experienced and the dreams they held for their future. Who deserves blame for this shortfall? Whoever it is becomes the scapegoat—the embodiment and focus of this white resentment.

Scapegoat theory argues that people project their frustration onto a symbolic representation of who or what they identify as the cause of their problem(s)—the source of that frustration (Ottati and Lee, 1995). Rather than seeking solutions to problems within themselves or through practical or logical avenues, people believe they are victims who lack control over their situation because of the scapegoat. Burke (1969) discusses how scapegoats can be used to rhetorically shift blame to another party for problems affecting a group. Scapegoating creates a distance between the victim and those responsible for this victimization. By distancing themselves from the "uncleanlinesses" (Burke, p. 406) of the victimizers, the victims are able to purify themselves as innocents—providing a rebirth of sorts. According to Ganesh (2007), "rhetorical critics argue that scapegoating as a tactic works only when it is able to tap into pre-existing, deep . . . collective anxieties and prejudices, and develop these anxieties into polar positions" (p. 80).

To the extent that political identities are ingrained within a culture, invoking these identities provides deep associations on which to base stereotypes that can be used to scapegoat. For example, Trump pilloried Hillary Clinton in order to undermine her perceived suitability to serve as President of the United States (he engaged in similar tactics running against Kamala Harris in 2024). However, this might not have been sufficient to secure Trump the election since people might have nonetheless voted for his opponent as the lesser of two evils in a two-party system. Rather, in 2016 Trump placed Clinton in the role of villain, responsible for the travails his growing pool of supporters had endured. According to Ganesh (2007), "positioning oneself as such a victim is both a means of accruing power and polarizing conflict" (p. 78).

In villainizing his opponent, Trump hit Clinton on countless matters large and small, including all manner of "vulgar" insults (Vitali, 2015). He went hard after her character. For example, in a June 22, 2016 speech he called her a "world class liar" (Politico, 2016). At the October 10, 2016 debate, Trump claimed that Clinton "has tremendous hate in her heart" (BBC, 2016). He also went after his opponent on more personal matters, calling her an "enabler" of her husband, President Bill Clinton—who had engaged in sexual behavior that was questionable at best—and accusing the Clintons of treating White House staff poorly (Johnson, 2016). At the October 10, 2016 debate, he pushed this theme further: "Bill Clinton was abusive to women. Hillary Clinton attacked those same women and attacked them viciously" (Bidgood, 2024a).

Trump's relentless verbal assaults on Clinton throughout the 2016 campaign centered on the epithet "Crooked Hillary"—emphasizing, like any villain, her evil nature—words he first uttered on April 16 of that year (Jamieson, 2016). Separate from job performance-related accusations (i. e., Benghazi[20]) he accused her of being corrupt in multiple ways, including that she had engaged in the "politics of personal enrichment" (Johnson, 2016)—and asserted many times that she belonged in prison. "Lock Her Up" was also a common audience chant at Trump rallies, and he explicitly agreed with that sentiment on at least one occasion that year. In June 2024, he falsely denied having ever called for Sec. Clinton's imprisonment (Alfaro, 2024). Then, on October 16, 2024, the twice-elected president declared: "You should lock them up. Lock up the Bidens. Lock up Hillary. [Audience chants "Lock them up"] Lock them up." (Roll Call, 2024a). Trump's charges of corruption cited decades worth of acts, ranging from the Whitewater scandal in Arkansas to the supposedly shady money taken in by the non-profit Clinton Foundation from foreign governments such as China, Iran, Saudi Arabia, and more. (McCammon, 2016). He accused her of taking bribes while serving as Secretary of State, claiming: "She ran the

---

20 This refers to the 2012 assault on U.S. government locations in Benghazi, Libya, committed by an al-Qaeda aligned militant group. The U.S. ambassador to Libya, J. Christopher Stevens, and three other Americans died.

State Department like her own personal hedge fund – doing favors for oppressive regimes, and many others, in exchange for cash" (McCammon, 2016). Trump slammed Clinton for money she earned delivering speeches to: "Wall Street banks and other special interests" (McCammon, 2016). Then there was the most familiar attack of all: "To cover up her corrupt dealings, Hillary illegally stashed her State Department emails on a private server" (McCammon, 2016). Trump, citing 30,000 or so emails that a Clinton staffer had deleted because they were not related to her work, invited Russia to take action—presumably through hacking or some other nefarious methods—to find the deleted emails, implying that his opponent was hiding something even more shocking (Schmidt, 2018).

The emails proved to be the most damaging scandal—not because Sec. Clinton ever faced criminal charges or was proven to have actually harmed national security. The damage was political. The matter appeared to be put to rest on July 5, 2016, when FBI Director James Comey made public his recommendation to the Department of Justice that, although Clinton had been "extremely careless," her actions did not warrant prosecution and that the matter be closed. As per *The New York Times*: "Mr. Comey's announcement was believed to be the first time that the FBI had ever publicly disclosed its recommendations to the Justice Department about whether to charge someone in any high-profile case, let alone a presidential candidate" (Landler and Lichtblau, 2016). Comey's criticisms stung, but they did not affect Clinton's standing in the polls.

But then, on October 28, 2016, Comey announced that the case against Clinton was being reopened after emails connected to the matter were found on a laptop belonging to Anthony Weiner, the husband of her top aide, Huma Abedin. On that day Trump employed one of his patented phrases (see Chapter 2) in order to emphasize his point: "Hillary Clinton's corruption is on a scale we have never seen before." The fairly large lead she enjoyed in the polls on that day, less than two weeks before Election Day, shrank significantly. Even though Comey announced 9 days later, on November 6, that the review did not reveal any new wrongdoing, and that the matter was (again) closed, that apparently was too little to reverse Clinton's slide in the polls. Trump greeted this second announcement with more charges of corruption: "Right now, she is being protected by a rigged system" (ABC News, 2016b). Clinton ultimately lost in the Electoral College, despite winning the popular vote by 2.1%, or just under 3 million votes. Trump hammering away at the theme of corruption and "her emails" for months beforehand prepared the ground for millions of Americans to believe that maybe his opponent really was corrupt and thus dangerous. The shock of Comey's last-minute announcements—even the second one—only served to reactivate many voters' thoughts on this, people whose votes shifted in the final days. The announcements had the impact they did at least in part because of the stereotypes Trump had long been communicating.

Through Trump's rhetoric, Clinton became the villain, and thus the scapegoat who stood at the head of the forces targeting Trump's supporters—of whom she famously (and foolishly, from a strategic perspective) declared that: "half" fit into a "basket of deplorables...racist, sexist, homophobic, xenophobic, Islamophobic—you name it" (Reilly, 2016b). He portrayed her as a ruthless, heartless, amoral enemy of America, one with tremendous hate in her heart for those who stood against her. Trump served as judge and jury, convicting Clinton in the court of public opinion. No wonder so many people wanted to lock her up.

Stereotypes are often activated through visually vivid and salient characteristics of age, gender, and race (Fiske and Taylor, 1984; Schneider, 1996; Hamilton and Sherman, 1994; Funder, 1995). In 2016, Clinton's gender, much like Biden's age in 2020 and especially 2024, and Harris's gender and race from July 2024 through Election Day served as prime fodder for Trump's attacks. Four aspects of a situation have been repeatedly demonstrated to activate stereotypes: the salience of target characteristics, the absence of individuating information, the ambiguity or uncertainty of the available information, and limited capacity to process information. To the extent that a situation consists of these elements, stereotypes may be triggered (Hamilton, Sherman, and Ruvolo, 1990). The social relevance of these attributes—as Trump invokes them—triggers stereotypes and expectations about associated attributes (Tajfel, 1969). These encourage Trump's base to make inferences that reinforce stereotypic beliefs and become the basis of judgments (Fiske and Taylor, 1984; Hamilton and Sherman, 1994; Hamilton, Sherman, and Ruvolo, 1990). This led to the election of Donald Trump as the 45th president in 2016, and the 47th president in 2024.

Socialization and gender stereotypes

When stereotypes are triggered, research from an information processing model (see Chapter 3) has shown that because individuals have a stake in their stereotypic assumptions, judgments are biased toward maintaining pre-existing belief systems and hypothesis confirmation (Fiske and Taylor, 1984). If communicated stereotypes serve information processing functions, then under similar situational constraints communicated stereotypes may be the basis of biased judgments that reinforce pre-existing belief systems and confidence in those beliefs. Stereotypes of women are widely prevalent in American culture. Many people accept them as fact.

Socialization (see Chapter 3) accounts for why there are repeated patterns of behavior among group members (Fausto-Sterling, 1985). Research studies have demonstrated that even as young as infancy, boys and girls are socialized into the ways they are expected to communicate in order to construct their gender identity. In one study (see Fausto-Sterling), a baby was dressed as either a girl or a boy at various times, and a participant in the study who saw and heard the baby crying offered a different response depending on the gender the baby appeared to be. If the participant thought a baby girl was crying, they articulated that she was scared, so we should hold her. If the participant thought a baby boy was crying, they articulated that he was angry, so we should leave him alone.

From that early age our society teaches females and males what emotions they are allowed to communicate, plus others communicate with them in ways that promote those gendered lessons. Women are stereotyped as weak as a result of this socialization, even though gender has been found to account for: "generally less than 10% of the variance in social behavior" (Aries, 1996, p. vii)—other variables play important roles in individual behavior as well. Despite this, gender stereotypes abound.

Biological essentialism

Biological essentialism is one way in which gender differences that have been used to discriminate against women are constructed. Specifically, biological essentialism refers to the use of biology as an explanation for behavior (Fausto-Sterling, 1985; Haste, 1994). This social construction presents itself as biological 'fact' and has been used to, for example, keep women from obtaining certain jobs, gaining access to educational opportunities, and even voting. Some prominent figures within the Christian nationalist right-wing have openly expressed that the U.S. should not have granted women the right to vote (Baker and Graham, 2024). Fausto-Sterling (1985) discusses, for example, how the belief that taxing women's brains too much took valuable energy from their other organs, threatening their health and their pregnancies, and was used to justify blocking women from getting an education. Biological essentialists constructed their arguments to make it in women's best interest not to educate themselves because of the impact on their unique ability to reproduce—seen in this view as their primary duty and higher calling (Fausto-Sterling, 1985). They required a paternalistic form of protection, one that ultimately prevented their professional and educational development. Trump's campaign website contains an official policy statement entitled "President Trump's Plan to Protect Children from Left-Wing Gender Insanity" that basically endorses biological essentialism:

> As part of our new credentialing body for teachers, we will promote positive education about
> the nuclear family, the roles of mothers and fathers, and celebrating rather than erasing the
> things that make men and women different and unique (Trump, 2023a).

Biological essentialism when applied to gender most often takes the form of associating women, due to their presumed ability to reproduce, with nurturing qualities that feed into and benefit from women's supposed and inherent emotionality
—something that can all too easily tip into hysteria (Fausto-Sterling, 1985), a term
whose origins suggest that this hyperemotional, crazed state is somehow essentially female in nature.[21] By extension, men are associated with impartiality and more
rational decision-making. Haste (1994) discusses the 'man as hunter' metaphor to
explain the historical legacy of constructed gender differences. Even now, many
presume gender is a binary "unique and absolute natural distinction" (Chodorow,
1979, p. 26). Consider how people, including women, jokingly claim that a woman
should not be president because she will potentially need to "push the nuclear button" during her menstrual cycle—a metaphor for having to make difficult decisions that require cool, unemotional analysis. Additionally, consider the frequency
of jokes we hear during everyday conversation about women and PMS or menstruation. Trump, who has communicated menstruation-themed stereotypes about female antagonists such as Megyn Kelly (see Chapter 1), draws on a long history of
these kinds of slanders against women in leadership or other high-profile positions
(Carmon, 2015).

Our society (stereo)typically rewards unemotional, ruthless leadership in corporate America. This is part of the male stereotype and hunter metaphor. This
characteristic becomes the norm (androcentrism). Men are viewed as better
able than women to be bosses or leaders (i.e., be in control) because the latter
are viewed as inherently over-emotional or, again, hysterical. Women are polarized and considered to be unable to handle this type of role (i.e., the glass ceiling)
(Isaac, et al., 2012). Because of these essentialist stereotypes, in 2016 Clinton had to
deal with the same double bind as many other women in leadership (Vedantam,
2016). On the one hand, women are often labeled too weak and/or emotionally unstable to succeed in such an important role. On the other hand, they are viewed as
cold and uncaring if they act otherwise, a criticism that, generally speaking, men
who behave similarly do not receive. Hillary Clinton faced this all-too-prevalent
double bind on a national stage as far back as when her husband was president.
Because critics labeled her unemotional for much of her campaign (Lind, 2016)—
Trump at one point referred to her as "Heartless Hillary" (Stokols, 2016)—she was

---

21 The word hysteria itself has its roots in female anatomy. It is derived from the Greek word for
uterus (Bailey, 1966).

cast easily into the role of villain. However, on another occasion her opponent slandered her as "unhinged" and "unstable" (Diamond, 2016). Trump hit her from both sides of the double bind.

Likewise, the double bind came into play for Kamala Harris in 2024 on the aforementioned matter of motherhood. On the one hand, women are emotional nurturers, juxtaposed to men as hunters/fighters/leaders. Harris, although she is a highly involved stepmother to two children from her husband Doug Emhoff's first marriage—who dubbed her "Momala"—does not have biological children of her own. For this, opponents have condemned her as being unfit to lead. During the campaign, video surfaced of JD Vance opining that the Democrats who "run . . . this country . . . are a bunch of childless cat ladies who are miserable at their own lives and the choices that they've made and so they want to make the rest of the country miserable, too" (Licon, 2024a). He specifically included Harris, along with Rep. Alexandria Ocasio-Cortez and Secretary of Transportation Pete Buttigieg—a gay man who had actually adopted children before Vance made his remarks (Licon, 2024a). Vance refused to apologize and pivoted to criticizing Harris's and Democratic policies as "anti-child" and "anti-family" (Licon, 2024a). Scholar of presidential rhetoric Jennifer Mercieca (interviewed in Sargent, 2024c) has tied Vance's comments to white nationalism/white supremacy and the related Great Replacement Theory (see Chapter 4).

The Trump campaign further attacked Harris for specific policy stances that it argued violate so-called traditional gender roles and norms. The campaign spent over $37 million—20 % of its overall advertising budget—on ads highlighting transgender-related issues, and that does not include similar ads run by other Republican candidates (Nagourney and Nehamas, 2024). It ran one ad that appeared over 55,000 times total, and aired in all seven of the most important battleground states—Arizona, Georgia, Michigan, Nevada, North Carolina, Pennsylvania, and Wisconsin (all eventually won by Trump)—proclaiming that "Kamala supports taxpayer-funded sex changes for prisoners" (Yilek, 2024). Note that the ad disrespects her position as vice president and as a leader by calling her only by her first name; it did so twice without ever using her surname. This is far more likely to happen with female than male candidates for office (Ryan et al., 2024). *The New York Times* summarized the ad's visual content: "The ad flashes to a photo of Ms. Harris, edited to look as if she is standing beside a bald, mustachioed person in a bright red dress and lipstick" (Bender, 2024b). The description continues:

> In one frame, a photo of Ms. Harris wearing an admiring expression is shown alongside one of Rachel Levine, the first openly transgender person confirmed by the Senate to a federal

position. Another photo, showing what look like orange-suited prisoners or detainees, is a publicity shot from the Netflix show "Orange Is the New Black."[22] The ad ends with video of Ms. Harris alongside a drag performer, Pattie Gonia, before cutting to scenes of Mr. Trump, flanked by men and a woman in suits, greeting uniformed blue-collar workers and then showing off his signature to workers in hard hats.

If the visuals were insufficient to drive home the message, the narrator's final lines removed any doubt: "Kamala is for they/them. President Trump is for you" (Bender, 2024b). The message is clear: Trump is a real man, and supports real men and women. "Kamala" is a radical who stands on the side of the freaks, and wants to destroy traditional understandings of gender.

Charlamagne Tha God, whose nationally syndicated radio show reaches 4.5 million listeners per week and is one of the leading black media figures in the U.S., saw the ad and responded on air: "When you hear the narrator say Kamala supports taxpayer-funded sex changes for prisoners, that one line I was like, 'Hell no, I don't want my taxpayer dollars going to that'." Going further, he added: "That ad was impactful . . . It made an impression" (Sourcestaff, 2024). Trump then turned that clip into another ad, one that Harris's top super PAC found moved the contest 2.7 points to the Republican nominee's advantage among people who saw it. The Trump campaign stated that the trans ad helped them with black and Hispanic men along with white suburban women who opposed trans females competing with cisgender females in sports (Goldmacher, Haberman and Swan, 2024).[23] Democratic pollster Cornell Belcher told *The New York Times* that the ad also helped the twice-elected president, well, rile up his base: "That's what Republicans do very, very well. They keep their vote energized and mobilized" (Nagourney and Nehamas, 2024).

On a similar theme, on September 17, 2024, Arkansas Governor and former Trump Press Secretary Sarah Huckabee Sanders took the stage with the Republican nominee in Flint, Michigan and went after Harris for not having biological children. Sanders offered that her own children are a "permanent reminder of what's important." She then added: "So my kids keep me humble. Unfortunately, Kamala Harris doesn't have anything keeping her humble" (Shalvey, 2024). The Trump team contends that because Harris rejects traditional values on gender both in her own personal life and the policies for which she advocates, she is somehow suspect and not fit for office.

---

22 This was a very popular show that gained widespread attention for having the first openly transgender actor playing a prominent transgender character.
23 Charlamagne sought to stop Trump from using the clip of him speaking, claiming it was misleading (Sourcestaff, 2024).

Relatedly, Trump has called Harris's running mate, Minnesota Governor Tim Walz, "Tampon Tim." This gender-related slur references a bill Walz signed in his home state that Trump claimed: "ordered tampons to be put into boys' bathrooms." He continued: "Do we have any children here? Please close your ears. He ordered tampons in boys' bathrooms. [Walz] signed a bill that boys' bathrooms—*all* boys' bathrooms in Minnesota—will have tampons" (Dale, 2024a). A CNN Fact Check found "Trump's claims are false," but the nickname drives home the contention that Walz, like Harris, rejects traditional gender norms and, in this case, favors transgender boys who might need a tampon because they remain biologically female (Dale, 2024a). This all connects to a larger, long-standing right-wing theme that stokes fear over trans rights blurring the lines between men and women as it relates to K-12 school bathrooms. Such blurring stands in direct contrast to the gender essentialism that Trump's rhetoric and governing policy has long featured.

Trump went even further on the theme of traditional gender norms and roles in an interview that aired on October 18, 2024, on a podcast hosted by a former professional wrestler whose audience, by every indication, almost certainly skews heavily male. First, the host opined that: "We need to see the fathers are capable of great things because we've dealt with it, especially in the last three and a half years, a complete dismemberment of what it is to be a man. We're under attack for everything" (Sullivan, 2024). The phrase "three and a half years" refers to the Biden-Harris administration. The twice-elected president replied: "We are. Well actually, manhood is under attack." Broadening his condemnation of his opponent, he added that religion is also under siege: "[religion is the] glue that kept this country together, and so many people are mocking it now. But it's absolutely under attack and under attack by [the Biden-Harris] administration" (Sullivan, 2024). On these, as with so many other 'culture war' issues, Trump and his allies paint Democrats like Biden, Harris, and Walz as seeking to destroy traditional values.

Authoritarian personality

As mentioned, Authoritarian Personality and Scapegoat Theory (Adorno, Frenkel-Brunswik, Levinson, and Sanford, 1950) fall under the umbrella of the Psychodynamic Approach to stereotypes (e.g., Allport, 1954/1979). According to this approach, people are motivated to stereotype because of a psychological need to reduce frustration (e.g., Tajfel and Wilkes, 1963). In Scapegoat Theory, the motivation is the need to project blame externally. People with an authoritarian personality desire to obey and be led by an authority figure.

Early stereotype research was grounded in a psychodynamic perspective that saw stereotypes as innately bad and presumed those who used them had a psychological need to do so (Kurylo, 2013). However, this approach has been replaced by a cognitive one (see Chapter 3), which is premised on the functionality of stereotypes for the individual who is inundated with information and must rely on stereotypes and other schema to cope with this information overload; thus, stereotyping is functional, automatic, unavoidable, and universal (though the content of the stereotype varies by culture and time). The cognitive approach literature on stereotypes is premised on the assumption that salient characteristics of an interaction (i.e., interactants or situation) rather than our own individual pathology or prejudice are what trigger stereotypes. Thus, the extension into communication contexts is logical. Contrasting the cognitive approach, the psychodynamic approach views individuals as motivated by psychological needs (Hamilton and Sherman, 1994) and stereotypes as "cognitive culprits in prejudice and discrimination" (Taylor and Fiske, 1984, p. 160). Pettigrew (1979), for example, labels stereotypes as bad and demonstrates how the psychodynamic perspective is "more concerned with prejudice than with stereotypes" (Leyens et al., 1994, p. 50).

Trump's behavior and rhetoric about Clinton invoked her gender and stereotypes thereof—including the double bind women endure—much as he has done with Harris (see Chapter 3). Separate from his aforementioned portrayal of Clinton as a ruthless villain, Trump also portrayed the former U.S. senator and Secretary of State as weak and unable to even help herself, let alone take on the most powerful position in the world. For just one example, see the September 27, 2016 presidential debate, where he derided her as not having "the look" or "the stamina" to be president (Lussenhop, 2016; see also Chapter 4)—in October 2024, the Trump campaign accused Harris, after she became the only one of the two to release her medical records, of lacking his "stamina" (Rogers et al., 2024).

At the second Trump-Clinton debate, on October 10, 2016, the twice-elected president also tried to show his dominance over his opponent by constantly interrupting and then—in an attempt to physically intimidate—hovering and even prowling behind her while she spoke. Clinton stated that she was shocked by the behavior; nothing like that had ever before occurred on a presidential debate stage. She explained: "He loves to humiliate women, loves to talk about how disgusting we are. He was hoping to rattle me" (Bidgood, 2024a). As Bidgood (2024) noted: "Mr. Trump has used his physical presence and body language to intimidate women, made veiled threats, complained that they were uniquely mean and belittled their qualifications in a way that many women view as open sexism." Trump aimed to make himself look like a strong man by constantly seeking to make Clinton look like a weak woman.

The authoritarian personality consists of personality dispositions interrelated to each other, including: a preference for the conventional; a penchant for rigid thinking, rules, and stereotypes; impatience with subjectivity; a desire to be submissive to an authority; aggression toward those who are not considered to hold authority positions; displays of power and toughness including through destruction and cynicism; projection of internal problems to external causes; and a focus on sex as an inherently omni-relevant concern (Adorno et al., 1950). Research has shown that conservative political preference is correlated with this personality type (Byrne and Przybyla, 1980) and specifically with support for Trump (Ingraham, 2020).

The twice-elected president appealed to supporters with this authoritarian personality many times, but perhaps none more directly than at a September 23, 2024 rally in Pennsylvania, when he spoke about what he would do for women, whom he claimed needed his protection as president:

> I am your protector . . . I want to be your protector. As president, I have to be your protector, You will no longer be abandoned, lonely or scared. You will no longer be in danger, you're not gonna be in danger any longer. You will no longer have anxiety from all of the problems our country has today. You will be protected and I will be your protector. Women will be happy, healthy, confident and free.

He added, in an incongruous aside: "You will no longer be thinking about abortion" (Mazza, 2024). Later, on October 30, Trump addressed the issue again, this time telling his audience that some of his staffers asked him to stop saying he would protect women because it was "inappropriate." He appeared to delight in rejecting that advice, along with any concern for how women might feel about his offer to protect them: "I said, well, I'm going to do it whether the women like it or not" (McDaniel, 2024). Karen Stenner, an expert on authoritarian political personalities, took note on Twitter of the "utter CONTEMPT in Trump's voice when he says 'women'" (Sargent, 2024c). *The Washington Post* reported that, although some supporters liked it, other women found this rhetoric "paternalistic or insulting" (LeVine and Knowles, 2024). Additionally, Trump here employed one of his favorite rhetorical tactics, namely saying that he is stating something that he's 'not supposed to say'—which signifies to his audience that he is a brave truth bringer, breaking through the boundaries of propriety to say what needs to be said (McCreesh, 2024c).

Returning to the 'protector' rhetoric, those who have an authoritarian personality need a leader to rule over them, and a savior to protect them from harm. Trump offered himself as both, presenting a kind of fantasy of an all–powerful father figure keeping women safe from harm like their daddies used to do. Sexism and traditional gender roles are clearly at play in these remarks, as Susan Faludi

(2024) explained: "Protection is an area of American culture that is resolutely gendered. The problematic dynamics that traditionally govern protection of home and hearth also govern our politics, an arena in which, historically, women have been granted neither protector nor protected status." In other words, if voters are thinking about their need for protection, that helps Trump and hurts Harris. Therefore, he ensures that they do think about it.

Power

A theme in this chapter has been the idea of power and the role stereotypes play in perpetuating divisions between groups on the basis of who holds power and who does not—as well as the related question of who deserves to. Through his rhetoric, Trump was able to trigger whites, men in particular, to follow his lead at least in part because he presented Clinton as a readily available villain and scapegoat. Moreover, for at least some of Trump's supporters, the Authoritarian Personality fit. This enabled the twice-elected president to surround himself with people who acted like sycophants. Those who did not yield to his authority as the leader of the party and/or country faced serious consequences.

Chapter 6
Muted Group Theory and Critical Race Theory: Weaponizing snowflakes

Regardless of the root cause of the stereotype use, the outcome of stereotyping can involve the silencing of targeted groups, something Trump successfully weaponized as a strategy. All groups, in theory, have the equal potential to communicate to ingroup members that their group is better and stronger than the other groups. Such communication stands at the heart of Social Identity Theory and Group Vitality Theory (see Chapter 4). We generally have the capacity and even the inclination to think the groups we belong to are special and, by extension, we are as well. Therefore, we may presume we deserve more, matter more, and should be more highly valued by society and other individuals. To be sure, this preference for ingroup members is not something we necessarily always act on in ways that hurt or silence others. This process is a survival tactic, to some extent, in which we look after those who we presume are most like us and are thus most likely to look after 'our' best interests. If we all do this equally effectively then, in theory, everyone's needs will balance out, and we can all survive and live relatively stable lives . . . if all else is equal.

The problem is that all else is not equal. As the U.S. Department of Treasury (Bowdler and Harris, 2022) documented in a detailed series on the impact of white racism in our country:

> Racial inequality in the United States today is rooted in long-standing behaviors, beliefs, and public and private policies that resulted in the appropriation of the physical, financial, labor, and other resources of non-white people . . . It is important to note the prominent role of inequitable and harmful policies—dating back to before the country's founding. These include attacks on Native Americans' political status and expropriation of their land, the reliance on slavery to underpin a significant portion of the colonial and then U.S. economy, and the Jim Crow laws and other formal and informal policies that enforced segregation and severely limited opportunities for non-white Americans.

> The millions of African Americans who left the southern United States to escape Jim Crow laws faced formal and informal employment, housing, and educational discrimination in destination cities in the North and West. Native Americans who survived the military conquests of the mid-19th century were subject to policies that disenfranchised them, forced their assimilation and relocation, and removed Native children from their households. Anti-Latino sentiment, which grew in the 19th century as emigration from Mexico to the United States increased in the years following the Mexican-American War, grew further following the Great Depression due to concerns that Mexican Americans were taking jobs from European-Americans.

https://doi.org/10.1515/9783111426327-009

Similarly, anti-Asian sentiment grew following the arrival of Chinese immigrants during the California Gold Rush, which was manifested in the Chinese Exclusion Act prohibiting the immigration of Chinese laborers beginning in 1882, and was ignited again after the bombing of Pearl Harbor, with the establishment of Japanese internment camps by executive order, which resulted in the forced relocation and internment of about 120,000 Japanese Americans.

Ingroups exercise tangible and substantial amounts of power that other groups do not, at least not in comparable quantities. In American society, white people exercise a disproportionate share of power. This is no doubt less so than in previous centuries, but power is nonetheless not yet distributed equally across racial and ethnic lines. In short, whites remain relatively dominant because they have the strongest group vitality (see Chapter 4) in the United States. Though their share of the population compared to minorities is gradually shrinking, whites in America still have considerably more status and institutional support than other groups.

We have had an African American president and vice president, the latter of whom also won the Democratic Party's presidential nomination. However, 75% of members of Congress (Schaeffer, 2023), and 75% of the members of state legislatures across the country for whom we have data—which is about 90% of them (National Conference of State Legislatures, 2023)—are white, even though the U.S. population is only about 60% white. These groups are also disproportionately male, wealthier than the average American, publicly straight (even if not always so in private), and Christian. It is easy to see, literally, who are the dominant groups in the United States. Because certain groups have disproportionate power and status (irrespective of simply having greater numbers), they control material resources in ways that often result in harsh effects on those groups who lack such power. These other groups or 'othered' groups include racial and religious minorities in the U.S., those in the LGBTQ community, Americans living in poverty, and, more often than not, women, among others. Those who are members of more than one of these groups face even more severe consequences because of the intersectionality[24] of their outgroups.

Once power is involved, this impact extends beyond how people perceive their identity or group alignment. With power, ingroup status can be weaponized. One need not look far for examples of how one group's power over another has historically enacted a high cost for the subjugated group; white supremacy was the law of the land de facto until 1865, and even de jure, in particular but not only in the South, during the Jim Crow century that followed. Most black Americans could not

---

24 As defined by Crenshaw (1989), "Intersectionality is a metaphor for understanding the ways that multiple forms of inequality or disadvantage sometimes compound themselves and create obstacles that often are not understood among conventional ways of thinking" (p. 149).

vote until the passage of the 1965 Voting Rights Act. Regarding that law, since the Supreme Court's 2013 ruling in *Shelby County v. Holder* that Section 4 was unconstitutional, various state governments—virtually all Republican-dominated—have implemented measures that impede access to voting in ways that disproportionately affect non-white Americans, the strong majority of whom, including about 90% of black voters, typically vote Democratic.

In terms of economic disparities, white households have on average approximately ten times the overall wealth of black households, and five times that of Latino households, with Asian households—which represent only 6% of the population—coming in just above white ones on average (Kochhar and Moslimani, 2023). To mention but one area of the economy, racial discrimination in housing was only outlawed in 1968. In spite of that, recent investigations have documented the continued discrimination black Americans face when trying to buy a home (Ferré-Sadurní, 2019). We also have documented evidence of continued racial discrimination in the job market (see Chapter 5). Regarding the criminal justice system, law enforcement, legal, and penal institutions disproportionately target and punish minorities—especially those with dark skin—resulting in a racism that permeates these systems. These factors disproportionately reduce members of those groups' access to the American Dream of pulling themselves up (from their metaphorical bootstraps) and getting ahead. Furthermore, some consequences of racial discrimination can be more subtle and harder to quantify or document. In the end, racial inequities—despite obvious and vitally important progress that advocates and leaders have fought and bled for over many long years—nonetheless remain.

When it comes to policy, although it is too simplistic just to say that all modern Republican presidents have harmed Americans of color and all Democrats have helped them, we can draw some distinctions in certain areas. The Republican approach shifted dramatically with the election of Ronald Reagan in 1980, moving in a much more conservative direction on socio-economic policy, with strongly negative outcomes for black Americans above all. As one historian wrote recently: "the sweeping Reagan Revolution . . . remade policy and American politics in ways that exacerbated the racial wealth gap and made closing it difficult, even today" (Schermerhorn, 2023).

Racism, prejudice and discrimination

Racism, prejudice, and discrimination have a wide-ranging impact on people's lives. Stereotypes are detrimental when they have undesirable consequences for those who use them (Hamilton et al., 1990) or for members of the groups they target (Allport, 1954/1979; Bar-Tal, Graumann, Kruglanski, and Stroebe, 1989; Zanna and Olson, 1994). These consequences may occur when stereotypes—as they almost always do—provide an inaccurate or false basis for judgment (e. g., Hinton, 2000; Judd and Park, 1993) and, therefore, are not useful for decision-making (de Longhe and Fernbach, 2019; Fiske and Taylor, 1984; Hamilton et al., 1990).

Moreover, stereotypes are most notably "cognitive culprits in prejudice and discrimination" (Fiske and Taylor, 1984, p. 160; see also Fiske, 1998). Stereotypes facilitate prejudice when they foster "an avertive or hostile attitude toward a person who belongs to a group, simply because he belongs to that group, and is therefore presumed to have the objectionable qualities ascribed to the group" (Allport, 1954/ 1979, p. 7). With whom do you do business? For whom do you have empathy? Whom do you perceive to be a member of your group? We are often unaware of our own prejudice because it need not look like overt discrimination. Rather, prejudice can often be subtle, and in some cases unconscious. As per the University of California San Francisco (n.d.): "Unconscious biases are social stereotypes about certain groups of people that individuals form outside their own conscious awareness."

Stereotypes that are communicated "matter because they have consequences" (Schaller and Conway, 2001, p. 163). Discrimination extends racially prejudicial thoughts that derive from inaccurate stereotypes and applies them to situations, resulting in harm to those targeted. Stereotypes facilitate discrimination when they extend prejudice into behavior by providing justification for "differential treatment" (Allport, 1954/1979, p. 52).

Though discrimination can occur anywhere, the workplace is a particularly important and consequential location to address because it affects who gets hired, promoted, given raises, or fired. In the professional world, the communication of stereotypes can permeate any workplace and at any level (Kurylo and Hu, 2024). DEI initiatives are intended to help with transparency, consistency, and an organization's overall ability to hire and shepherd those from groups with less power through the pipeline to senior level positions in order to increase all forms of representation at every level.

Kurylo and Veeramani (2024) note:

> Given the potential for prejudice and discrimination, unpredictable or poor work-life balance, lack of transparency in decision-making, necessity to accede to dominant cultural norms, and dearth of inclusivity that minoritized employees may experience in these organizations, it should not be surprising that those who are minoritized may at times prefer to work outside majority White owned or led corporations (Lynch, 2002; Zheng, 2019, p. 17)

In other words, rather than be subject to the norms, whims, and exclusion minorities may face in white-majority organizations, they may choose to opt out. However, for many if not most Americans of color, this is not a realistic option.

In 2011, President Obama signed Executive Order 13583 "Establishing a Coordinated Government-wide Initiative to Promote Diversity and Inclusion in the Federal Workforce." A first of its kind, this required that government agencies develop and implement DEI initiatives. In 2020 Trump revoked this initiative with Executive Order 13950, "Combating Race and Sex Stereotyping," which banned federal employees and contractors from presenting certain kinds of content often associated with DEI when conducting diversity-related trainings. President Biden reinstated DEI through Executive Order 13985 "Advancing Racial Equity and Support for Underserved Communities Through the Federal Government," which revoked Trump's EO 13950.

On a related note, in his first term Trump also removed all LGBTQ-related content from the White House website (O'Hara, 2017), further silencing the voice of this marginalized community. He did so again upon taking office in 2025 (Wong and Ma, 2025). Beyond the website, Trump issued an executive order on Inauguration Day, January 20, 2025, that took particular aim at the rights of transgender Americans. In line with traditional, gender essentialist concepts, it all but declared that transgender and nonbinary people do not exist as far as federal policy is concerned, among other actions (Arkin et al., 2025).

In his 2024 campaign, Trump made clear that his antipathy to DEI will motivate his policy approach on these issues (ACLU, 2024), and, as per an Axios report, his "close allies want to dramatically change the government's interpretation of Civil Rights-era laws to focus on "anti-white racism" rather than discrimination against people of color" (Thompson, 2024). Survey data indicate that the twice-elected president is in sync with Republican voters on this, as a 2024 CBS poll found that about two-thirds of Republicans believe that "efforts to promote racial diversity and equality" were "going too far," with only one in ten saying that such efforts were "not going far enough." Among Democrats, over 50% said "not going far enough," while a bit over 10% said "going too far" (Bump, January 15, 2024).

In the opening weeks of his second term, Trump has railed against DEI almost daily, aiming to eliminate any trace of DEI programs or principles from the executive branch (Alfonseca, 2025), and indeed any institution that receives federal funding, in particular schools (Binkley, 2025). He cites DEI's supposedly harmful effects even when there is no evidence that it relates to a given topic or incident—such as with the January 30, 2025 mid-air collision between a military helicopter and a passenger jet over the Potomac River jet that killed 67 people, leaving no survivors (Bumiller, 2025).[25]

---

25 This fits a general pattern, as Baker (2025) noted: "Mr. Trump often moves to place any crisis into his own political or ideological narrative, regardless of the facts. He tied the California fires to

Traditional DEI training is not in itself a panacea. Kurylo and Veeramani (2024) note that: "communicated stereotypes can undermine DEI initiatives and hurt customer relations, sales, and a company's brand reputation. Understanding the role stereotypes play in thwarting DEI is, therefore, integral to carrying out DEI initiatives effectively" (p. 18). They continued: "When DEI initiatives fail, successful employee recruitment, employee satisfaction, and staff retention decrease while recruitment costs and employee turnover increase (Bach, 1995)" (Kurylo and Veeramani, 2024, p. 15). Nonetheless, DEI has faced a severe backlash, due at least in part to its perceived over-reaching and lack of rigor, as well as some research that suggests it may in fact: "promote rather than ameliorate intergroup hostilities" (Network Contagion Research Institute, 2024). These problems provide an opening for the right-wing to discredit DEI initiatives and, more importantly, the concepts that underlay its ideology (Detrow, 2024). DEI has become one more tool wielded to fit the narrative that white people are under attack, as critics argue that it is patently unfair or reflects, to use the right-wing phrasing, "reverse discrimination" (Guynn, 2023).

Systemic racism and generational wealth

White supremacy has, despite progress in combating it, created an America in which whites hold disproportionate power at almost every level of society; non-whites have been left out to a significant degree. Without access to the same material resources as whites, most black Americans, Latinos, and American Indians in particular have had a more difficult time gaining access to power. Truly significant wealth—that is generational wealth that provides the kind of resources and advantages many families use to preserve or expand their positions—remains concentrated largely in the hands of white Americans (Federal Reserve Bank of St. Louis, 2024). This is true even as many white families continue to struggle as well in a system where economic inequality exists within as well as across racial lines. Trump's exceptional generational wealth, for example, gave him a tremendous head start—the aforementioned many millions of dollars (see Chapter 1) which he received from his father that began and sustained his business career.

Systemic racism is the idea that various institutions in American society predictably and consistently—even if not intentionally or with deliberate malice—

---

wrongheaded environmental and water policies, assertions that experts disputed. After the New Year's Day terrorist attack on Bourbon Street in New Orleans, Mr. Trump blamed immigration, even though the attacker was a U.S. citizen born in Texas."

mistreat Americans of color, thus preventing them from achieving the same level of success as whites. White generational wealth—even to the extent seen among the middle class—exacerbates racial disparities, giving the appearance that anyone can achieve success based solely on talent and hard work when it is simply not as easy as that. For the most part, this systemic racism is not intended or planned by the people who benefit from it today. There is no wide-scale conspiracy per se standing behind these systems, nor is such a conspiracy required to maintain their operation. The status quo needs only inertia to function effectively. Indeed, systemic racism is difficult to see unless you have experienced it. Because of its invisibility, ingroup members that benefit from it regularly fail to see outside their own perspective. Instead, they all too easily view themselves as having *earned* privilege that resulted from their own hard work and initiative. The ingroup then uses that narrative to discredit the outgroup's lived experience with systemic racism, criticizing them for supposedly not putting in the necessary effort to earn such success.

Post-affirmative action

Affirmative action, a kind of legal precursor to DEI initiatives, was enacted to address injustices and other obstacles that hampered the ability of racial minorities and women to achieve equality in school admissions and jobs. Affirmative action's intent was to counteract the privileges and opportunities afforded to those in the dominant group—i. e., white male privilege. Some criticize affirmative action as inherently unfair because it takes race and gender into account rather than be "blind" to them. The critics argue that it privileges certain groups and is therefore not treating groups equally under the law. Supporters contend instead that affirmative action attempts to rebalance what was long the unofficial or, in some cases, official policy by which preference for white men permeated the systems of employment and education in America.

Trump had in 2018 reversed official guidance the Obama administration had given schools encouraging them to use race in admission decisions. Then, the U.S. Supreme Court ruling in *SFFA v. Harvard* (2023) and *SFFA v. UNC* (2023) completely banned race-based affirmative action from the admissions process. Rensselaer Polytechnic Institute, a well-respected competitive STEM school on the East Coast, felt the need to acknowledge this change in their application system, posting the following on its admissions website FAQ's:

> In the past, a student's race/ethnicity has been just one aspect of a holistic review process at Rensselaer. Moving forward, in accordance with the recent U.S. Supreme Court Decision . . .

Rensselaer will be suppressing all student race/ethnicity data (collected in the recruitment and application phases) during the application review process.

Some cheered the court's ruling and argued that it restored fairness to college admissions after long periods that favored whites and then people of color respectively. Some argue that the United States no longer needs affirmative action because racism is no longer a problem. However, there is blatant evidence to the contrary.

Critical Race Theory

A mere ten years ago Critical Race Theory (CRT) was a niche academic field that was only familiar to those on a college campus, even mostly those within related departments. Critical Race Theory studies systemic racism in order to raise awareness of the problems that racial minorities disproportionately face. The area of Critical Studies, in which Critical Race Theory resides, originated in the 1930s at the Institute for Social Research in Frankfurt, Germany, and its influence grew thanks to Jürgen Habermas along with others in the 1960s and 1970s. Of course, few people know of Habermas or the Frankfurt School because relatively few outside academia take a critical approach or study Critical Race Theory in depth. This is an important point. The only reason millions of Americans have come to hear about this niche field is because the right-wing has turned those who study it into a scapegoat. The right-wing misrepresentation of this field of thought has consequences, and not surprisingly these harm racial minorities.

Critical Race Theory came under attack from the right after garnering attention outside of academic circles. Trump-supporting Republicans and activists in a number of conservative-run states have led an effort to ban the teaching of CRT in K-12 public schools even though, according to available evidence, curricula do not include it and students are not learning its tenets in any kind of organized fashion (Sawchuk, 2021). In 2024, the American Historical Association conducted a nationwide survey of 3,000 middle and high school teachers. James Grossman, the head of the AHA, explained the findings as follows:

> The divisive concepts legislations that have been introduced by lawmakers make assumptions about what teachers are teaching. We always knew that teachers don't really teach Critical Race Theory in their classrooms. But not one [piece of legislation] had any data on what's being taught . . . We found that teachers don't use materials from contentious sources, so the accusation that teachers are teaching kids to hate America is simply untrue (Banerji, 2024).

Through misrepresenting Critical Race Theory, Trump and his allies on the right can further argue that whites are under attack and being blamed and scapegoated themselves (see Chapter 4). One critic, Tennessee Republican Senator Marsha Blackburn (2021), criticized: "the left's effort to brainwash our children by injecting CRT into public school curriculum" (Blackburn, 2021). She spoke of a white child in her state who attended a school that supposedly presented CRT-influenced content and came home saying: "I'm ashamed that I'm White. Is there something wrong with me? Why am I hated so much?" (Blackburn, 2021). Blackburn contended: "this child's distress was the desired result of her lessons. If left unchecked, this mental and emotional trauma will worm its way into every classroom in America" (Blackburn, 2021). Arguments like these undergird the push by Trump and like-minded people on the right to teach our history the way they want it taught.

These critics argue that just because a person is white does not mean they are to be blamed for systemic racism. But this is a straw man argument because CRT agrees. The existence of systemic racism does not impugn individual white people but, instead and literally by definition, the systems that are in place. The anti-CRT narrative places whites in the role of victims who are innocent but helpless against the unsubstantiated attacks from Critical Race Theory. This allows the right to take victimhood away from racial minorities and redefine it as something experienced by whites because of their race. Coupled with the 'browning' of the United States, conservatives cite the supposedly anti-white positions espoused by Critical Race Theory as 'evidence' that whites both individually and collectively are being threatened. This mentality, along with the rhetoric that accompanies it, views resources for minorities and majorities as a zero-sum game wherein resources are finite and if one group gets something then by default the other group loses something. In reality, there are a variety of ways to increase or reapportion the pool of resources to benefit members of all racial groups, if leaders choose to do so.

As added benefits of this redefinition of victimhood, the right can delegitimize a field that helps people become aware of systemic racism and the role they may inadvertently play within it, as well as paint academia as a haven for those seeking to attack white people. The irony is that, despite the aforementioned evidence from the American Historical Association and elsewhere, the right focuses on banning CRT from K-12 education. They have succeeded in passing laws in 18 states ranging across the South, Plains, and Mountain West that, according to Education Week: "restrict teaching Critical Race Theory or limit how teachers can discuss racism and sexism" (Schwartz, 2021). In 26 other states, similar measures have been proposed, or passed by the legislature but vetoed or blocked in some other way.

Right-wing alternate history

Some right-wing dominated states have gone even further. For example, the required public school curriculum in states like Florida now has redefined slavery as providing some level of protection for enslaved black people who would otherwise not have been able to survive on their own (Peoples et al., 2023). They were being taken care of, the argument goes, by a 'cradle to grave' social safety net. Redefining enslavement in this way essentially praises the institution that stands at the root of the systemic racism Critical Race Theory is exposing—albeit at the level of college and beyond. Thus, it is no surprise that the right-wing aims at erasing the influence of CRT. This kind of right-wing, alternate history is designed to foment racial division by erasing awareness of systemic injustice. Misinformation and disinformation represent the largest threat the world faces in 2024 (World Economic Forum, 2024). For the right, a less educated populace is more convenient, especially one that knows less about the impact of systemic racism on Americans of color, and has an incorrect view of who is the real victim of racism in the U.S.

Beyond the officially mandated curriculum, six states, including Florida, have entered into a relationship with PragerU in which their history-themed videos become available as optional materials for teachers to show their students. PragerU states that its purpose is to push back against what it calls: "the dominant left-wing ideology in culture, media, and education" (Natanson and Meckler, 2024). The president of the Arizona Education Association expressed concern: "PragerU's materials are hyperpartisan to the point of propaganda, inaccurate and incredibly substandard" (Natanson and Meckler, 2024). One video features a wholly made-up segment in which noted abolitionist Frederick Douglass explains that the Founders made compromises when drawing up the Constitution that allowed slavery to continue because it was necessary to create a unified country. That is not a totally unreasonable historical argument. However, putting it in the mouth of an animated Frederick Douglass is misleading at best because it essentially suggests that the leading African American figure of the 19th century defended the preservation of slavery after the American Revolution, giving the so-called peculiar institution a kind of black seal of approval. Princeton history professor Kevin Kruse summed up PragerU's approach to history thusly: "There's a constant effort to spin atrocities in the past as not so bad" (Natanson and Meckler, 2024). A comprehensive analysis of their materials done by researcher Adrienne McCarthy found that PragerU: "mimics much of the extreme right-wing ideology in a way that is more readily digestible" (Natanson and Meckler, 2024). This is true especially for young minds.

Florida's anti-DEI and anti-CRT laws make more than just a political impact; they may be causing psychological harm as well. One psychologist (Fialk, 2021) explained that:

> The pushback against teaching CRT, and an inaccurate portrayal of black history in schools, communicates to people of color that their lived experience, perspective, and daily struggle, past and present, in a white supremacist society does not matter and will never matter. When kids believe they do not matter, it impacts identity, esteem, efficacy, and the ability to succeed. The debate and pushback could even represent yet another racial trauma that brings with it an intense emotional and mental injury.

> Hiding historical trauma prolongs and amplifies present trauma and deepens its impact. The cumulative emotional and psychological wounds are carried across generations leading to higher rates of mental and physical illness, substance use, and the decimation of families and communities.

The growing right-wing indoctrination of children in K-12 schools is evidence of why this is a concern. Under the Trump-led Republican Party, students are taught a deeply biased version of American history and learn that colleges are havens of false liberal ideology. The lack of historical understanding among students learning this material results in new generations believing that white people are victims, that systemic racism does not exist, and that slavery was not an abhorrent institution (Ede-Osifo, 2024).

Relatedly, others have expressed similar sentiments. CNN reported that some years earlier former North Carolina Lt. Gov. Mark Robinson, Republican nominee for governor in 2024 (he ultimately lost his race by a resounding 15 points), had posted the following online: "Slavery is not bad. Some people need to be slaves. I wish they would bring it (slavery) back. I would certainly buy a few." Robinson, who is African American, identified himself online as a "Black Nazi" and also stated that he would rather have Adolf Hitler than Barack Obama leading the U.S. (Kaczynski and Steck, 2024). Here's what Trump has proclaimed about Robinson: "This is Martin Luther King on steroids. I told that to Mark. I said: 'I think you're better than Martin Luther King. I think you are Martin Luther King times two,'" and called him "one of the great stars of the party, one of the great stars in politics" (Balk, 2024a). Here we see, in one individual, the connection on the right between the denial of slavery's evil and pro-Nazi sentiments. Among white nationalists, the connection is even stronger.

Trump has made clear that in his second term he will use the power of the Federal Government to block funding for K-12 schools that refuse to adopt his right-wing ideology on race and beyond—a radical ramping-up of presidential interference in America's public education. In March 2024 he laid out his intentions in clear language:

> On Day 1, I will sign a new executive order to cut federal funding for any school pushing Critical Race Theory, transgender insanity and other inappropriate racial, sexual or political content onto our children. And I will not give one penny to any school that has a vaccine mandate

or a mask mandate. I will keep men out of women's sports, 100 % (New York Times Editorial Board, 2024).

Going beyond K-12 education, Trump as well as Vance have also evinced a deep hostility to mainstream higher education, with their opposition to the DEI and CRT they see as entrenched in those institutions serving as a core element thereof. Trump has laid out plans for his second term that would fundamentally alter college in the U.S. (Dahlkamp, 2024). He would create what he defines as: "a revolution in higher education," in which the government would "take the billions and billions of dollars that we will collect by taxing, fining, and suing excessively large private university endowments, and we will then use that money to endow a new institution called the American Academy," at which "there will be no wokeness or jihadism allowed." In Trump's second term he has launched a wide array of attacks on American institutions of higher education (Goldberg, 2025).

Trump also disparaged the aforementioned colleges as "plagued by antisemitism" (Trump, 2023b), and in early 2025 threatened to cut billions in funding to schools who, in his mind, failed to combat antisemitism. Along similar lines, in a 2021 speech entitled *The Universities Are The Enemy*, Vance declared: "The universities tell us that so long as we're trailblazing on diversity, equity, inclusion, it doesn't matter if normal people get screwed . . . They care more about identity politics . . . than they do their own society and they do the people who live in it" (Damiano and Burns, 2024). Actually, Trump and his allies also practice identity politics (Reifowitz, 2019), namely the oldest and most powerful form thereof in American history: white identity politics (see Chapter 5).

The power wielded by this ingroup enables a state government to tell public colleges they cannot offer courses where certain topics are taught, for example again in Florida (Coghill, 2023). Power gives a state government a virtual veto over the content of courses, as seen in that state's rejection of a proposed AP African American History course, with the caveat that: "if the course comes into compliance and incorporates historically accurate content, [the Florida Department of Education] will reopen the discussion" (Alfonseca, 2023). Power enables a state to enact legislation—the law in Florida is named "Stop WOKE"—that removes curricula, for example about slavery, developed from the consensus among historians and taught in schools for generations, and replaces it with ideologically-driven substitute histories. Such changes render Americans of color voiceless by erasing their history and experience. Power enabled Trump, during the first 100 days of his first term, to dismantle many of his predecessor's achievements as president (ABC News, 2018). Likewise, we are already seeing that in a second term Trump will use his power to reverse whatever progress the Biden-Harris White House has achieved on matters of racial justice.

A bully wielding modern concepts as weapons

Trump and his MAGA allies' use of Critical Race Theory as a straw man and scapegoat aims at silencing racial minorities and other marginalized people. Another word further aids this endeavor: snowflake. Drawing on a term that appears to have grown out of a remark in the 1996 novel *Fight Club*—later a hugely successful movie—(Konerman, 2017), right-wingers deride those who point out various forms of oppression in American society and culture as hypersensitive "snowflakes," that is, weak people easily tweaked and agitated by the slightest provocation (McIntosh, 2020).

This name calling represents bullying as well as an attempt to silence Trump's political opponents and their supporters. Doing so enables the twice-elected president to discount and dismiss any concern, regardless of its legitimacy, with a single word. For example, a Trump campaign website offered tips on how supporters can rhetorically defeat "that liberal snowflake relative" (Allyn, 2019). As Schwartz (2017) writes: "Snowflake is an ad hominem attack, a taunt of a schoolyard bully by way of Ayn Rand. You're a wuss, and so your argument is invalid . . . It's [sic] purpose is dismissing liberalism as something effeminate, and also infantile, an outgrowth of the lessons you were taught in kindergarten." Though doing so does not often change the opinion of those who oppose Trump's rhetoric or ideology, using or hearing the word "snowflake" against opponents empowers his ingroup to further view their leader as strong, as the alpha. This reinforces his value as an ingroup member; it enhances both the group vitality of Trump's ingroup—because he possesses multiple forms of strength and power—as well as his status as a strong leader among those drawn to him at least in part because of their authoritarian personality style (see Chapter 5).

Showing liberals and their ideological values to be weak and derived from hypersensitivity makes it that much easier to effectively scapegoat them as the cause of the unfair problems white people face. Granted, some of the more progressive approaches to fostering greater equality have perhaps overcorrected. Trigger warnings, it turns out, actually do not help much (Bridgland et al., 2023). Some of the left's preferred language choices to describe groups are often viewed as overly paternalistic or infantilizing by members of the groups they are intended to describe inclusively. For example, there is the term Latinx (see Chapter 2), which progressive academics, students, and activists often use, but which an overwhelming majority of actual people of Latino/Hispanic heritage utterly reject (Newport, 2022; Falcon, 2023). It is this type of over-correction, much like the concept of microaggressions, that has helped Trump garner support by putting off centrists who might otherwise back Democrats—in particular older generations who were raised to have a thick skin and let perceived insults and slurs roll off their back.

Trump's rhetoric weaponizes this one little word, snowflake, to do some heavy lifting.

Muted Group Theory

Muted Group Theory helps explain how dominant perspectives silence or suppress minorities, making them invisible. When it comes to race in the United States, doing so is a potent way of enhancing white privilege. When groups in power prioritize their own needs, expectations, histories, and so on, they render those of marginalized groups muted, that is to say voiceless. Although we are focused here on right-wing attempts to silence such groups, it is important to recognize that attempts to silence happen on the left as well. For one example, on abortion, some on the far left tell men essentially to stay out of the debate, as this issue directly affects women's bodies (Fetters, 2019). The motivation for this is to prioritize marginalized voices, but the effect is nonetheless to mute a specific group of people. As seen here, the extremes on both sides of the political spectrum display some parallels in how they operate—demonstrating a willingness to silence anyone who disagrees in the name of winning an argument. There is an expression that captures some of this idea: the ends justify the means. Those wielding power have the choice to either encourage a healthy and vigorous public discourse, or instead silence marginalized voices. Republicans—with Trump at the lead— have demonstrated they will not hesitate to do the latter.

In the case of the LGBTQ community, initiatives from the right literally seek to silence their perspectives. In 2022, Florida (and other states which copied Florida's legislation) barred teachers in public schools from presenting "instruction on sexual orientation and gender identity"—which led many schools to remove books or even cut material from songs sung in school musicals that included LGBTQ themes. Some teachers feared that the law—dubbed "Don't Say Gay" by opponents—meant they could not reveal their own sexual orientation, meaning they could not have pictures of their family on their desk. In one particularly harsh example, the school board in Miami-Dade County, which in 2021 had formally recognized LGBTQ history month, feared that doing so again in 2022 would run afoul of the law. Ultimately, the settlement of a lawsuit over this legislation clarified what could be discussed in schools (Associated Press, 2024a). The consequences on this marginalized group of exercising power in such a way include permanently silencing students, as evidenced by the high attempted suicide rates of this significantly at-risk population: "41% of LGBTQ+ young people seriously considered attempting suicide in the past year, including roughly half of transgender and nonbinary youth" (The Trevor Project, 2024). This is twice the rate for teens overall (Pappas, 2023).

The term "snowflake" provides yet another way to mute and, ultimately, ignore marginalized voices. Trump's attacks on Kamala Harris's laugh (see Chapter 3), for example, attempted to mute her. By focusing on her laugh as stereotypically female, Trump was able to distract his supporters from appreciating her skills, experience, and expertise. Harris refused to alter her presentation or tone it down in some way in order to please others. She used her vocal presence in the public arena and was heard by millions of Americans. Yet, the media can amplify, distort, or further mute voices as well.

Voices and voting choice

Trump is far from the first right-wing politician to use rhetoric that plays into prejudice and fear. Most white working-class people used to vote Democratic until about 75 years ago. To clarify, most African Americans, who were overwhelmingly working-class at that time, lived in the South and could not vote until the Voting Rights Act of 1965. Yet now most of the white working-class votes Republican (Cohn, 2021). Major cracks in their support for Democrats started to appear when South Carolina Governor Strom Thurmond broke from the Democratic Party in 1948—after a pro-Civil Rights plank was adopted at that year's National Convention—and ran for President on a third-party ticket as an open, avowed segregationist. During the campaign he declared: "There's not enough troops in the army to force the Southern people to break down segregation and admit the Nigra race into our theaters, into our swimming pools, into our homes, and into our churches" (Noah, 2002). He carried four states—all in the Deep South—which had previously been among the most consistently Democratic states going back to the Civil War.

In 1964, Arizona Senator Barry Goldwater became the first Republican presidential nominee to actively oppose major civil rights legislation. Strom Thurmond became a Republican and supported Goldwater's candidacy, serving as a vanguard of the almost total shift of Southern white Democrats to the Republican Party. Goldwater won the same four states Thurmond had 16 years earlier, along with Georgia, also in the Deep South—and no others besides his home state. Democratic Alabama Governor George Wallace—who was most famous for in 1963 having declared himself in favor of: "segregation now, segregation tomorrow and segregation forever" (Elliott, 2003), and subsequently standing in the doorway of a building at the University of Alabama to physically prevent its integration by two black students seeking to enroll—ran for president in 1968 as another third-party candidate in the mold of Thurmond circa 1948. Wallace won four of the five Southern states Goldwater had won, along with Arkansas, which is also in the Deep South.

Most importantly in terms of long-term impact, Republican nominee Richard Nixon in 1968 implemented the so-called Southern Strategy—aiming to appeal to white working-class voters in the South in particular, but beyond as well. This strategy garnered significant increases in support for Republicans among white working-class voters, support that has grown ever since. Lee Atwater, who worked on campaigns for Thurmond early in his career, then was deputy director and political director for President Ronald Reagan's 1984 re-election campaign, and then ran George H.W. Bush's presidential campaign in 1988—which included the infamous Willie Horton ad (see Chapter 1)—explained how the Southern Strategy worked and how it morphed over time:

> You start out in 1954 by saying, 'Nigger, nigger, nigger! By 1968 you can't say 'nigger' —that hurts you. Backfires. So you say stuff like forced busing, states' rights and all that stuff. You're getting so abstract now [that] you're talking about cutting taxes, and all these things you're talking about are totally economic things and a byproduct of them is [that] Blacks get hurt worse than whites (Herbert, 2006).

As Bob Herbert (2006) wrote, the strategy has been "working beautifully for the GOP for decades." White working-class support for Republicans in the South and across the country reached a new high when Trump was the party's nominee in 2016, with only a slight drop-off in 2020 (Dilulio, 2024), and appears, based on initial exit polls, to have reached another new high in 2024 (NBC News, 2024). As this shift in voting patterns reflects, people often vote against their material interest as defined by universally applicable, objective metrics such as income/wealth, health/life expectancy, etc.

The primary innovation in Trump's approach to winning white working-class voters is that, unlike his predecessors, he adds fear of immigration and the browning of America into the mix. Largely because it suited the needs of business owners, Republican presidents and nominees before him spoke relatively positively about immigrants and at times supported measures to help undocumented immigrants become citizens. Trump, on the other hand, following the path laid out by Limbaugh, Fox News, and others in right-wing media (Reifowitz, 2019) broke from the Reagan-Bush-McCain tradition on immigration. The twice-elected president plays and preys on white people's racial anxiety about their collective status at a time when America's demographics are shifting rapidly. One of his rhetoric's primary effects is to convince working-class whites to vote on their perceived racial interests as white people, rather than their economic interests as working-class people.

Jonathan Metzl, in *Dying of Whiteness: How the Politics of Racial Resentment Is Killing America's Heartland*, interviewed Trevor, a 41-year-old white Tennessean, whose story personifies this aspect of Trump's impact. Trevor adamantly endorsed Republican officials' rejection of the option to expand Medicaid eligibility in his state as provided for by the Affordable Care Act, aka Obamacare, an expansion that would have given him health care coverage he could not otherwise afford (Metzl, 2019, p. 20). Trevor saw America as the aforementioned racial zero-sum game in which anything that benefits a person of color must harm him, thus exemplifying the LBJ quotation about the wealthy picking the pockets of poor whites by distracting them with racial resentment (see Chapter 5). Despite being near death thanks to liver disease and hepatitis C, Trevor told the author: "Ain't no way I would ever support Obamacare or sign up for it," and added "I would rather die." As to why, Trevor offered: "We don't need any more government in our lives. And in any case, no way I want my tax dollars paying for Mexicans or welfare queens" (Metzl, 2019, p. 20). Here we see the extent of the influence of classic right-wing stereotypes around supposedly undeserving Americans of color on welfare (see Chapter 2)—some of which Trump has engaged in as well (see Chapter 5), along with anti-immigrant sentiments. These ideas further demonstrate the intersection between racial identity and economic issues.

Trumpism ultimately encourages white Americans to identify with their perceived racial interests over other kinds of interests, such as those relating to class (Reifowitz, 2019). As Ian Haney López argued:

> On the right, the story that creates a common sense of identity is rooted in race. Who are we? We are decent, hard-working people who are threatened by (implicitly Black and Brown) violent, lazy, pestilent "others." Donald Trump embodies this identity that Republicans have constructed for themselves for the last 50 years—an identity of white victimization and endangerment (Karma, 2020).

Although this book focuses on analyzing the twice-elected president's rhetoric on stereotypes rather than countering its effects, López has conducted research that points to a particular direction on that front. He proposes what he calls the Race-Class Narrative, according to which candidates and campaigns who oppose this Trump vision should put forth a message that confronts its content directly, by arguing that Americans of different races are, in fact:

> Working families that have more in common than differences between us, but we are being divided by economic elites who seek profit, division, and conflict. And the way forward is to build social solidarity across lines of division. This is a story of identity more than it is one of ideology or policy" (Karma, 2020).

López has tested this message in field surveys, and it outperformed three other commonly used political messages, including not only two other standard left-leaning messages—i.e., a colorblind economic populist one, and one that emphasizes racial justice—but also a Trump-style "racial fear" message (López, 2019; Karma, 2020). So perhaps there is hope for us after all. Unfortunately, any success in the future will arrive too late for Trevor.

Returning to *Dying of Whiteness*, Metzl summarized the now deceased Tennessean's thinking thusly: "Trevor voiced a literal willingness to die for his place in [the racial] hierarchy, rather than participate in a system that might put him on the same plane as immigrants or racial minorities." More broadly, the author explained: "Trump supporters were willing to put their own lives on the line in support of their political beliefs . . . make tradeoffs that negatively affect their lives and livelihoods in support of larger prejudices or ideals" (Metzl, 2019, p. 22). Stereotype-laden rhetoric distracts working- and middle-class people from feeling oppressed by an economic elite that exercises great power over them. In academic terms, it is a snow job.

Chapter 7
Elaboration Likelihood Model and Agenda Setting Theory: "The true enemy of the people"

Donald Trump both loves and hates the media. The twice-elected president attacked journalists relentlessly, and even threatened to harm the interests of media outlets and companies he thought treated him unfairly, including CNN, *The Washington Post,* and Meta, which owns Facebook (Bassin and Potter, 2024) —even as he relied on them to amplify his stereotype-laden message. For example, according to MediaQuant, during his 2016 White House run he received the equivalent of $5.6 billion worth of coverage—what is known as "earned media"—far greater than his opponent Hillary Clinton (Stewart, 2016). Trump almost certainly could not have become president without the unprecedented amount of attention the mainstream media lavished upon him.

Elaboration Likelihood Model (ELM) postulates about the central and peripheral routes through which media messages can persuade people. Petty and Cacioppo (1985) posits that: "We can be persuaded by the *central route*, which involves a thoughtful consideration of the issues involved . . . On other occasions we might be persuaded by the *peripheral route*, where learned expectations or simple strategies such as 'don't miss out on a bargain' can be used to persuade us" (Hinton, 2000, p. 61). When most of us think about how persuasion works, we think of one person actively attempting to change the mind of another and sometimes succeeding. As it turns out, this is a fallacy. Persuasion is an internal process. While others can play a role by providing the prompt necessary to prime us to be persuaded in a certain way, ultimately we persuade ourselves. In this way, persuasion is an internal cognitive process. Communicating a stereotype provides such a prompt. As discussed in Chapter 2, stereotypes are not factual. Instead, they are essentially prompts through which we convince ourselves of their accuracy, depending on the assumptions we already have available to us cognitively, as per our heuristics and other cognitive schema (see Chapter 3). Boss (1979) demonstrates the process through which stereotypes prompt someone to persuade themselves about the accuracy of the stereotype.

Implicit stereotypes

Although stereotypes can be communicated explicitly in language (Maas and Arcuri, 1996; Mackie et al., 1996), Boss (1979) argues that a communicated stereotype

https://doi.org/10.1515/9783111426327-010

need not be expressed explicitly in a conversation to be understood and, thereby, persuasive. One just needs to hint at the stereotype (e.g., the Willie Horton ad discussed in Ch. 1). This is because, when communicated, stereotypes take the form of an enthymeme, which is a rhetorical tool used to persuade (Boss, 1979; Kurylo, 2013). An enthymeme is a logical argument in which one component remains unstated. This missing component is key, because through it the individual fills in the information needed to understand the meaning of the stereotype. Without filling in this missing component internally, the stereotype would make no sense and would be rejected as nonsensical to think or say. However, by filling in the missing component, individuals persuade themselves internally, through their own cognitive process, of the veracity of the stereotype.

We can use what is known as a syllogism, another rhetorical tool, to understand the missing stereotypical information. A syllogism contains the information needed to understand the unstated portion of the enthymeme. A syllogism includes three components: major premise, minor premise, and conclusion. Through his example of a stereotype of a Jewish person, Boss (1979) identifies these components. The major premise of Boss's example is: "Jews are shrewd" in which the content referencing both the stereotyped group "Jews" and stereotyped trait "shrewd" are explicit. Boss continues his argument by stating that the syllogism containing this major premise involves the enthymemes "Joe is Jewish" (i.e., the minor premise) and Joe is shrewd (i.e., the conclusion).

The minor premise "Joe is Jewish" is an enthymeme because it is incomplete. To understand this minor premise, a person must have familiarity with the major premise, which is the stereotype "Jews are shrewd". Similarly, the conclusion that "Joe is shrewd" is also an enthymeme, because it omits the information from the major premise that is necessary for this enthymeme to be understood. The implication is that Joe's shrewdness is derived from his being Jewish. In communicating these enthymemes to another person, either the minor premise—which involves the stereotyped group—or the conclusion—which involves the stereotyped characteristic—is unstated.

Omitting this information when communicating an enthymeme is not necessarily problematic for a speaker. As Lau et al., (2001) note, communicators "have some prior knowledge of what their addressee knows and does not know before they engage in communication" (p. 355). Moreover, this missing information is not problematic for the listener because in conversation "often . . . sentences that are produced are not complete [and] sometimes things that are not said convey more meaning that [sic] do those that are said" (Semin, 2000, p. 599). The listener's cultural knowledge base that enables them to fill in missing information. In this way, as Boss (1979) argues, someone hearing either enthymeme in the above scenario would be able to infer the major premise based on hearing the minor premise or conclusion and, notwithstanding missing some information, be readily able to complete the syllogism.

In sum, Boss (1979) argues that, when communicated, stereotypes can take any of three forms corresponding to their role within a syllogism.

- Explicit Group(s) and Explicit Characteristic(s) = major premise in the syllogism
- Explicit Group(s) and Implicit Characteristic(s) = minor premise in the syllogism
- Implicit Group(s) and Explicit Characteristic(s) = conclusion in the syllogism

A fourth form is suggested by the coding scheme provided by Boss (1979), a form not mentioned in the syllogism comparison he presented. Consider that in the previous hypothetical scenario if someone said, "Joe, you are like that," it is feasible that someone in the interaction would be able to interpret the message as referencing the stereotype and major premise that: "Jews are shrewd" based on a shared cultural knowledge base and other situational factors in the moments in which the stereotype is communicated. Therefore, communicated stereotypes may take the following fourth form not discussed by Boss that, nonetheless, also invokes the major premise:

- Implicit Group(s) and Implicit Characteristic(s)

Collaboration

As Boss argues (1979), and as a result of the implicit form in which stereotypes may be communicated, the stereotype message is not the product of the speaker alone, but the product of the involvement of both the speaker and the listener collaborating to produce the message by: "work[ing] together to arrive at mutually acceptable representations in the communicative process" (Lau et al., 2001, p. 366). This collaboration implicates both the speaker and listener in the process of producing and reproducing a stereotype that draws on the American cultural knowledge base without either having had to explicitly state the stereotype. Boss (1979) notes that when we communicate stereotypes implicitly, others in the interaction participate to complete the stereotype meaning, and adds that this little-explored process, along with other characteristics, may play a significant role in the persistence of stereotypes.

Boss (1979) explores the idea of stereotypes as a collaborative process by comparing stereotypes to enthymemes. He suggests that the stereotype need not be explicit, but if it is implied, then the hearer's mind processes and completes it. Thus, the meaning of the stereotype is not inherent in its communication but rather created in the specific interaction. In other words, stereotyping is a collaborative process (Maass and Arcuri, 1996; Haslam et al., 2002; McGarty et al., 2002). Without this collaboration, there would be no consensus among those in the interaction on the meaning of the implicitly communicated stereotype, and its content may not be perpetuated.

In this way, Boss (1979) explains a fundamental process that facilitates stereotype maintenance within a cultural knowledge base. Change in stereotypic knowledge, then, is potentially in the hands of any person in each interaction where a stereotype is communicated. The listener can forestall the perpetuation of an implicitly communicated stereotype by challenging its meaning to make clear to the stereotyper that they are not on the same page. Imagine if, in this hypothetical scenario, the response was: "I'm not sure what you mean." In this way, the listener would challenge the seemingly nonsensical meaning of the stereotype rather than collaborate on it with the stereotyper. The communication of stereotypes in implicit forms provides one explanation of how stereotypic knowledge is maintained over time, but also provides an opening for people to challenge them (Boss, 1979).

Mindlessness

Devine (1989) alludes to this opportunity to challenge stereotypical assumptions by arguing that there are two steps in the processing of stereotypes. The first automatic step occurs when we encounter a trigger (salient characteristic) that primes the stereotype (Fiske and Taylor, 1984). The second step occurs when our processing (within our awareness) can choose to refute or ignore this automatically triggered stereotype. However, when we are cognitively busy because there is an overwhelming amount of data to contend with, or if we are otherwise disinterested as in the case when relatively routine, habitual, or scripted interactions take place, such as small talk, the mindless automatic process is more difficult to override (Fiske and Taylor, 1984). Mindlessness is a state of reduced attention paid to the information we process actively in a given interaction (Langer et al., 1978).

One famous example used to test the concept of mindlessness is referred to as the copier study conducted by Langer et al. (1978), which took place in an office copy room. Colleagues who were actors 'in' on the research made one of three requests to others on the line waiting to make copies.

1. "Could I cut in front? I'm in a rush." = request with legitimate reason
2. "Could I cut in front?" = request only
3. "Could I cut in front? I need to make copies." = request with irrelevant reason

It might be unsurprising that people would be willing to allow a colleague who made the first request to cut them in line. We might also expect that participants were more likely to deny the second request. The surprising result of the study was the reaction to the third request. In these cases, the researchers found that regardless of its legitimacy, as long as the request included a reason people were willing to accede. Essentially, people responded based on autopilot, such that they agreed to the request as long as it fulfilled their expectation that such a request should include a reason. The persuasiveness of the message was not in what was said per se, but rather in the cognitive (and mindless) interpretation of the message that was communicated. Mindfulness is a state of alert and lively awareness involving active information processing, an appreciation for the distinctiveness of messages communicated in a given moment, and the creation of new categories into which to process information. While we can choose to be mindful when someone communicates a stereotype (Devine, 1989), doing so is not easy. Langer et al. (1978) demonstrate that our typical default is to be mindless.

There are numerous theories that elucidate our mindlessness. Implicit personality theories help to explain that people have preconceived notions of what to expect about personality types and the way their related traits appear together (Bruner and Taguiri, 1954). For example, the halo effect and horn effect (Thorndike, 1920) are specific implicit personality theories that predict: "if a person judged another highly on one particular personality characteristic [good/bad], they might also rate the same person highly on a range of other [related good/bad] characteristics" (Hinton, 2000, p. 39). Illusory correlation occurs when we make associations between things that are not necessarily associated in the presumed way. Chapman (1967), for example, found that in a semantic association test, participants presumed that pairs like hat and head, or lion and tiger were more likely to co-occur than other word associations. Katz and Braly (1933) found that, because of assumptions gained from a shared cultural knowledge base, participants associated characteristics with groups despite not having had contact with group members. We need not have someone convince us of these associations. Instead, we convince ourselves through our own cognitive processes.

Processing information passively may produce various negative consequences. Arguably, most important among these is that we may inadvertently misperceive randomness in consistent and predictable ways (Hinton, 2000). When we process information mindlessly, we make assumptions in the absence of evidence, such as with the illusion of control bias. In this bias, we overestimate our influence or control of a situation. For example, many people are more scared of flying than driving and more scared of sharks than dogs. Donald Trump for example seems to be obsessed with the danger sharks pose, having gone off on shark-related tangents during multiple campaign rallies (Parker, 2024a). As with much of what Trump tells people to be scared of, research shows those fears are quite misplaced. Gilovich (1991) articulates several ways people maintain false associations in his eloquently titled book, *How We Know What Isn't So*, including: Gambler's Fallacy, Clustering Illusion, Hot Hand Fallacy, and the Barnum Effect. The last one is perhaps the most relevant when it comes to a showman like Trump, who bears some resemblance to the great P.T. Barnum, to whom people attribute the famous quote: "There's a sucker born every minute." Processing information mindlessly—by Elaboration Likelihood Model's peripheral route—can lead to the triggering of our fears and the sparking of our hopes in easily manipulatable ways.

Trump's stereotypes of migrant crime

When it comes to successfully triggering people's fears and manipulating them to one's own political benefit, no public figure can top Trump. Since that famous ride down the escalator in 2015, his primary focus has been scaring Americans about undocumented immigrants. This fearmongering reached a new level of intensity in the final dozen weeks of the 2024 campaign. Near the end of August 2024, Trump started repeating a specific story—a flat-out falsehood. In his telling, a criminal gang of Venezuelans had supposedly taken full control over an apartment building—The Edge at Lowry Apartments in Aurora, Colorado—and was terrorizing its residents. The twice-elected president angrily condemned this non-existent development and connected it to his larger argument: "You haven't seen even the beginning of this migrant crime," and added: "And you know, they have a hat that said, 'Trump was right about everything,' and I have to say, I pretty much was right about everything." Trump often cites unnamed other people (i.e., "they," "many people," or "everyone") who attest to the accuracy of his stereotyping rhetoric (see also Chapter 2).

Meanwhile, Heather Morris, Aurora's interim police chief, issued a statement flatly denying that this had happened: "Gang members have not taken over this complex" (Olmsted, 2024). Residents confirmed this, and noted that their primary problem was poor conditions resulting from the management's failure to take care of the building properly. Furthermore, major crimes in Aurora were actually down 17.2 % year-to-date in 2024 compared to 2023 (Anastasio, 2024). This fact contradicts Trump's falsehoods regarding a supposed migrant crime wave. The twice-elected president, meanwhile, continued to peddle the story even after the police and residents had debunked it, talking about: "tough young thugs" carrying "big rifles" moving in and "taking over buildings" (Olmsted, 2024). Likewise, on September 7, 2024, in Wisconsin, Trump went beyond the Aurora non-incident, even as he hinted at it by mentioning Venezuela to fearmonger even further: "If you think you have a nice house, have a migrant enjoy your house, because a migrant will take it over. A migrant will take it over. It will be Venezuela on steroids" (Richardson, 2024b). This kind of simplistic, repetitive message persuades its audience using ELM's peripheral route.

Trump returned again to these themes of "migrant crime" in the September 10 debate with Harris, and also brought up a bizarre, debunked tale going around the internet—spread by Blood Tribe, a neo-Nazi outfit—about Haitian immigrants in Springfield, Ohio eating the residents' pet cats and dogs. Christopher Pohlhaus, the head of Blood Tribe, crowed that, with Trump's help, they had "pushed Springfield into the public consciousness." On Gab, an online forum where extremists frequent, one Blood Tribe member proclaimed: "[President Trump] is talking about it now. This is what real power looks like" (Zadrozny, 2024). The day before the debate, a campaign official contacted Brian Heck, the Springfield City Manager, about these claims. Heck told the official that they were in fact baseless (Maher et al., 2024). Obviously, that had no effect on Trump's use of these appalling stereotypes, to which JD Vance, in a CNN interview, added: "Communicable diseases like HIV and TB [tuberculosis] have skyrocketed in this small Ohio town. This is what Kamala Harris' border policies have done" (Wiggins, 2024). PolitiFact reviewed the claim and judged it "mostly false," noting that (excluding COVID-19, which had no cases in the U.S. before 2020) the communicable disease rate in Springfield had fallen since 2018, and in 2023 reached the lowest level since 2015 (Uribe, 2024a). The twice-elected president went even further than his running mate, declaring on October 11 that bringing in disease was an intentional Biden-Harris policy: "People come in, they're very sick. Very sick. They're coming into our country, they're very, very sick with highly contagious disease. And they're let into our country to infect our country" (Ulloa, 2024b).

A sociology professor, Anthony Ocampo, told *The Guardian:* "this is low-hanging fruit to rally xenophobia in a very quick way" (C. Wang, 2024). As Serwer (2024a) noted, all these slanders are: "long-standing staples of anti-immigrant rhetoric." A number of scholars have expressed similar sentiments (Ulloa, 2024b). Karl Racine, who came to the U.S. from Haiti at age 7 and was Attorney General for the District of Columbia from 2015 to 2023, lamented that this kind of rhetoric: "may seem like just politics. But it's serious business, with the real possibility of violence" (Jordan, 2024). More broadly, political science professor Yonatan Lupu, who heads a group keeping an eye on approximately 1,000 online hate communities, told *The New York Times:* "I certainly don't remember in my lifetime the rhetoric against immigrants ever getting this strong during an election." He also stated that the amount of hate speech had increased by 50 % in the past four years (Qin, 2024).

Trump, for his part, has a long history of denigrating Haitian immigrants, including his October 7, 2021 comment on Sean Hannity's Fox News show: "We have hundreds of thousands of people flowing in from Haiti. Haiti has a tremendous

AIDS problem. Many of those people will probably have AIDS, and they're coming into our country. And we don't do anything about it" (Shear, 2024). He repeated this dangerous stereotype more than once. According to *The New York Times*, Trump's falsehoods about Haitians and AIDS reflect:

> A pattern that goes back years and appears to have its roots in the early 1980s, when the Centers for Disease Control stigmatized Haitians as a particular threat in the spread of AIDS, driving years of panic about the newly discovered disease. Mr. Trump, a self-described germophobe, has persisted in that debunked belief even though it was formally abandoned by the C.D.C. nearly four decades ago (Shear, 2024).

Further lamenting the fact that Haitians immigrate to America, Trump added to Hannity: "We let everybody come in. Sean, it's like a death wish. It's like a death wish for our country" (Shear, 2024).[26] Additionally, in 2018, while meeting in the White House with Republican legislators, the twice-elected president asked aloud: "Why do we want people from Haiti here?" given that it, along with African nations, were, as mentioned previously (see Chapter 4), "shithole countries" (Shear, 2024). Trump also informed his fellow Republicans that he would never back a bipartisan effort then moving through Congress that would create more pathways for Haitians to legally immigrate here (Shear, 2024).

Returning to the September 10, 2024 debate, moderator David Muir informed Trump (and the tens of millions watching) that the aforementioned Mr. Heck had told ABC News that there were no credible reports of immigrants eating pets. This reality did not deter the twice-elected president, who replied that he had learned of these developments from: "the people on television saying my dog was taken and used for food" (Ulloa, 2024a). Springfield's mayor, Rob Rue, reported that two days post-debate someone sent an email threatening to blow up City Hall that included: "negative language toward immigrants" and "Haitian folks" (Sargent, 2024a). The threats caused Springfield to close schools and city buildings for multiple days, and two colleges were forced to close temporarily as well. Ohio Governor Mike DeWine, a Republican, reported that the town had received: "at least 33" bomb threats, and reminded anyone listening that the Haitian immigrants in Springfield were not undocumented, but were, in fact, there legally (Breuninger and Rozzelle, 2024). Vance rejected this fact, claiming that the Biden-Harris executive branch actions that granted legal status to Haitian immigrants are themselves somehow outside the bounds of the law: "Well, if Kamala Harris waves the wand illegally, and says these people are now here legally, I'm

---

26 Violating basic journalistic standards, Hannity campaigned on a stage with Trump prior to the 2018 midterms (Darcy, 2018).

still going to call them an illegal alien. An illegal action from Kamala Harris does not make an alien legal" (Rashid, 2024b). Invoking the notion that Harris is a witch —a woman who waves a magic wand—also draws on long-standing sexist tropes. Vance again pushed this false logic about the legality of Haitian immigrants in his vice-presidential debate with Tim Walz (Svitek, 2024b).

Vance has acknowledged being deeply influenced by what he has read on the immorality of scapegoating, yet he, along with his boss, has gone down the path of depicting a person of color as dangerous or even inhuman in order to rile up the Trump base (I. Ward, 2024). Kathleen Belew, an expert on white supremacy, characterized this kind of rhetoric as follows: "It's straight-up fearmongering. It's incredibly efficient to demonize people and make others scared of them, and it's always carried a huge and violent cost" (Bender, 2024a). Likewise, Jardina and Piston (2023) found that: "Racially dehumanizing attitudes can be influenced by political elites," and that "Trump supporters expressed more racially dehumanizing beliefs toward black people after the 2016 presidential election." Put simply, candidates for the White House employing this kind of language is not only breathtakingly reckless, it is morally repugnant.

Mayor Rue, asked about what Trump and Vance had said about his town, replied: "When a federal politician has the stage and they don't take the opportunity to build up the community, instead of inadvertently not understanding what their words are gonna do . . . it can really hurt the community." He continued: "we've been punched . . . it was their words that did it" (Sargent, 2024b). When asked if he denounced the Springfield bomb threats, Trump again turned to the same lies about crime: "I don't know what happened with the bomb threats. I know that it's been taken over by illegal migrants and that's a terrible thing that happened. Springfield was this beautiful town and now they're going through hell (Marsden, 2024). Trump and Vance repeated this despicable pet-eating claim again multiple times even after the debate. On September 12, at an Arizona rally, Trump declared:

> Twenty thousand illegal Haitian immigrants have descended on a town of 58,000 people, destroying their way of life. Residents are reporting that the migrants are walking off with the town's geese. They're taking the geese. You know where the geese are, in the park. And even walking off with their pets (Bouie, 2024a).

More dehumanizing rhetoric

Furthermore, the twice-elected president employs this dehumanizing rhetoric in order to justify his policy proposals—in particular his call to forcibly deport up to 20 million undocumented immigrants, which he acknowledges will be "bloody" (Blake, 2024c). He made the connection explicit on September 13: "We're going to have the largest deportation in the history of our country. And we're going to start with Springfield and Aurora" (Bouie, 2024a). Under what legal authority? Trump declared: "I will invoke the Alien Enemies Act of 1798 to target and dismantle every migrant criminal network operating on American soil."[27] He added, approvingly: "Those were the old days, when they had tough politicians" (Treisman, 2024). Scholar of authoritarianism Ruth Ben-Ghiat, in a Politico interview, laid out how 10 years of stereotypes brought Trump to the precipice of winning the support and power—which he ultimately did win on Election Day—necessary to implement an action that would require the U.S. to become a virtual police state in order to fully implement:

> He's been taking Americans and his followers on a journey since really 2015 conditioning them . . . step by step instilling hatred in a group, and then escalating. So immigrants are crime. Immigrants are anarchy. They're taking their jobs, but now they're also animals who are going to kill us or eat our pets or eat us. That's how you get people to feel that whatever is done to them, as in mass deportation, rounding them up, putting them in camps, is OK (M. Ward, 2024).

On his mass deportation, Trump further elaborated in a post to Truth Social shortly after the September 10 debate:

> As President I will immediately end the migrant invasion of America. We will stop all migrant flights, end all illegal entries, terminate the Kamala phone app for smuggling illegals (CPB One App), revoke deportation immunity, suspend refugee resettlement, and return Kamala's illegal migrants to their home countries (also known as remigration). I will save our cities and towns . . . all across America (Mathias, 2024).

One word in this post stands out. Jakub Kuhl of the Institute for Strategic Dialogue told the Huffington Post that: "Trump's rhetoric about 'remigration' has its origins in the international far-right... [It] was popularized by groups adhering to Identitarianism, a pan-European ethno-nationalist movement, as their policy to reverse the so-called 'great replacement'" (Mathias, 2024). The twice-elected president's use of the term "remigration" caught the attention of those same anti-immigration extremists. Martin Sellner, head of the Austrian branch of the white supremacist or-

---

27 On March 15, 2025, the Trump White House issued an executive order citing the Alien Enemies Act as the source of his authority to expel members of Tren de Aragua, a Venezuelan gang (Treisman, 2025). The U.S. government relied on this law—which gives a president sweeping authority only during wartime—to send approximately 120,000 people of Japanese descent to internment camps during World War II.

ganization Generation Identity tweeted his unrestrained glee at Trump's post, declaring that the word had now become the "term of the hour" in the U.S. Remigration, for Sellner and his ilk, is essentially code for ethnically cleansing people of color from majority white countries. He created a channel on the Telegram app —which caters to right-wing ideology—called the "European Compact for Remigration," which also included a call for the "de-Islamicization" of Europe (Mathias, 2024). Back in the U.S., Pat Buchanan, a former aide to President Nixon and serious contender for the Republican nomination in 1992 and 1996 who in many ways presaged the takeover of the GOP by Trump's brand of white identity politics, had written about the need for "remigration" as part of his call to remove non-whites from America as early as his 2006 book *State of Emergency: The Third World Invasion and Conquest of America* (Mathias, 2024).

Trump attacked Haitian immigrants who had been moving to another town, Charleroi, Pennsylvania, in a series of false statements in late September 2024. He claimed that the Haitian arrivals had left the town "virtually bankrupt" and had brought "massive crime to the town and every place near it." As with Springfield, Ohio, local town officials denied just about everything Trump said. Here's the town's borough manager, Joe Manning, who was interviewed by KDKA-TV local news: "It hasn't been a drain on borough resources, we haven't seen a spike in crime, we haven't seen any major problems. They have been a benefit to the town" (Taylor, 2024). Manning also told the *New Republic:* "There's what the former president is saying and then there's easily observable reality" (Sargent, 2024b).

At a rally on Long Island on September 18, eight days after the debate with Harris, Trump went on a rant about migrants and the border, falsely declaring that under Biden, the "border is 25 times worse" (Bender, 2024a). In fact, by July 2024, after the White House had implemented new policies, undocumented border crossings dropped in half compared to the previous month (Aleaziz, 2024). The twice-elected president continued by fearmongering about undocumented immigrants in starkly racial terms, stereotyping them as non-white people trying to destroy the America his supporters know and love:

> They're coming from the Congo. They're coming from Africa. They're coming from the Middle East. They're coming from all over the world—Asia. A lot of it coming from Asia. What's happening to our country is we're just destroying the fabric of life in our country. We're not going to take it any longer. You got to get rid of these people. Give me a shot (Bender, 2024a).

The anti-immigrant rhetoric continued, with Trump opining that his opponents wanted to "inundate" communities in Pennsylvania with large numbers of migrants, "changing the character of small towns and villages all over our country and changing them forever" (Svitek, 2024a). He again spoke of the so-called migrant invasion, citing "migrants attacking villages and cities throughout the Midwest" (Corn, 2024). He proclaimed: "We are going to totally stop this invasion. This invasion is destroying the fabric of our country." This type of rhetoric does not operate along the central route of persuasion described by ELM; it would not hold up under careful analysis. It can only succeed through the peripheral route, which is more mindless.

On the eve of the election, Trump condemned both the undocumented immigrants in Aurora and the migrants here legally in Springfield, characterizing their effect on the U.S. as "military invasions without the uniforms. That's all it is" (Bradner and Sullivan, 2024). These remarks and many others (M. Ward, 2024) parallel the dark themes pushed by Buchanan, Limbaugh, and other right-wing precursors to Trump on how demographic change will bring about the fundamental transformation of America into something his supporters will no longer recognize (Reifowitz, 2019).

Then the twice-elected president repeated a lie he had told many times: "Every job in this country produced over the last two and a half years has gone to illegal aliens—every job" (Bender, 2024a). Likewise, Vance also attacked undocumented immigrants as:

> People who shouldn't be here, people who are competing against you and your children to buy the homes that ought to be going to American citizens. Our message to Kamala Harris is: Stop giving American homes to foreigners who shouldn't be in this country. Start giving them to American citizens who deserve to be here (Bender, 2024a).

One Trump voter, interviewed on September 23, 2024, by the right-wing outlet Newsmax, said that: "illegal immigration" was his most important issue. Not because it was hurting him directly, he acknowledged, but because: "It's just the principle of everybody coming in and getting free stuff and taking stuff away from hard-working Americans" (Rupar, 2024). This clearly echoes campaign rhetoric.

On October 13, 2024, Trump brought together many of these false claims in a single statement: "The mass migration invasion has crushed wages, crashed school systems—your systems are a disaster—wrecked the standard of living and brought crime, drugs, misery and death" (Qiu, 2024a). Trump and Vance have blamed undocumented immigrants coming across the Mexican border, and thus Kamala Harris, for a number of other real or imagined problems, including: increased hospital and emergency room wait times; a (non-existent) increase in the inflow of illegal guns; the weakening of Social Security and Medicare's finances—on this, the opposite is the truth because undocumented immigrants pay taxes into those systems and cannot receive benefits; unaffordable home prices; and fentanyl overdoses. As Linda Qiu (2024a) noted: "seldom is unauthorized immigration the actual cause of the problems [Trump and Vance] say plague the country." *The New York Times* debunked each of these claims (Qiu, 2024a).

Throughout the 2024 campaign, the twice-elected president falsely connected undocumented immigrants with crime specifically in order to buttress his attacks on the Biden-Harris administration's border policy. Corn (2024) explained:

> Not merely peddling a series of lies, Trump is knitting together a full story that is utterly bogus, trying to convince tens of millions of a reality that does not exist: They're living in a dangerous hellhole in which they're imperiled by barbarians, who happen to be people of color. And Trump then accuses Harris and President Joe Biden of purposefully orchestrating this purportedly deadly situation and the collapse of America.

On September 26, 2024, Trump talked about "Kamala's migrant invasion" and accused Harris of supporting "amnesty for all illegal aliens . . . even if they're murderers and drug dealers, human traffickers" (C-SPAN, 2024). Even though she was vice president and did not wield the powers of the presidency, Trump accused Harris of ordering a "halt" to "the removal of virtually all criminal aliens, including MS-13 gang members, the worst gang anywhere in the world . . . evil gang" (C-SPAN, 2024). Finally, he claimed that his opponent had: "lost 325,000 children. They are either dead, being sold into sex slavery or just plain missing." (C-SPAN, 2024). On September 27, Trump again revisited this theme, and claimed VP Harris had: "delivered these horrors," adding: "She unleashed these atrocities, and blood is on her hands at a level that, probably, nobody's ever seen in this country" (Bradner, 2024). On October 16, he proclaimed: "Kamala has imported an army of illegal alien gang members and migrant criminals from prisons and jails and insane asylums and the worst mental institutions anywhere in the world" (Ulloa, 2024b).

Taking his rhetoric to another level, Trump accused his opponent of the worst crime public servants, acting in their official capacity, can commit against their own citizens—treason. He did so with an accusation the right-wing has long used against Democrats on immigration (Reifowitz, 2019): "What Kamala Harris has done is unforgivable. It's a crime what she did. There's no greater act of disloyalty than to extinguish the sovereignty of your own nation" (Associated Press, 2024b).[28] Sovereignty is a key term for Trump; in a 2018 UN speech he spoke of: "confront[ing] threats to sovereignty from uncontrolled migration." By accusing

---

[28] The twice-elected president has also accused other political opponents of treason, including Hillary Clinton, Rep. Liz Cheney, long considered one of the single most conservative Republicans (she voted with Trump 93% of the time, and held the number three position in the House Republican caucus), and in fact the entire bipartisan House Select Committee on the January 6 Attack. More broadly, an NPR investigation found that: "Trump has issued more than 100 threats to investigate, prosecute, imprison or otherwise punish his perceived opponents" (Dreisbach, 2024).

Harris of weakening U.S. sovereignty, he is contending that she would turn over control of our country's fate to outside forces with whom she is conspiring, and who want to do Americans harm.

On September 28, Trump offered that immigrants were going to "walk into your kitchen, they'll cut your throat," and added: "your towns, your cities, your country is being destroyed" (Wisconsin Politics, 2024). On October 1, Trump made a specific accusation that beggars belief, even more so than most of his others. He again cited: "Kamala's phone app," and claimed it is: "meant for the cartel heads. The cartel heads call the app, and they tell them where to drop the illegal migrants" (Corn, 2024). If this baseless claim were true, it would represent a conspiracy theory of the highest order. On November 1, Trump predicted that if he lost: "every town in America will be turned into a squalid, dangerous refugee camp" (Rogers et al., 2024). The twice-elected president also took a more general approach to fearmongering about Harris, predicting that if she became president: "you won't have a country anymore." He continued: "You're pretty close to not having one. You better hope I get elected" (Gold, 2024c).

On the other hand, Trump contended that if he won, our country would experience a "liberation day," on which we could finally throw off the yoke of what he called an occupation, and reverse the so-called migrant invasion. He made that remark on October 27, 2024, at a day-long Madison Square Garden campaign rally during which various speakers made so many offensive remarks—including calling Puerto Rico an "island of garbage" along with racist jokes about Jews and money, as well as black people and watermelons—that *The New York Times* ran a headline describing it as: "A closing carnival of grievances, misogyny and racism" (Goldmacher et al., 2024). These so-called jokes were part of the prepared remarks, and were loaded into the speaker's teleprompter by Trump campaign staff (Zinoman, 2024). For his part, the twice-elected president called the event an: "absolute love fest" (Samuels, 2024a). Finally, in a breathtaking display of hypocrisy, shortly after the MSG event he slammed Biden for responding to the joke about Puerto Rico by saying: "The only garbage I see floating out there is his [i.e., Trump's] supporter's—his—his demonization of Latinos is unconscionable." Trump claimed Biden was saying that the garbage was: "his supporters" rather than "his supporter's," which the White House denied, but either way the Republican nominee himself had called Harris supporters "absolute garbage" as well as "scum" (see Chapter 4) only a few weeks earlier (Alba and Terkel, 2024).

Stereotype school for persuasion tactics

Trump relies on the existing cultural knowledge his supporters possess—prejudices he himself has helped inflame over the years—to maximize the persuasiveness of his stereotypes. He employs this rhetoric in order to rile up those not yet sufficiently motivated. We have seen, as discussed in Chapter 1, violent acts committed by people who believed and echoed his anti-immigrant and anti-minority stereotypes (Levine, 2020). As part of their education as Trump supporters, they are indoctrinated as to how to think about the topics he teaches them to care about most. Social Learning Theory (Bandura, 1963) argues that people learn what to think and how to behave by observing, imitating, and modeling. For the most part: "humans internalize social values and norms and are largely motivated to seek social approval by conforming to these values and norms" (Ashmore and Del Boca, 1981, p. 23). Trump's rhetoric provides a (mis)education that forms the basis of a highly persuasive, self-perpetuating loop for his base.

As mentioned previously, Elaboration Likelihood Model presumes that messages persuade along either the central or peripheral route. To the extent that we have a high desire to elaborate—think mindfully about—the persuasive messages we receive, we logically evaluate those messages using the central route. When we have a low desire to elaborate—think mindlessly about—persuasive messages, we evaluate those messages using the peripheral route, which involves less scrutiny and greater acceptance of premises that we might otherwise have closely examined and critiqued.

A premise of this model is that a desire to be correct, or to be persuaded that something is correct, is a motivating factor for people. However, people determine what is correct based on a variety of individual and situational factors. These moderate whether we have a desire for higher or lower elaboration (Note: these are not dichotomous points but rather exist on a continuum). These factors include our investment in or motivation to elaborate on a topic, our ability to engage in an understanding of the topic, and our opportunity to do so. Because of the familiarity and resulting believability of Trump's stereotypes, members of his base do not actively process them using the central route, but instead use the peripheral route whereby they ultimately persuade themselves of the 'truth' of Trump's views on immigration and other topics. His supporters internalize his stereotypes of immigrants along with the many other stereotypes he communicates. A person may incorporate any of the following seven tactics along with stereotypes in order to prompt listeners to process a message using the peripheral rather than central route, and thereby think less logically and with less scrutiny about that message (Cialdini, 1984).

1. Reciprocation involves the desire for people not to be perceived as owing someone but rather that there exists a mutual benefit.
2. Scarcity refers to the idea of supply and demand. If we think something is scarce we may be more likely to desire it.
3. Authority refers to the credibility of those who are perceived to be knowledgeable and/or credible.
4. Consistency (and Commitment) highlights the need for a person to deem their future behavior as consistent with their current behavior, or with how someone else perceives it.
5. Liking refers to the idea that people are more persuaded by those they like (e.g., charismatic people).
6. Consensus (or Social Proof) is the desire to conform to what one understands others are doing.
7. Unity refers to the desire people feel to belong.

Trump's effectiveness in communicating stereotypes, in particular to those in his ingroup, relies heavily on many of these. For example, his constant refrain that immigrants are taking the jobs of Americans (see Chapters 1 and 2) reflects the theme of *scarcity*. On *authority* and *likability*, the twice-elected president has clearly established himself as a credible 'truth bringer' (see Chapter 3) with a certain charisma among his followers. *Consensus* and *unity* relate to the desire of people to be part of a group with a coherent set of shared values (i.e., MAGA). To be sure, he does not incorporate all seven strategies into his rhetoric. For one, Trump does not utilize consistency as a persuasive strategy. Rather, he has become known for *not* being consistent when switching a position would benefit him (Astor and Levien, 2024).

The Elaboration Likelihood Model helps to explain much of the success of product advertising, social media influencers, and politicians—not just Trump's —in getting good people to persuade themselves to make poor decisions. However, there is some good news. Persuasion accomplished through the peripheral route is less enduring, less likely to affect behavior, and less resistant to change than when we have elaborated on such decision-making through a central route which necessarily took more time and effort, and, thus, was inherently more convincing. Overall, persuasion accomplished through our use of a peripheral route is less likely to 'stick'; however, in the short term there can be high costs, especially when the messaging comes not just from one source. Not surprisingly, there are other strategies.

Media amplification

Agenda setting argues that the media can shape public opinion through what topics they address in their programming. In this way, people come to care about what the media emphasizes in coverage (Iyengar, 2022). Sometimes this amplification can come under the guise of providing equal time for 'both sides' of an argument, even when both sides are not equally truthful. In this way, the media serves as a megaphone for celebrities, politicians, and other personalities who spread falsehoods. As more different outlets repeat the messages more often, they reach a wider audience.

Politicians are well aware of how the media operates in this regard. Conservatives in particular will 'work the ref'—repeatedly denounce the mainstream media as 'liberal' to the point they often end up treating Democrats unfairly in order to disprove this characterization. In 1992, Republican National Committee Chair Rich Bond actually admitted this is what they do: "I'm a coach of kid's basketball and Little League teams. If you watch any great coach, what they try to do is 'work the refs' [meaning the media]. Maybe the ref will cut you a little slack next time" (Cohen, 2001). And it worked splendidly in 2016—an election decided by about 77,000 votes in three states—to Trump's benefit, according to a detailed analysis of mainstream media coverage by the *Columbia Journalism Review:*

> [CJR researchers] found roughly four times as many Clinton-related sentences that described scandals as opposed to policies, whereas Trump-related sentences were one-and-a-half times as likely to be about policy as scandal. Given the sheer number of scandals in which Trump was implicated—sexual assault; the Trump Foundation; Trump University; redlining in his real estate developments; insulting a Gold Star family; numerous instances of racist, misogynist, and otherwise offensive speech—it is striking that the media devoted more attention to his policies than to his personal failings. Even more striking, the various Clinton-related email scandals—her use of a private email server while Secretary of State, as well as the DNC and John Podesta hacks—accounted for more sentences than all of Trump's scandals combined (65,000 vs. 40,000) and more than twice as many as were devoted to all of her policy positions (Watts and Rothschild, 2017).

The CJR report also explained that this media coverage reached and influenced far more people than did, for example, fake news spread across social media by Russian bots or right-wing influencers.

Likewise, observers have noted a severe double standard in media coverage in 2024. Robinson (2024) laid out the contrast in stark terms, describing how, on the one hand: "Trump rants about mass deportations and claims to have stopped 'wars with France,' after being described by his longest-serving White House chief of staff as a literal fascist," and on the other: "commentators debate whether Vice President Kamala Harris performed well enough at a CNN town hall to 'close the deal.'" Or, as Van Jones (CNN, 2024b) put it: "He gets to be lawless, she has to be flawless."

Even as conservatives relentlessly attack the media, they also use it expertly to spread their preferred messages. After the Republican campaign's lies about the fate of Springfield's dogs and cats had been debunked, Vance said the quiet part out loud. He acknowledged that it was necessary for him: "to create stories so that the American media actually pays attention." Vance later clarified that he still believed this story was true, and was talking about doing whatever it takes to draw more media attention to the story—in other words, he doubled down on a proven lie (Astor, 2024a). Even though the mainstream media reporting typically refuted the lies, the simple volume of attention paid helped amplify the Trump-Vance message that these immigrants are dangerous. Plus, as the old saying goes: "a lie can travel halfway around the world while the truth is still putting on its shoes."

Along similar lines, Steve Bannon, who served as the Trump campaign's CEO in the final months of the 2016 campaign and was White House Chief Strategist and Senior Counselor to the President for most of Trump's first year in office, summed up the Trump/MAGA approach not long after leaving the White House: "The Democrats don't matter. The real opposition is the media. And the way to deal with them is to flood the zone with shit" (Stelter, 2021). Regarding this approach, Richardson (2024c) noted:

> Keeping listeners constantly trying to defend what is real from what is not destroys their ability to make sense of the world. Many people turn to a strongman who promises to create order. Others will get so exhausted they simply give up. As scholar of totalitarianism Hannah Arendt noted, authoritarians use this technique to destabilize a population.
>
> Trump is that strongman.

In return for amplifying messages, the media benefits from increased audience and engagement metrics that enable them to sell more advertising and, ultimately, increase revenue. All too often, decisions on what to air on news or news-like programming are not inherently altruistic or based on the public good, but instead are data-supported business decisions that for-profit corporate entities make for their own benefit. The media will follow the dollar (e.g., Bond, 2016). The result of this reciprocal process is that there is an almost parasitic motivation for both the personality and the media to work in conjunction such that as long as one thrives, the other will as well. To the extent a personality can get the attention of the audience, and the media can predict that will be the case, then the decision-making about airtime will reflect that audience preference. Trump's stereotypes have an impact—and that impact is measurable in terms of sales and votes. The democratic process is not just about who votes or is officially disenfranchised, or even whether the election is fair or rigged. The media's choices also have an impact. In a 24-hour news cycle, those choices could result in a lot more airtime for Trump, and a lot less for everything else that is going on in the world, as if little other news of note exists.

All Trump, all the time

Trump has devoted much time and energy to working the refs as well as simply bombarding journalists with one rhetorical attack after another. For a couple among countless examples (Bassin and Potter, 2024; Reilly, 2024), see Trump's February 17, 2017 tweet where he called out specific media sources—"the 'failing' New York Times, NBC News, ABC, CBS, and CNN"—as "fake news" and characterized them as "the enemy of the American people" (Grynbaum, 2017). More recently, at an August 31, 2024 rally, the twice-elected president again went on an extended rant criticizing CNN over an interview it had just aired with Kamala Harris and Tim Walz: "It was a very weak interview from the standpoint of CNN. I think CNN should be ashamed of themselves." He then slammed *The New York Times:* "Truly they are the enemy of the people. They are the enemy of the people. They tell false stories about me—that's all they do is they write false stories." This time, a few minutes after that statement, a rallygoer climbed the barrier separating the audience from journalists covering the event in an attempt to attack them. The police had to apprehend and tase him in order to subdue him. Trump, meanwhile, seemed to be watching these events unfold and repeatedly said: "he's on our side" (Herchenroeder, 2024). Finally, the twice-elected president mused directly about violence against the press at a rally two days before the 2024 election: "I have this piece of glass here. But all we have really over here is the fake news, right? And to get me, somebody would have to shoot through the fake news. And I don't mind that so much. I don't mind" (Krieg and Sullivan, 2024).

On October 10, 2024, after CBS had aired an interview with Harris that upset Trump, he accused them of having selectively edited her answers to make her look better. He proclaimed: "CBS should lose its license, and it should be bid out to the Highest Bidder, as should all other Broadcast Licenses, because they are just as corrupt as CBS—and maybe even WORSE" (L. Reilly, 2024). The twice-elected president also promised that if he became president again: "We're going to subpoena their records" to discover whatever CBS might have done to help Harris (Collinson, 2024). As for actions taken while president, observers generally believe that he directed his Justice Department to sue in an ultimately unsuccessful attempt to block the merger of AT&T and Time Warner—the parent company of CNN—because he wanted to retaliate against what he saw as negative coverage (Mayer, 2019). This approach to the media parallels the "autocratic technique" employed by Hungary's Prime Minister, Viktor Orbán, whom Trump himself in 2016 cited as a model, and who visited him at Mar-a-Lago in 2024. The Trump/Orbán technique is: "intended to chill a free press in violation of the First Amendment" (Bassin and Potter, 2024).

Trump tailors his message, streamlines his communication channels, and eliminates competition in messaging from different sources in order to push the media to spread his agenda to the public. He has been incredibly successful in getting both right-wing media and other right-wing politicians to repeat that message directly, in particular to his own supporters, who then echo his claims (Searcey and Alban, 2024). Here are just a couple of examples of Republican politicians parroting the twice-elected president: then-New York Rep. Marc Molinaro shared a post describing pets being "carved up" and eaten by Haitian immigrants in Springfield, Ohio, and refused to disown the lie even after it was debunked (Ashford, 2024). Louisiana Rep. Clay Higgins echoed and even embellished upon the aforementioned lies and hateful rhetoric Trump spewed about Haitians: "These Haitians are wild. Eating pets, vudu, nastiest country in the western hemisphere, cults . . . slapstick gangsters . . . All these thugs better get their mind right and their ass out of our country before January 20th"—the next Inauguration Day (Levien, 2024). Higgins took down the offending post, but then in an interview with CNN declared: "It's all true" (Grayer et al., 2024).

Separate from those fellow Republicans who parrot Trump are others who simply deny the reality of what he says. On October 14, 2024, when Virginia Gov. Glenn Youngkin appeared on CNN, host Jake Tapper asked (CNN, 2024a) if he supported the twice-elected president's call for using military force against domestic opponents, including a specifically named elected official, Adam Schiff (see Chapter 4). Youngkin retorted that, although he "can't speak" for Trump, he did not believe that Trump meant what he clearly appeared to have said. The governor also said that he thought Tapper was: "misinterpreting and misrepresenting [Trump's] thoughts." After some more back and forth, Tapper pushed again: "I'm talking about Donald Trump saying that he wants to use the National Guard and the military to go after the left." Youngkin replied: "I don't believe that's what he's saying." Incredulous, Tapper retorted: "I played the quote and I just read it to you!" (CNN, 2024a).

Reacting to Youngkin's performance, a number of political observers cited a passage from George Orwell's *1984:* "The Party told him to reject the evidence of his eyes and ears. It was their final, most essential command" (Nichols, 2024). It is worth noting that on October 20, Republican Speaker of the House Mike Johnson of Louisiana, the most powerful member of his party in Congress, parroted Youngkin's false interpretation of Trump's remarks in an interview with Tapper, even after the host played Johnson a tape of Trump mentioning Schiff and Pelosi (Maher and Krieg, 2024). On that same day, Trump was asked again about the remarks, and replied that "of course" Schiff represented an enemy within. In an interview with Tapper that aired on October 27, JD Vance likewise echoed Youngkin and Johnson on the "enemy within" line (Maher and Krieg, 2024).

Beyond those that were already on his side, Trump also successfully used mainstream media platforms to deliver his messages at key moments—such as the "but her emails!" coverage in the final days of the 2016 election—even as he simultaneously undermined their credibility. The twice-elected president's communication of stereotypes fueled his ability to curate his media appearances on select channels (i.e., Fox), while nonetheless garnering constant attention from the 24-hour news cycle of most media organizations.

As Poerksen (2024) explained:

> The fact is: The man has discovered a decisive trick for steering the media system. It is a trick that can best be described using a term from behavioral biology: *supernormal stimuli.* The term refers to outsized, central stimuli that are almost impossible to resist. Fierce conflict, sex, drama, humiliation and struggle. Trump is the hyper-stimulus incarnate of the entertainment culture. And he delivers—day after day, hour after hour. Until there is almost no other issue under discussion. Just: Trump said . . . And: Trump wants . . . And finally: Trump is trying . . .

The appropriation of the media for political gain is intentional, with executives in boardrooms deciding in what directions to take media platforms in order to maximally monetize messaging. This does not only happen on overtly partisan outlets like Fox but also on presumably neutral media platforms without an obvious political agenda. The head of CBS, Leslie Moonves, openly admitted in early 2016 that his network benefited from Trump's candidacy—it increased ratings as well as political ad spending, and thus improved his company's bottom line: "Donald's place in this election is a good thing . . . It may not be good for America, but it's damn good for CBS . . . Man, who would have expected the ride we're all having right now?" Moonves added: "I've never seen anything like this, and this is going to be a very good year for us. Sorry. It's a terrible thing to say. But, bring it on, Donald. Keep going . . . The money's rolling in and this is fun" (Bond, 2016).

Fox News

Of course, the partisan media, including social media influencers, play an outsize role in spreading Trump's message. Pillai et al. (2023) found that:

An increase in the number of repetitions of a falsehood corresponded with increased belief among Republicans but decreased belief among Democrats . . . The effects of repetition were larger when people consumed more right-leaning cable news and when falsehoods were mostly repeated on Twitter.

In fact, since Elon Musk, a top Trump donor, high-profile campaign surrogate, and perhaps his closest adviser at the outset of his second term—he runs the uniquely powerful Department of Government Efficiency (DOGE)—purchased Twitter (since renamed X), it has evinced a "new pro-Trump bias" (Mahler et al., 2024).

As for Fox News, the most-watched cable news channel and a sharply partisan media outlet, there are thousands of examples of their pro-Trump bias. For just one, multiple programs on Fox News repeated, thus amplifying, the twice-elected president's lies about the Biden-Harris administration's response to Hurricane Helene (which devastated the Southeast in late September 2024) almost word for word —even as one intrepid Fox reporter tweeted about receiving information from House Republicans debunking that disinformation. This debunking information appeared in a single, lone story on FoxNews.com (never on television), in the final paragraph of a post that ran under a completely unrelated headline: "Resurfaced video shows FEMA worrying about faith-based partners' treatment of trans migrants at border" (Bump, 2024c). This is what the field of media criticism calls a 'cover your ass' move—now Fox can say "see, we report the facts on Fox!"—even as they buried the information so that as few Trump supporters saw it as possible. As historian Nicole Hemmer told *The New Yorker*, Fox during the Trump presidency is: "the closest we've come to having state TV." She added: "Fox is not just taking the temperature of the base—it's raising the temperature. It's a radicalization model" (Mayer, 2019).

Beyond this kind of open, on-air bias, Fox also helped Trump in more duplicitous ways. In January 2024, someone at the network apparently leaked to his campaign all the questions the hosts planned to ask him at an Iowa Town Hall, giving them time to prepare answers beforehand (Ramirez, 2025). This deceit makes the aforementioned accusations and threats the twice-elected president leveled in October 2024 at CBS for supposedly favoring Harris all the more outrageous.

In terms of how it treats Trump compared to his various opponents, Fox News also consistently puts its thumb on one side of the scale. For example, on October 16, 2024, the network broadcast a town hall event for Trump where he answered questions from an audience that, as per CNN's reporting, Fox had selected and which: "was packed with local Republican supporters" (Gold and Reilly, 2024). Furthermore, Fox "edited its broadcast to remove some of their vocal advocacy of Trump" so as to conceal the audience's pro-Trump nature, making it appear to be simply a representative group of Georgia voters (Gold and Reilly, 2024). The

Fox personality who introduced the event, Harris Faulkner, made no mention of the audience's partisan makeup or Fox's role in selecting it, and a Fox News press release stated simply that Trump's event was: "held with an audience entirely composed of women" (Gold and Reilly, 2024). This is not how a fair and balanced news network is supposed to operate.

Likewise, we can compare the one-on-one interviews Fox News anchor Bret Baier (i.e., not an opinion host like Sean Hannity) conducted with Trump in 2023 and Harris a few weeks before the 2024 election. Trump's began with a softball question: "What do you think is the most important issue facing the country right now?" (Stelter, 2024b). The twice-elected president spoke for 45 seconds, uninterrupted. The second question, submitted by a Trump supporter, was similarly designed to let him say what he wanted to say: "What is the first thing you will do to turn this country around if you get elected?" (Stelter, 2024b). By contrast, Harris's interview began with Baier asking an accusatory, narrowly focused question: "How many illegal immigrants would you estimate your administration has released into the country in the last three and a half years?" (Stelter, 2024b). The anchor then interrupted Harris after she had spoken for only 11 seconds. This set the tone, as Baier broke into a Harris response once every 42.6 seconds, but did so only once every 77.1 seconds with Trump—barely more than half as often (Stelter, 2024b). Finally, although Baier did press Trump on a few matters, virtually all the questions he asked Harris were drawn straight from Republican talking points, with some of the same specifics—for example, naming victims murdered by undocumented immigrants—Trump uses at his own rallies (see Chapter 2).

Beyond right-wing cable news, pro-Trump conservatives (e. g., Sinclair Broadcast Group) are increasingly buying local stations, which despite the new ownership continue to present as neutral and non-partisan, and seemingly neutral national media platforms such as Newsweek (Dooley, 2014; Rouhandeh and Jamali, 2023). The right is buying up once-neutral sites, platforms, and media known for straight journalism, and then misleadingly presenting content as non-partisan while all the while utilizing the brand's politically independent history to bolster that content's credibility and facilitate the neutrality charade.

Matthews (2018) explained how this works in depth through one specific example:

> The 193 local TV affiliates owned by the Sinclair Broadcast Group began running a series of promotional segments, warning of a scourge of "fake news" promoted by "members of the media [who] use their platforms to push their own personal bias and agenda to control 'exactly what people think.'"

The segments, which echo the Trump administration's anti-media rhetoric, are eerily uniform across all Sinclair affiliates, so much so that Deadspin's Timothy Burke was able to edit them together into a supercut showing dozens of Sinclair anchors saying the exact same words.

The video is just the most recent example of Sinclair stations' strong partisan tilt. A recent paper by Emory University political scientists Gregory Martin and Josh McCrain found that when Sinclair buys a local station, its local news program begins to cover more national and less local politics, the coverage becomes more conservative, and viewership actually falls—suggesting that the rightward tilt isn't enacted as a strategy to win more viewers but as part of a persuasion effort.

In this and similar cases, the reality is far from how these outlets portray themselves. They use the Trojan horse of their advertised neutrality to bring something into people's homes that can be far from neutral. The American public may well remain largely unaware of the role the media plays in this process, which enhances Trump's ability to rile up the millions of people who make up his base. He does so by getting them to process his messages mindlessly using the peripheral route as described by the Elaboration Likelihood Model. This manipulation has a significant impact on public opinion, and thus on the outcome of elections.

Chapter 8
Semiotics and social construction: Trump's creation of an alternate reality called "TrumpWorld"

A friend named John has a cat. It is the cutest cat in the world. John's cat is a striped tabby with big green eyes. You can probably imagine what it looks like. However, that cat does not exist. We just made it up. We were able to get you to conjure up a reasonably detailed picture of this cat in your mind because we have words at our disposal. These words have shared meaning among people who speak the same language. Because you do not know John, ascertaining whether he has a cat would require a good bit of research. Confirming the veracity of some statements is simple. For example Trump stated on October 7, 2024, that he had visited Gaza—which his campaign subsequently backed up, without providing details. It is relatively easy to search public records and media coverage to find that, in fact, the twice-elected president has never been to Gaza; his claim was untrue (Dale, 2024e).[29] Confirming others can be more difficult.

Words seem to exist independently of the person who speaks them and the person who hears them. After all, there is a dictionary in which words appear, printed in black and white. Merriam-Webster defines a word as something that: "symbolizes and communicates a meaning usually without being divisible into smaller units capable of independent use." Essentially, words come "with" meaning. Like a pregnant mother is "with child." They are a combined unit.

Semiotics

Semiotics explains the association between words and their meanings, and draws attention to communication codes as signs. Each sign—which is a communicative unit of meaning—consists of two parts. First, the signifier is the form that the sign takes. For example, "cat" takes the form of a word spelled c-a-t. Second, the signified is the meaning of that sign. For example, a cat is a small, furry, domesticated animal that meows. Together, the signified and the signifier create the sign "cat."

---

29 It is worth noting that Trump's false claim about visiting Gaza generated far less attention than Gov. Walz's misstatement about having been in Hong Kong during the Tiananmen Square massacre in Beijing (MSNBC, 2024). He had been there, but was off on the timing by a couple of months.

https://doi.org/10.1515/9783111426327-011

Some signs have a universally accepted meaning. This meaning is called analogic because the meaning (i.e., signified) is closely related to the code used to represent it (i.e., signifier). People can interpret a sign that is an analogic code no matter what language they speak. "Meow" is an analogic code. Though different languages may have a slightly different spin on this sound that a cat makes, a person's interpretation of "meow" will, nonetheless, be relatively universal. Analogic code, however, has its limitations. Not all code can be analogic and, indeed, most codes (verbal or non-verbal) are not.

Although meow is analogic, for example, the word "cat" is not. While cat is used in the English language, other languages use different codes like *gatto* in Italian, *kissa* in Finnish, and *neko* in Japanese. As it turns out, "cat" is a digital code. In contrast to analogic code, digital code involves an arbitrary relationship between the signifier (i.e., meaning) and the signified (i.e., code). This arbitrary relationship is consequential because it means that the word is not tied to or grounded in what it represents. Verbal communication is predominantly composed of digital code, while non-verbal communication is more likely to be analogic code—such as a smile. Research has shown that a smile is an evolutionary response involuntarily triggered when people feel happy and is, therefore, analogic, although people can fake it voluntarily (Frank and Ekman, 1993; Kurylo, 2021). While meow does sound like a cat's typical verbal stylings, the form of the word "cat" has nothing to do with the animal called a cat. Actually, a cat could have been called anything, even "dog." There is nothing inherently "cat" about a cat. We need not have a cat to imagine the fictitious cat mentioned earlier. Indeed, no individual cat has to exist in our lives for us to discuss cats. That is the beauty of digital code. People can use it to create wholly new things from our imagination, as in Dr. Suess's "Whoville" or, more recently, the world of Harry Potter; whereas, analogic code represents what observably exists in the world. Because we can create with digital code, we can also use digital code to invent lies.

Lying

Lying is not foreign to Donald Trump. It is a trait that long predates his entry into politics. One deposition from 2007 saw him tell a minimum of 30 lies: "mostly over mundane facts about his businesses such as the size of his workforce, a payment for speaking fees and the cost of his golf membership" (Contorno, 2024). Separately, as per CNN, Trump: "once claimed that he stood on the rubble at ground zero after the 9/11 terrorist attacks and that he paid his workers to clear away the debris, neither of which is backed by public record" (Contorno, 2024). As for the four years he spent in the White House, according to *The Washington Post*, he made 30,573 false or misleading statements (Kessler et al., 2021). At a single news conference, on August 8, 2024, NPR documented 162 Trump lies and distortions. CNN laid out a dozen "wholly imaginary tales" that the twice-elected president simply made up over a one-month period in late summer 2024 (Dale, 2024b). *The New York Times* compared speeches given on September 13, 2024, by the two presidential candidates. They determined that in a 23-minute speech Harris made one false statement, one misleading statement, and one exaggerated statement. Trump, over 63 minutes, made 23 that were false, six that lacked evidence, 15 that were misleading, and 16 that were exaggerated (Qiu and Shao, 2024).

Here is one representative example, a straight-forward lie the twice-elected president told on October 15, 2024, to back up his claim that his aggressive approach to tariffs worked. He stated:

> John Deere, great company. They announced about a year ago they're gonna build big plants outside of the United States. Right? They're going to build them in Mexico . . . I said, 'If John Deere builds those plants, they're not selling anything into the United States.' They just announced yesterday they're probably not going to build the plants, OK? I kept the jobs here (Dale, 2024f).

Here is what CNN fact-checker Daniel Dale (Dale, 2024f) found:

> A search of news articles and corporate press releases showed nothing about any such John Deere announcement the day prior. And in response to Trump's story, a John Deere spokesperson told The Wall Street Journal and Bloomberg News that it had not changed its plans or announced any such changes. The Trump campaign did not respond to a CNN request for any evidence for the former president's story.

One of the most egregious instances appeared in Trump's remarks on August 30, 2024: "Uh, the transgender thing is an incredible thing. Your kid goes to school and comes home a few days later with an operation. The school decides what's going to happen with your child, and you know, many of these childs [sic], 15 years later say, what the hell happened, who did this to me?" (C. Graham, 2024). He repeated this lie many times, including on September 7, 2024, in Wisconsin: "Can you imagine you're a parent and your son leaves the house and you say, Jimmy, I love you so much, go have a good day at school, and your son comes back with a brutal operation. Can you even imagine this? What the hell is wrong with our country?" (Richardson, 2024b). On September 10, during his debate with Kamala Harris, he repeated another lie he had told many times, going back to the 2016 campaign, namely that his opponent and the Democratic Party broadly support: "abortion in the ninth month" as well as a baby's "execution after birth" (Hoffman, 2024). As multiple fact-checkers reported, this claim is completely baseless (McCammon, 2024).

After Hurricane Helene (see Chapter 7), Trump's response earned the following characterization from the Associated Press: "Donald Trump repeatedly spread falsehoods Monday about the federal response to Hurricane Helene," including that President Biden was "sleeping" and ignoring the pleas for help from governors (Licon et al., 2024). On September 30, the twice-elected president also accused Biden and Democratic governors of: "going out of their way to not help people in Republican areas." The governors of North Carolina and Georgia—one Democrat, one Republican—both debunked the claims Trump made about the Biden-Harris administration's failures to help, as did other local Republican officials (Cochrane et al., 2024; Dale, 2024e; Dixon et al., 2024).

Tying together disparate lies, Trump claimed on October 3:

> The Harris-Biden administration says they don't have any money [for hurricane relief] . . . They spent it all on illegal migrants . . . They stole the FEMA [Federal Emergency Management Administration] money just like they stole it from a bank, so they could give it to their illegal immigrants that they want to have vote for them (Kessler, 2024).

He has repeated this falsehood multiple times as well. Fact-checker Glenn Kessler (2024) characterized this claim as: "completely wrong," and further noted: "when [Trump] was president, he did exactly what he claims Biden did—take money from FEMA's disaster fund to fund migrant programs at the southern border." Trump continued to tell more lies, including that FEMA would only provide $750 in total to each hurricane victim, even after his initial ones were debunked (Bidgood, 2024b).

One former Trump official, Olivia Troye, stated that her boss's first response to the outbreak of massive wildfires in 2018 in California—which had voted overwhelmingly for his opponent—was to tell the head of FEMA not to provide "any money." The twice-elected president also did not want to provide aid to Puerto Rico after severe hurricanes hit, according to Troye: "We saw numerous instances—[California] was just one—where it was politicized. It was red states vs. blue states." Former Trump White House Press Secretary Stephanie Grisham recalled Trump consistently taking that same approach: "[Trump] did that basically if there ever was a disaster and a state needed disaster aid. One of his first questions would be: Are they my people?" (Balk, 2024b). His projection of his own misdeeds onto his opponents is something he does on a regular basis.

Returning to the example of Hurricane Helene allows us to see the consequences of his lies. FEMA actually created a web page in order to: "Respond to Rumors and Confirm the Facts Related to Hurricane Helene Response and Recovery" (FEMA, 2024). Furthermore, local personnel have explained that these right-wing lies and conspiracy theories about the response made it more difficult to deliver aid to the most-affected areas such as western North Carolina (Stelter, 2024a), and eastern Tennessee (Wadhwani, 2024)—which are, ironically enough, disproportionately Republican. Regarding North Carolina, *The New York Times* reported: "Aaron Ellenburg, Rutherford County's sheriff, has spent days refuting baseless claims about lithium sales or communities being bulldozed to cover up bodies left behind by the storm." Ellenburg told the Times: "I've never seen anything like it. I'm sick and tired of this crap" (Cochrane et al., 2024).

More specifically, FEMA has had to evacuate rescue workers from Rutherford County because of violent threats against them. One federal official reported that members of the National Guard: "had come across x2 trucks of armed militia saying they were out hunting FEMA" (Blake, 2024e). Trump has promoted specific conspiracy theories on social media about FEMA using the recovery efforts to steal residents' property and otherwise harm them. The Institute for Strategic Dialogue stated that these wild claims fueled: "calls to send militias to face down FEMA for the perceived denial of aid, or to shoot and/or harm FEMA officials and the agency's emergency responders" (Blake, 2024e). As *The Washington Post* reported: "it's not just social media users promoting this underlying theory. It has also been Trump" (Blake, 2024e). Whatever the reality on the federal response to Hurricane Helene, Trump's supporters heard that Democrats like Harris do not help Americans because they only care about 'illegal immigrants' and stealing elections.[30] When given an opportunity to condemn the threats FEMA rescue workers were facing—threats exacerbated by his rhetoric—the twice-elected president refused, instead replying: "Does that mean that if they're doing a poor job, we're supposed to not say it? I think you have to be able to speak." He then repeated the aforementioned lies about FEMA funding going to support undocumented immigrants (LeVine and Arnsdorf, 2024).

Separately, there are Trump's lies about the 2020 election—collectively known as "The Big Lie"—in which he claimed to have won an election that he clearly and decisively lost. That lie ultimately resulted in the violent insurrection of January 6, 2021—a day that the twice-elected president on October 16, 2024, referred to as a "day of love" (Reston, 2024). That was also a lie, among others he has told about that day's events—including that no one who stormed the Capitol that day was armed (Astor, 2024b). On October 18, 2024, on Truth Social, Trump promoted a conspiracy theory-laden post offering that January 6 was, in fact, an inside job in which: "the government staged a riot to cover up the fact that they certified a fraudulent election" (Haberman et al., 2024). He has lied repeatedly about the events that flowed from The Big Lie: "You had a peaceful transfer of power," he contend-

---

30 We explore this lie and its implications in greater depth in Chapter 4.

ed, and noted that he had: "left the morning that I was supposed to leave." Thus, it was "a very peaceful transfer" (Lerer and Gold, 2024). On the other hand, two days before the 2024 election Trump seemed to regret his departure, musing "I shouldn't have left, honestly" (Gold et al., November 3, 2024). Furthermore, Trump pretends as if the January 6 insurrection, and his role in inciting it, is a figment of our collective imagination. The transfer of power only occurred after police officers defeated a violent attempt to block it from happening. That is not peaceful.

Trump does not limit himself to backward-looking election lies. Throughout the 2024 campaign he issued lies and unfounded accusations about anticipated future election fraud. The twice-elected president regularly claimed, without evidence, that Democrats were going to cheat on a massive scale in the 2024 election (Itkowitz, 2024). As with the threats against FEMA workers his rhetoric has stoked, these election fraud claims have inspired supporters to take threatening actions that have terrorized election workers, both in the aftermath of the 2020 election (Wines, 2020) and in the run-up to the 2024 contest (Riccardi, 2024). Regarding these and conspiracy theories more broadly, *The New York Times* examined six months' worth of Trump's Truth Social posts and reposts during the 2024 election campaign, and discovered that: "at least 330 of them met two tightly defined and striking criteria: They each described both a false, secretive plot against Mr. Trump or the American people and a specific entity supposedly responsible for it" (Bedi et al., 2024). It is worth noting that once he won the 2024 election, the talk of election fraud came to an abrupt halt.

Trump's moral compass, such as it is, poses no barrier to telling lies. As a result, he intentionally incorporates lying into his political strategy to a degree no other national figure comes close to matching. The twice-elected president's approach to lying, therefore, poses some particular challenges for opponents as well as voters seeking the truth. Although this is far from the only time he has done so, in his single 2024 debate with President Biden on June 27, 2024, Trump engaged in a tactic known as the Gish Gallop. The next day, Richardson defined this as a:

> rhetorical technique in which someone throws out a fast string of lies, non-sequiturs, and specious arguments, so many that it is impossible to fact check or rebut them in the amount of time it took to say them. Trying to figure out how to respond makes the opponent look confused, because they don't know where to start grappling with the flood that has just hit them. It is a form of gaslighting (Richardson, 2024a).

It is an understatement of vast proportions to say that this kind of lying by a major party nominee for president—let alone an actual President of the United States—is wholly unprecedented, as journalism and public policy professor Bill Adair told *The New York Times:*

> No one in American politics has ever lied on this scale. His impact is not just in the volume and repetition of lies that he tells but also in the way that he has affected the culture of the Republican Party. He has made it more acceptable to lie, and that's clear when you listen to debate on the House floor and you hear his lies get repeated, or you watch Fox and you hear his lies get repeated (Baker, 2024b).

Meaning

As the example of the cat suggests, meaning is not as cut and dried as a dictionary would have us believe. While there are dictionary definitions, these are only part of how people come to understand the words another person speaks. In this way, the meaning that a code has for one person is not necessarily the identical meaning it has for another. For example, absent from the definition of the aforementioned cat is that a cat is cute. Although cat lovers may view this as fundamental to any proper definition of a cat, someone with a cat allergy or even just a simple aversion to cats may disagree and not necessarily see cuteness as an integral part of that definition.

Meaning is something that we work together to create. Elements of Trump culture demonstrate this point. The red MAGA hat provides a visible symbol that signifies the alignment between Trump and his base. Moreover, there has come to be a default uniform for candidates and elected officials (Lewis, 2023) who want to show their absolute fealty to the twice-elected president, but for whom a MAGA hat might seem too informal and/or perhaps not a strong enough statement: a dark blue suit, white shirt, and red tie, the symbolic colors of America that Trump himself often wears in this fashion. By copying his outfit, people are also able to create new meaning for existing symbols in our culture (Houghtaling, 2024). In Trump's 'uniform' example, Jennings (2024) opined:

> I think Republicans are wearing the bright red tie to signal that they're a Trump Republican as opposed to a Romney Republican. It's not just the bright red tie, it's that they're often wearing satin red ties, a very shiny material that Trump wears. Historically for men, it's usually the tie you'd wear in the evening. But Trump wears a satin red tie even in afternoons and mornings, because it's the strongest, punchiest way to wear a red tie. Other Republicans have picked up on that and bought essentially the same tie when you see them coming out in support of Trump.

Jennings continued:

> The first time I really noticed that was the very first Republican primary debate for this presidential campaign. So many came out in bright red ties, and the only men that didn't were Chris Christie and Asa Hutchinson, both of whom said they wouldn't support Trump if he were the party's nominee. They were totally scorched by Republicans for that. As everyone has noted, Trump has taken over the party. It's this kind of careful thing where candidates want to stand up to him and say that you're an alternative, but then you also have to court his base of diehards.

Rewards and punishments

Social Exchange Theory helps explain why Trump's behavior motivates his base to align with him on matters ranging from clothing choices to stereotype use and more. This theory argues that people learn acceptable behaviors based on the benefits they receive for engaging in them (Kelley and Thibaut, 1978). Through increased social media traffic for his posts, among other metrics, the twice-elected president receives rewards in real time for invoking stereotypes. By contrast, the media would traditionally have punished a politician for this behavior, as happened with Virginia's George Allen (see Chapter 1). Compared to previous presidents, Trump has to a good degree shunned traditional, sanctioned, and journalistically moderated communication channels with the general public, and has received positive reinforcement that encourages him to continue largely communicating with his supporters in non-traditional ways. Of course, the for-profit media environment benefits from his outlandishness as well (see Chapter 7).

Moreover, Trump models the behavior he expects to see in his supporters by demonstrating the perceived rewards and punishments they can expect based on whether they engage in similar behavior, or in behavior he otherwise endorses. For one example, at a February 1, 2016 rally, then-candidate Trump gave the following instructions as to how his supporters should deal with protesters they saw, and also offered a pledge of support for any consequences that following his instructions might bring: "Knock the crap out of them, would you? Seriously. OK? Just knock the hell – I promise you, I will pay for the legal fees. I promise, I promise" (Wright, 2016).

In particular, the stereotypes Trump uses can lead those who take them as truth to carry out violence, which has happened already. ABC News found: "at least 54 criminal cases where Trump was invoked in direct connection with violent acts, threats of violence or allegations of assault." And that was only as of May 2020 (Levine, 2020). After a 2015 attack on a homeless Latino man in Boston during which the attackers used his name as justification, Trump praised them as patriots:

"They love this country. They want this country to be great again. But they are very passionate." (Bouie, 2024b). After a protester spoke out during a 2015 rally in Alabama, the twice-elected president thundered as his supporters beat and kicked the person: "Get him the hell out of here! Throw him out!" The next day he appeared to endorse that violence: "Maybe he should have been roughed up, because it was absolutely disgusting what he was doing" (Bouie, 2024b).

After the outbreak of the COVID-19 pandemic, Trump used racist language, talking about the "Chinese Virus" and the "Kung flu." A research study found: "Anti-Asian sentiment depicted in [Trump's rhetoric] likely perpetuated racist attitudes and parallels the anti-Asian hate crimes that have occurred since" (Reja, 2021). The number of anti-Asian/Asian American hate crimes and racist tweets jumped in the first week after Trump first tweeted about the "Chinese Virus" on March 16, 2020 (Reja, 2021). The worst of these crimes saw six Asian American women murdered in Georgia, although the perpetrator denies that racial animus played a role.

Moving into the 2024 campaign, at an October 7 rally in Juneau, Wisconsin, the twice-elected president spoke casually about his supporters hypothetically committing violence against Harris backers: "Is there anybody here that's going to vote for lying Kamala? Please raise your hand, please raise it," Trump asked, before he changed his mind. "Actually, I should say, don't raise your hand—it would be very dangerous. We don't want to see anybody get hurt" (Bidgood, 2024b). At an October 12 rally, he took verbal aim at a protester, declaring that she should: "go back home to Mommy" and "get the hell knocked out of her," and then described how her mother—in this scenario a "big fan of ours"—would beat up her own daughter (Associated Press, 2024c). When it comes to Trump's language, in particular at his rallies, politics and violence go hand in hand. In fact, one study found no major party nominee for president has ever matched the level of violent rhetoric he employed in the 2024 campaign (Kivovitz and Kung, 2024)

The twice-elected president's communications often include both stereotypes and violent rhetoric. On May 29, 2020, in the aftermath of the murder of George Floyd, Trump stereotyped those who took to the streets nationwide to protest as "THUGS" and added: "when the looting starts, the shooting starts" (Haberman and Burns, 2020). Twitter appended a message noting that the tweet violated the site's rules on "glorifying violence" (Haberman and Burns, 2020). In 2021, he essentially called for police brutality: "When you see these thugs being thrown into the back of a paddy wagon, you just see them thrown in, rough, and I said, please don't be too nice" (Bouie, 2024b). Trump echoed these sentiments just over a month before the 2024 election, offering: "we have to let the police do their job [crowd cheers]. And if they have to be extraordinarily rough [crowd cheers louder]" (Nicholls, 2024). He blamed liberal politicians for putting restrictions on what the police can do, and continued:

> The police aren't allowed to do their job. They're told if you do anything, you're gonna lose your pension, you're gonna lose your family, your house, your car . . . You know, if you had one day, like one real rough, nasty day. One rough hour, and I mean real rough, the word will get out and it will end immediately. End immediately. You know, it'll end immediately (Nicholls, 2024).

Sometimes Trump uses violent language or seemingly encourages supporters to commit violence even without stereotyping. For example, there is his suggestion on August 9, 2016, that "Second Amendment people" could solve the problem of a potential President Hillary Clinton picking judges who would take away people's guns. Please note that this remark referred to what they could do after she was elected, thus, it was not an attempt to encourage voting or otherwise participate in the upcoming election that fall (Corasaniti and Haberman, 2016). Another example is Trump's 2020 attacks on Michigan Governor Gretchen Whitmer, who became the target of a kidnapping plot—after which he portrayed the perpetrators in a sympathetic light (Vazquez and Carvajal, 2020). Additionally, there is the bombardment of election workers with death threats from those energized by Trump's lies that the 2020 election was stolen (So, 2021). In 2023, after a man broke into the home of Nancy Pelosi with the aim of killing her, and instead badly wounded her husband with a hammer, the twice-elected president told a joke and chuckled about it in a speech to California Republicans (Bouie, 2024b). Many other examples abound. Higher support among Republicans for political violence shows up in survey data. The Public Religion Research Institute (2024) found: "Nearly three in ten Republicans (29%) believe that true American patriots may have to resort to violence to save the country, compared with 16% of independents and 8% of Democrats." Ruth Ben-Ghiat told *Mother Jones:* "[Trump] is running a radicalization campaign, using his rallies since 2015 to change the way people perceive violence, to build his leader cult. It's unprecedented even among most autocrats on the rise" (Corn, 2024).

A study found that in 2016 assaults on a given day jumped by 12% in a city when Trump held a rally there, whereas Hillary Clinton rallies produced no such effect (Morrison et al., 2018). On a related note, the assassination attempts on July 13, and September 15, 2024, on the twice-elected president remind us all that violent acts unfortunately continue to profoundly impact our country's electoral politics—as they have going back to the murder of Abraham Lincoln. However, the fact that Trump was a victim of political violence in no way absolves him of responsibility for the violent rhetoric he himself has employed (Young, 2024), instances of which are "legion" (Schoenfeld, 2024). Trump's reaction to the second attempt on his life reflected more of the same:

> "He believed the rhetoric of Biden and Harris, and he acted on it," Mr. Trump told Fox News on Monday [September 16]. "Their rhetoric is causing me to be shot at, when I am the one who is going to save the country, and they are the ones that are destroying the country— both from the inside and out."

> Even as he complained that the Democrats had made him a target by calling him a threat to democracy, he repeated his own assertion that: "these are people that want to destroy our country" and called them: "the enemy from within"—certainly language no less provocative than that used about him (Baker, 2024a).

Sen. Vance also blamed Democrats, and offered this disturbing thought: "No one has tried to kill Kamala Harris in the last couple of months, and two people now have tried to kill Donald Trump in the last couple of months. I'd say that's pretty strong evidence that the left needs to tone down the rhetoric and needs to cut this crap out" (Allen et al., 2024). Likewise, from the stage at Trump events Elon Musk has repeatedly talked about Harris being assassinated. Jennifer Mercieca told *The New York Times* that doing so "obviously . . . gives people the idea that someone ought to do that," and added: "We've really taken a turn here. It's really dark" (Fahrenthold, 2024).

Going even further, Trump blamed Biden and Harris in more direct terms for the closeness of the July 13 attempt on his life—not just because of their rhetoric, but because they, in his words: "did not properly protect me, and I was forced to take a bullet for Democracy" (Haberman and Swan, 2024). Trump's language— heard by millions of Americans—at least leaves open the possibility that his opponents deliberately failed to protect him, that his opponents wanted him dead. Finally, Trump's son Eric made the accusation explicit at an October 5 rally for his father in Butler, Pennsylvania, at the site of the first assassination attempt: "They impeached him twice, and then, guys, they tried to kill him. They tried to kill him, and it's because of the Democratic Party. They can't do anything right" (McCarthy, 2024). When asked about this highly explosive, irresponsible charge coming from a son of the former president, Republican House Speaker Mike Johnson refused to condemn it, replying merely: "I'm not going to parse the language of what people say at rallies" (McCarthy, 2024).

Modeling 'good' behavior

When it comes to fellow politicians, those who support Trump receive praise and rewards while he rhetorically eviscerates—often with a demeaning nickname (see

Chapter 3)—those who dare to speak against him. This occurs even if you claim to be a member of his party—which is increasingly difficult to do if you violate the prevailing norm of kowtowing to Trump. The list of such people is long and includes many previously considered staunch Republican icons. The aforementioned John McCain (see Chapter 1) stood up to the twice-elected president on multiple occasions. These include his 2015 accusation of Trump "firing up the crazies" by hurling stereotypes about immigrants, and when—after the aforementioned Trump Access Hollywood tape ("Grab 'em by the pussy") emerged a month before the 2016 election—McCain declared that this "make(s) it impossible to continue to offer even conditional support for his candidacy." He added that "no excuses" exist, and that: "[Trump] alone bears the burden of his conduct" (BBC News, 2018). Trump attacked the Arizona senator repeatedly, calling his July 27, 2017 vote against the repeal of Obamacare "disgraceful" (Cillizza, 2019). Trump's attacks on McCain went beyond the political: In 2015 then-candidate Trump offered: "He's not a war hero. He's a war hero because he was captured? I like people who weren't captured" (Cillizza, 2019). One might think that Trump—someone who avoided going to war due to his father reportedly calling in a favor from a doctor who was also a real estate customer (Eder, 2018)—might be hurt politically by going after a powerful Republican war hero. Far from it.

Mitt Romney, former U.S. Senator from Utah and Massachusetts Governor, and 2012 Republican presidential nominee, became a prominent Trump critic, and voted to convict the twice-elected president at the end of both of his impeachment trials. Romney's first vote made him the first senator ever to vote to convict a president of his own party. He also declined to endorse Trump in 2024. Trump slammed him many times, for example in 2023 calling him a "total loser" (Pengelly, 2023). Trump's own former vice president, Mike Pence, refused to endorse either candidate for president in 2024, another unprecedented development. Trump never forgave Pence for rejecting the demand that he, in his role as vice president on January 6, go along with Trump's unconstitutional scheme to block Congressional certification of Joe Biden's 2020 electoral victory. His former boss called Pence "delusional" (Iyer, 2023), among other insults.

Rep. Liz Cheney became one of Trump's strongest critics after the January 6 insurrection, serving on the bipartisan House Select Committee that investigated the event. That service cost her a leadership position among House Republicans, and later, after she lost the 2022 Republican primary, her seat as representative from Wyoming. Trump called for Cheney to be sent to jail because of her service on the committee (Gabbatt, 2024). She and her father—former Vice President Dick Cheney, another staunch conservative—denounced Trump and endorsed Kamala Harris for president in September 2024, and Rep. Cheney campaigned in person with Harris. No former vice president (or president) in American history had ever endorsed the other party's candidate for president (Robillard, 2024). Afterwards, Trump called Vice President Cheney "irrelevant" and the: "King of Endless, Nonsensical Wars, wasting Lives and Trillions of Dollars, just like Comrade Kamala Harris," and slammed Rep. Cheney as having committed: "unthinkable" acts (Irwin, 2024). On November 1, 2024, the twice-elected president criticized Rep. Cheney as a "radical war hawk"—a legitimate, policy-based statement—before turning to some of the most violent rhetoric he had employed to that point: "Let's put her with a rifle standing there with nine barrels shooting at her, OK? Let's see how she feels about it. You know, when the guns are trained on her face" (Gold and Nagourney, 2024).

Attacks like these reflect Trump's success in utterly and completely redefining the very meaning of the Republican Party in a way no other political figure has done. As Klein (2024) put it:

> What Donald Trump has done is remarkable. It is historic. It is unique in the entire history of American politics. To run as an outsider to a political party and capture that political party totally. Break its fundamental consensus. Slander its previous standard-bearers. To then become president having never held elective office or served in the military, while saying things and doing things that, until you, everybody believed you could not do or say in politics.

By contrast, part of Trump's redefinition of the GOP was that the sole criteria for being a good Republican was simply being on his side. Unreservedly. Either you are with him, or you are beyond the pale. His former Chief of Staff Gen. John Kelly explained that loyalty to Trump above everything else: "is virtually everything to him," and anyone who fails to demonstrate absolute loyalty would soon find: "your time is short" as a member in good standing of Team Trump (Schmidt, 2024). There is no better example of the value the twice-elected president places on loyalty than JD Vance, who went from characterizing himself as a: "never-Trump guy" and harshly and publicly criticizing Trump as unfit in 2016, to becoming his running mate by 2024 (Demissie, 2024). How? Because he had first flip-flopped and transformed into a virulent supporter and supplicant of Trump. Other one-time harsh critics also made a 180 degree turn and were welcomed back into the fold. These include, to name a few prominent examples, former Florida Sen. Marco Rubio (see Chapter 3)—who became Trump's Secretary of State at the start of his second term, South Carolina Sen. Lindsey Graham, and even Megyn Kelly (see Chapter 1). On the night before the election, she embraced Trump on stage and made a rousing speech on behalf of the man who had once called her "nasty" and said of her: "She's not very tough and not very sharp. I don't respect her as a journalist" (Cooper, 2024). Through tight control over who gains entry into his inner circle (i.e., those who pledge their undying fealty) at the political level, Trump is able to control the message that goes out to his base. Additionally, modeling this kind of ruthlessness in dealing with those who oppose him has an important impact—it further exacerbates the polarization of society by encouraging his supporters to ostracize anyone with whom they disagree. They see that their leader reaps rewards from acting this way, and they also fear that ostracization if they themselves step out of line.

What happens at the level of leadership models what should happen at the individual/supporter level. At the individual level, people persuade each other and motivate each other to join a particular cause, movement, or campaign. As discussed in Chapter 4, that strategy of persuasion is necessary for a strong group vitality that keeps the group's demographic numbers and perceived status high. Rewards make this easier to achieve. In turn, being a part of the ingroup is in itself a reward. Seeing Trump evade retribution despite committing the (once) unforgivable sin of overtly communicating stereotypes gives hope and pride to the base, and fosters their own desire to finally be free to do the same after years of suffering under the yoke of political correctness. These shared feelings enhance the process by which Trump's base views itself as a cohesive community (i.e., ingroup) that is well-taken care of, protected, and nurtured by their leader.

Creation of TrumpWorld

TrumpWorld essentially possesses its own fully formed culture, one that the twice-elected president has carefully crafted. His base thoroughly understands this culture, which centers around a fear-based worldview, and which tells its adherents exactly who are the heroes—primarily Trump himself—and who are the villains—most prominently Obama, Clinton, Biden, and most recently Harris, among others. The hero wants to Make America Great Again, while the villains threaten to destroy it (e.g., Kurylo, 2018). Indeed, threats are everywhere in TrumpWorld, a world he has created both literally through his policies as president and figuratively through his language choices and, in some cases, outright lies. This culture includes stories, rituals, inside 'jokes' or other shorthand/inside information that his fans immediately recognize—this was an art Limbaugh had perfected over the years (Reifowitz, 2019)—artifacts (e.g., the MAGA hat), values, metaphors (e.g., 'the swamp'), and performances (e.g., the campaign rallies).

For one example of such inside information, across the campaigns Trump has told and retold a particular tale about a kind woman who saves a badly wounded snake.[31] In the end, the snake kills his rescuer with a fatal bite. Trump tells his audience that this story is a metaphor for U.S. immigration (Pinchin, 2019). The undocumented immigrants are, of course, the deadly snake. No one in American politics uses metaphors to fearmonger more effectively. Through these elements of a culture (Kaye, 1995), Trump is able to both rile up his base and provide a sense of cohesive identity to its members.

On January 6, 2021, the twice-elected president relied on the shared cultural knowledge of TrumpWorld's members to motivate some of them to march on the Capitol. After repeating the Big Lie about a stolen election, he thundered: "We fight like hell. And if you don't fight like hell, you're not going to have a country anymore," and added: "I know that everyone here will soon be marching over to the Capitol building to peacefully and patriotically make your voices heard" (Naylor, 2021). However, like "Critical Race Theory" (Chapter 6) and "sovereignty," (Chapter 7) the word "patriotically" may well have served as a dog whistle in that Trump had previously defined patriotism for his base as sometimes involving violent means to justify patriotic ends, such as in the aforementioned anti-immigrant assault in Boston. Dog whistles like these index other knowledge within Trump-World's culture of which his base would be well aware (Blake, 2024a).

Social construction

A perspective known as social construction helps explain Trump's worldbuilding. Social construction provides a unique lens through which to view, expose, and understand how multiple 'realities' coexist (Gergen, 1992) as well as the various dynamics and consequences for society that the existence of these differing realities cause. Mokros (2003) defines a constitutive, or social construction approach when he states, "a constitutive view of communication . . . takes seriously the centrality of communication for making sense of personal and social being" (p. 4). Three aspects of a social construction approach are worth noting.

First, cultural communication research from a social construction approach does not concern itself with generalizations about differences among groups. A social construction approach focuses instead on the way we communicate culture in context. Carbaugh (1990) clarifies: "communication is everywhere 'contextualized,' locally designed, situationally managed and individually applied" (p. xvi). In this way, generalizing behavior to a cultural group is neither accurate nor appropriate

---

[31] Trump once incorrectly cited Al Wilson as the writer of this story, but credit actually goes to Oscar Brown Jr.

because the message is given meaning by virtue of the interactional moment, rather than because a large number of people voice that message. From a social construction perspective, people are viewed as active participants in their conversations who work collaboratively to produce shared meaning in the moments of our interactions with each other (Condor, 2006; Galanes and Leeds-Hurwitz, 2009; Mokros, 2003; Tracy and Robles, 2013). Communication "constitutes purposeful social interaction, takes place in a social context, and is regulated by social rules and conventions (e.g., regarding language use) that are deployed to establish a 'shared reality' and to attain individual goals" (Semin, 2000, p. 598). Therefore, we do not merely share pre-existing meaning through communication. Rather, communication produces meaning.

Second, a social construction approach is not concerned with an individual's level of awareness of their behavior or intent. Instead, researchers from this perspective have essentially pushed Sapir's understanding of culture further to argue that regardless of the individual's level of awareness, culture is something an individual does, engages in, or actively participates in the production thereof (Carbaugh, 2005, Deetz, 1994; Mokros, 2003; Philipsen, 2002). From a social construction approach we might:

> Think of any particular identity as a set of communicative practices that is more noticeable or salient in some social scenes than in others. Just as an individual is more adept at some identities (e.g., being a teacher, or an Argentinean) than others (e.g., being a business executive, or a Russian), so too are social scenes designed for some identities more than others. This is a way of . . . moving the site of identity from the individual into actual scenes of communicative action. (Carbaugh, 1996, p. 25).

Communicated stereotyping works as an interactive process in which individuals collaborate on the stereotype and understand it as produced through an interactional process.

Third, this production and reproduction requires the assistance of others, that is collaboration. Through people working together to communicate in culturally relevant ways, they collaborate to produce cultural identity. After all, if you walk into class dressed as the President of the United States, your classmates will likely respond to your altered identity with incredulity or laughter, and ultimately reject it. If, however, you do this while you act in a play about current politics, the audience will suspend their disbelief and allow you to inhabit that identity in the moment. In this way, as Mokros (2003) explained: "identity [is] an emergent property of communication and . . . [is] relational, a property not of the individual but of interaction itself" (p. 12). Because we produce identity—our own and others—in interaction rather than it just pre-existing, in different communication contexts an individual might wish to construct different cultural identities for themselves and others. Carbaugh (1996) refers to this when he notes that "any social scene supports some communicative performances more than others, some identities more than others" (p. 26). Cultural communication: "generally looks at . . . the role of communication in the creation and negotiation of shared identities" (Gudykunst, 2002, p. 20).

Collaboration

TrumpWorld could not exist without his base, but neither could it exist without collaboration from the media to help him spread his vision to the American people. Novelist Jodi Picoult (2005) wrote: "It takes two people to make a lie work: the person who tells it, and the one who believes it." This idea that lying requires collaboration is so mainstream that even TV's Homer Simpson famously impugned his wife's innocence by saying: "Marge, it takes two to lie. One to lie and one to listen." Indeed, with regard to Trump there are two constituent groups who collaborate with him when he lies—which, as documented, occurs quite often.

First, the American public, specifically his base of supporters, participate actively in listening to and believing Trump's rhetoric, all too often regardless of how outlandish. Second, the media are complicit by platforming and providing airtime for even the most outrageous statements, so long as doing so can help with ratings and, ultimately, selling advertising. Furthermore, the media have generally proven unable to provide a fact check in real time, while Trump is actually speaking (the Trump-Harris debate on September 10, 2024, was a partial exception), so that the entire audience will see it—especially given that many watch such nationally broadcast remarks on Fox News or other right-wing outlets that typically do not contradict him.

He "tells it like it is"

As the hero in his world, Trump possesses a king-like authority through which he can seemingly shift policies at his whim. For example, Trump's desire to use the U.S.-Mexico border to whip up fear and create anger toward the Biden-Harris White House in the 2024 campaign led to his blocking passage of a painstakingly negotiated, bipartisan immigration law that might have resolved much of what he has repeatedly called a deadly serious crisis (Kapur and Thorp, 2024). In this way, through his communication—and with the support of his base and help, in some cases unwitting, from the media—the twice-elected president socially constructs a world in which threats are rampant from liberal politicians, the elite universities, as well as immigrants and refugees among others.

In Trump's world of threats, he can shift his already vocalized and widely reported stances without the retribution other politicians have faced. In 2004, not only did the campaign of President George W. Bush memorably call Democratic presidential nominee John Kerry a "Flip-Flopper," but the media also adopted Bush's framing, for one example among many in this CBS News article titled: "Kerry's Top Ten Flip-Flops" (Roberts, 2004). In 2024 Vice President Harris endured greater and more sustained scrutiny about changing her positions (Thomas and Nichols, 2024) on fracking and various other issues than did Trump—whose positions sometimes shifted radically. For example, on abortion he even publicly changed his take multiple times within 24 hours (Price, 2024).

The ecosystem of Trump's world is a closed loop wherein his base need not look outside for information, support, or truth. As he has said repeatedly, the media are fake. Supporters receive rewards while naysayers, as the twice-elected president has amply demonstrated, end up as outcasts. In the stories Trump and his followers tell, he is the god-like hero—the only one who can save his base and their version of America and its culture. Trump's supporters continue to see him as expressing key societal truths, as *The New York Times* explained:

> At his rallies, Mr. Trump's fans tell reporters that they recognize that he may not always have the details just right or that he's exaggerating to make a point. But in what they consider a buttoned-down, overly sensitive, "woke" world, they find his willingness to confront the establishment bracingly honest in its own way. His certainty is appealing even if his facts are off (Baker, 2024b).

Ironically, many of his supporters believe he speaks the truth about the problems our country faces, yet do not believe he will carry out many of the most extreme solutions he has proposed to solve those problems (McCreesh, 2024b).

Indeed Trump has garnered a reputation for being a truth bringer. One supporter, interviewed after the February 23, 2016 Republican caucuses in Nevada, praised Trump because he: "tells it like it is" (Markovits, 2016). In exit polling from the South Carolina primary, held three days earlier, voters were given four choices and asked which one was the top quality they were looking for in a Republican presidential nominee. Seventy-eight percent of those who picked: "tells it like it is" voted for Trump, with the next strongest candidate getting a mere 8 % among those voters (Gamio and Clement, 2016). Likewise, in 2024, a Wisconsin Trump voter related: "The first time I saw Trump, I couldn't believe it. Everything I'd been thinking in my head came out of his mouth" (Searcey, 2024). From the stage at the October 27 Madison Square Garden rally, Tucker Carlson offered that his candidate had: "liberated us in the deepest and truest sense. And the liberation he has brought to us is the liberation from the obligation to tell lies. Donald Trump has made it possible for the rest of us to tell the truth about the world around us" (Goldberg, 2024).

The twice-elected president often talks about how he's saying something that other people, such as his opponents in politics, or the media, or sometimes just a generic "they" refuse to say (Time, 2017; Bickerton, 2024)—typically, Trump argues, because they are politically correct and cower before the power of snowflakes. Doing so reinforces the notion that he tells hard truths that those who stand against him dare not speak, making his audience feel even more of a bond with him. After telling a particularly crude story about the golfer Arnold Palmer's genitalia, the twice-elected president added: "I had to tell you the shower part of it because it's true. What can I tell you? We want to be honest" (Gold, 2024e). Furthermore, even just talking about someone else's male sexual potency reminds the audience that Trump himself is a powerful man. Dowd (2024b) referred to him as "phallocentric."

Likewise, Trump has evinced a strong preference for proclaiming he is saying or proposing something "nobody has even seen before"—another way for him to demonstrate what David Graham (2024) called his "novelty," and thus the unique value that accrues to supporters. Trump told a Florida audience on August 30, 2024, that he discussed the issue of transgender women competing in sports against cisgender women because he refused to be politically correct, whereas on the other side: "everyone's afraid to talk about it" (McCreesh, 2024a). Here are four more similar statements from voters (Brown et al., 2016):

- "I backed Trump from the beginning. Because he calls things out. He does not allow lies to live. He just exposes things. Pastors sometimes need to be politically correct, and Donald Trump is not politically correct, and I love that about him" – Crystal Myers, California, May 2016
- "He's outspoken. Other candidates wouldn't tell you how it is, but he does." – Betty Tully, August 2015
- "I like that he's over the top. My president needs bravado . . . somebody who is big and loud, strong and powerful." – Victoria Wilen, Orlando, Florida, November 2015
- "He doesn't hold back. You get what he really believes in, even if everything that he says isn't what is the right thing exactly." – Nicholas Poucher, Florida, December 2015

A 'terrifying' world

In building out TrumpWorld's culture, the twice-elected president co-opts themes that already existed on the right-wing, from sources ranging from Limbaugh to Fox News and beyond. This is to say, Trump did not invent talking about the specific fears he exploits (Kurylo, 2018). But he has taken doing so to a new level. Through his rhetoric, Trump creates the 'reality' in which his followers live, and embedded there is a fear-based control mechanism that keeps them on a tight leash. In the alternate reality of TrumpWorld, immigrants are literally monsters who would eat your pet—and who knows what else they are capable of?

TrumpWorld is a terrifying one for its denizens, one in which the leader creates new enemies and hurls stereotypes that ultimately serve, as planned, to motivate supporters to act on his behalf. This is not a world that Democrats or liberals inhabit. Indeed, this world often contradicts the empirical reality derived from statistical data. But to his base, TrumpWorld reflects their perceived reality. Others might call it an ideology, a movement, or even a cult (Dickinson and Suebsaeng, 2024). Regardless of the descriptor, the twice-elected president has created a coherent and complete worldview that covers every aspect of American society—even if some details come straight from Trump's imagination. Nevertheless, he has run for president three times now with that worldview at the center of his bid, and won twice.

Chapter 9
Conclusion and future directions: The "greatest" argument

Trump's use of stereotypes created the coalescing, combustible force that convinced his base to view him with such adoration. Doing so enabled him to take over the Republican Party by allowing him to stand out against the other candidates battling for the 2016 nomination (see Chapter 1). Without first controlling the party—having been vaulted to that leadership position by a riled-up base who has kept him there in all the years since—he could not have won the presidency in either 2016 or 2024. Stereotypes also helped him garner the media attention and public-facing visibility he needed to motivate his base (see Chapter 7). Trump's constant use of stereotypes has become the dominant form of rhetoric on the American right-wing at every level of government, with Republican candidates and elected officials parroting his language (see Chapter 7). Furthermore, Trump not only won support from people who already agreed with his stereotype-laden rhetoric, that rhetoric pushed some percentage of his white supporters to have increased hostility toward other racial and ethnic groups (Chapter 3). These developments have corroded our public discourse. The distance between Republican nominee John McCain standing against the stereotyping of Barack Obama in 2008 (see Chapter 1) and Donald Trump only eight years later is just breathtaking. And not in a good way.

The ultimate argument each chapter has made reduces to the idea that core supporters of the twice-elected president have been motivated, coerced, and manipulated by his utilization—knowingly or not—of strategies explained by well-established scholarly theories. Each individual theory describes, explains, or predicts how stereotypes might attract supporters to him. Taken as a whole, these theories form a complex labyrinth from which there appears no way to escape. Trump's rhetoric, in particular its heavy incorporation of stereotypes, places his supporters into a vicious cycle that includes:

1. rewards and punishments (social identity theory, psychodynamic approach)
2. inevitable bias of our perceptual lenses (cognitive approach)
3. historical lead-in to current times (political correctness)
4. seemingly unlimited reach of traditional and social media (elaboration likelihood)
5. constructed division (interactional dilemma, social construction)

https://doi.org/10.1515/9783111426327-012

This is not about blaming members of the base for getting riled up. Once someone enters TrumpWorld, getting out is no easy feat. Others cannot extract you. No one can pull the curtain back for you—but you can do it for yourself. The website Republican Voters Against Trump collected hundreds of video testimonials from people like Lori McCammon (Gunn, 2024) who once backed the twice-elected president and have since decided to oppose him. One ex-supporter said that Trump "disgusts me to my core" (Levin, 2024). In TrumpWorld, supporters digest misinformation and disinformation (i. e., lies) aimed at scaring and, ultimately, controlling them. The twice-elected president, along with other right-wing provocateurs, employs strategies to accomplish this goal. Social media algorithms amplify the message, while traditional media provide the appearance of credibility and extend the reach exponentially. This encourages Trump's base to travel further down an extremist rabbit-hole into an alternate reality akin to the setting of Lewis Carroll's *Alice's Adventures in Wonderland.* These adventures are a force out of Alice's control. They act on her, compel her choices, and, to paraphrase Trump's already infamous remark, do what they do whether she likes it or not (see Chapter 5). Alice's desire to get back home remains pure, innocent, and relatable. Ultimately, she succeeds after battling the Queen of Hearts.

Members of the Trump base, even the January 6th insurrectionists, are on their own self-defined quest to return to an imagined version of the past their leader has often invoked—a comfortable place and time when America was "great" that only he can bring back. TrumpWorld residents, in their telling of this tale, are the innocents fighting the forces of change surrounding them so they can regain a sense of normalcy and control that the twice-elected president tells them is their birthright.

The idea of the innocent battling all sorts of obstacles in order to return home is a common trope in American culture. Dorothy in *The Wizard of Oz* experiences a similar fantastical journey to get back to Kansas. This trope includes villains, helpful heroes, and the innocent victim/protagonist on a quest they have not chosen, fighting against odds and oddities to return to a familiar place. Taken as a whole, the theories explored in each chapter present a story no less fantastical than the tales that invoke this common trope. We are not suggesting the members of Trump's base are innocent in the same way Dorothy or Alice are, nor do we deny that they chose to join the cause of their own free will. Nevertheless, we hope to shed light on their journey into TrumpWorld, as they experience a place that acts upon them as they try to restore and return to the MAGA version of America—with Trump as the "Wizard of MAGA Oz," as Mika Brzezinski (MSNBC, 2024a) referred to him.

Trump, on the other hand, views his supporters differently. In his telling they are not innocents subject to the bewildering environment that is TrumpWorld. To the last hours of the campaign, his rhetoric aimed to empower those who follow him, to put them in control. The twice-elected president has consistently reinforced this. "The only way we can blow it is if you blow it," Trump said the night before Election Day (Samuels, 2024b). These words aim to motivate, but also shift both responsibility and, by extension, blame. A negative outcome of the election, as with so many other of his endeavors, would not be *his* fault, but would instead rest on the actions of his supporters—although he has also said he would blame Jewish Americans for not supporting him if he lost (see Chapter 1). Either way, Trump himself bears no responsibility for a negative outcome.

If, however, the outcome is positive then the praise knows no bounds. In the early morning hours of November 6, 2024, Trump claimed victory in the election that made him the 47th President of the United States of America. He stood at the head of what he described as a movement of a kind: "nobody's ever seen before . . . this was the greatest political movement of all time." His running mate called Trump's win: "the greatest political comeback in American history" (Steinhauser, 2024). This is in keeping with the kind of rhetoric Trump has used for decades (see Chapter 8). Remember that upon accepting the Republican nomination in 2016 he declared: "I alone can fix" what ails America (Jackson, 2016). Hyperbolic superlatives like these both center Trump and puff up the chests of that same base, enabling its members to bask in his reflected glory. If he is the greatest, then—to some degree at least—so are they. This is just one more way his rhetoric strengthens the bond of community between leader and led.

There is a point of intersection between the narrative that we have made in the previous chapters and Trump's own narrative. In the story laid out in this book we also view his supporters as possessing latent power, despite the ways his rhetoric on stereotypes acts on them. Alice, fighting the evil queen, realizes that her opponent does not actually have the support of those around her. In fact, they genuinely resent her. Alice ultimately defeats the villain, despite the queen's repeated assertions of: "Off with her head." Along with her traveling companions, Dorothy is an innocent on a search for a wizard who will solve all their problems and get her back to Aunt Em and Uncle Henry. In the end, Dorothy had the power all along.

Innocent does not mean without power. The question is: how do you use it?

The power of stereotypes

To recap, this book takes the approach that: "stereotypes are learned, maintained, and potentially changed through the language and communication of a culture" (Stangor and Schaller, 1996, p. 11). In this way, stereotypes function within contexts of interaction (McGarty, 2002) through which they are maintained and perpetuated. Because stereotypes are communicated within interactions, they are products of coordinated and collaborative communication processes (Haslam et al., 2002; McGarty et al., 2002; Schaller and Latané, 1996). This understanding allows us to view stereotypes:

1. Not as fact, but as creations of a culture such that stereotypes are social constructions.
2. Not merely as inherently bad and inevitably prejudicial, but also as functional for individuals who choose to wield them.
3. Not as a problem solely for the targeted people, but as a process involving all those participating in the interactions in which they are communicated.
4. Not as a weapon used to victimize people viewed as incapable of helping themselves or unable to act effectively. Instead, people, regardless of whether they are the target of the stereotype. should be empowered through their own agency to combat stereotypes and those who use them. (Macrae, 1996).

As Schaller and Conway (1999) explained:

> Although a psychological understanding of stereotypes demands that stereotypes be defined as individual level knowledge structures represented in individual minds, the stereotypes that really matter are more than that: they are shared knowledge structures that are represented similarly in multiple minds and across broad populations of people (p. 820).

The distinction between viewing stereotypes as individually held or as shared is integral to how we discuss stereotypes in this book (Kashima, 2000; Semin, 2000). Because stereotypes are a shared mental representation, we can use them as tools for communication purposes in political rhetoric, through media channels, and in our everyday talk. Communication can be viewed as a: "tool to implement cognition" (Semin, 2000, p. 601) and also as an "interactive" process through which individuals produce meaning (Mokros, 2003, p. 265; Guerin, 2003; Hopper, 2003; Lee, 1996; Tracy, 2002). That stereotypes are *shared* representations is the start, not the end, of how we must use them to understand their role in Trump's political successes.

Mokros (2003) discusses how one individual in his study communicated the stereotype of Jews as cheap to explain the undesirable behavior of another individual being too selective in picking out produce at a market. In the interaction that Mokros analyzed, this stereotype justified the person in the study fighting, verbally and physically, with the other individual. In this example, the stereotyper attempted to negotiate his identity by trying to control the situation through scapegoating. The stereotype allowed the attention and blame to be shifted to the other individual so that the stereotyper would be seen as justified in the altercation. Through his discussion, Mokros (2003) begins to draw scholarly attention to how stereotypes are used as a tool to negotiate identity and solve practical interactional problems.

Similarly, Hopper (2003) looked at transcripts of interpersonally communicated stereotypes to understand how people construct and collaborate on gendered identity in the communication process. His examples show that, through communication, gender stereotypes can 'formulate' differences where none exist (p. 116). For example, Hopper (2003) discusses a heterosexual romantic couple who assign "household chores" according to gender stereotypes (p. 109). By communicating these gender stereotypes, the couple works together to construct and reinforce gender differences as meaningful distinctions between people in ways that allow them to assign tasks without conflict.

Kurylo (2013) discusses examples in which interpersonally communicated stereotypes can provide enjoyment for people who communicate them. For example, ingroup members may communicate stereotypes to make ingroup or outgroup members laugh (Lee, 1996). Doing so may put others "at ease," for example, by using self-effacing stereotypes (Lee, 1996, p. 94). Ethnophaulisms (i.e., racial slurs) can act similarly. For example, Tracy (2002) notes: "although terms such as [n-word] and wop are insults when communicated by someone who is not a member of the group, they can become friendly address forms between members of the same ethnic group" in a particular interaction (italics in original; p. 175). In this example, people can construct their shared identity as ingroup members by communicating ethnophaulisms. A similar example is the reclamation of "queer"—once generally understood as a slur aimed by heterosexuals against members of the LGBTQ community—by members of that community (Rocheleau, 2019).

Revisiting political correctness

Although communication processes are potentially valuable for understanding stereotypes, their communication has historically been discouraged because using stereotypes is generally stigmatized. Beginning in the 1960s: "the Civil Rights Movement and feminism fostered work in how stereotypes, prejudice, and discrimination could be reduced" (Liberman et al., 1998, p. 156). The political correctness movement, begun in the 1970s and expanded in recent years to focus on microaggressions, has heightened awareness of the stigma associated with stereotypes. These movements have encouraged sensitivity to the issues affecting diverse human populations (Williams, 1995) while also, inadvertently, making discussion of stereotypes verboten and fostering a resentment that Trump has been able to use to his advantage during his campaigns and time as president. If stereotypes hamper social cohesion in a diverse society—and virtually all societies are diverse to some degree—because they exacerbate prejudice and discrimination (Allport, 1954/1979), then using them as communication tools seems absurd and paradoxical. Worse yet, if we avoid discussing stereotypes at all because of political correctness we have essentially thrown the baby out with the bathwater.

The regular communication of stereotypes in conversation and political rhetoric traps the people who experience them into viewing them as absolute and fixed categories. This results in mindlessness (see Chapter 7), producing a state of reduced attention in which we behave passively when we hear them (Kurylo and Robles, 2015). As a result, people can lack the ability to think in complex ways about groups, exhibit emotional and cognitive rigidity when confronted with stereotypes, and find it difficult to adapt to new communication situations that counter stereotypical assumptions.

The 2024 election

We have emphasized that white racial anxiety about demographic change and white Christian nationalism more broadly are central to Trump's appeal to his base—which we define as his core supporters, a subset within the broader universe of those who voted for him. 2024 exit polls (Wolf et al., 2024; Washington Post, 2020; Washington Post, 2024) showed that, by slightly different degrees in each poll, Trump performed a few points better with Asian American voters than he had four years earlier, and improved by a great deal with Latino voters —even winning a 12-point majority among Latino men after losing them by 23 points in 2020. By comparison, black and white Americans both voted for Trump by virtually the same percentage as they had in 2020.

Separate from any racist attitudes these Asian American and Latino Trump voters might have either shared with the twice-elected president, or simply grew willing to tolerate from him, some may have decided that his rhetoric attacking recent asylum seekers or others crossing the border without authorization does not target them or their loved ones. As Arizona Democratic Senator Ruben Gallego—who in 2024 won his open seat race by 2.4% while Harris lost the state by 5.5% —explained about Latino voters who support a pathway to citizenship for some undocumented immigrants already in the U.S.: "It's very simple: [they] don't identify with those people that are coming over right now" (Browning and Medina, 2024).

Irrespective of broader identity-related issues, some of these immigrant voters of color, including Latinos, may have come to resent what they perceive as lenient treatment the Biden-Harris administration has offered to undocumented newcomers, particularly asylum seekers. Rosa, an undocumented immigrant from Mexico who has lived in Whitewater, Wisconsin for three decades, expressed anger that new arrivals who were awaiting a verdict on their asylum case could apply for a driver's license and a permit to work, but she could not (Sanchez and Rosenberg, 2024). She said simply: "It's not fair. Those of us who have been here for years get nothing." One Fresno, California voter who arrived from Mexico over 25 years ago, José Pérez Gómez, switched from being a Biden 2020 voter to a Trump voter in 2024 for exactly this reason. He explained: "Suddenly in one year, millions of people come in with all the rights without having contributed anything to the country. So a lot of people feel defrauded" (Mayorquín and Morales, 2024). The especially dramatic shift toward Trump in formerly heavily Democratic counties along the Texas-Mexico border appears to reflect these developments and sentiments. Trump voters from the region interviewed by *The New York Times* said that one reason they supported him was "out of a concern over uncontrolled immigration" (Goodman et al., 2024).

In this book, we do not use the breakdown of how various racial groups voted in order to make a fine-grained, data-driven analysis of why Trump won the presidency in 2024. After all, we know that high inflation during the Biden-Harris administration—inflation that, to be sure, all developed countries experienced after COVID-19 (see Chapter 3) mattered to a great number of voters, something totally separate from our subject matter. In the end, we aim to explain how stereotyping—which was a core element of Trump's rhetoric—works, and how it helped him to rile up his base and become the 45th and 47th President of the United States. As for the impact of his rhetoric, Baker (2024c) offered the following analysis the day after the election:

> Mr. Trump's testosterone-driven campaign capitalized on resistance to electing the first woman president . . . Rather than be turned off by Mr. Trump's flagrant, anger-based appeals along lines of race, gender, religion, national origin and especially transgender identity, many Americans found them bracing. Rather than be offended by his brazen lies and wild conspiracy theories, many found him authentic.

Moving forward?

For others who reject the ideology that underlies Trump's messaging and its stereotypes, and who are looking for optimism, Social Identity Theory demonstrates that people can be united as easily as they can be divided. Mindfulness, active listening, central route messaging, education, and legislation can help change narratives to combat disinformation and misinformation as well as societal polarization. Indeed, Harris spent the end of her campaign stumping on this inclusive messaging. In the end, she won only 1.47% fewer votes than her opponent. In her "Closing Argument" speech—delivered October 29 at the Ellipse, the same park where on January 6, 2021, Trump had incited an insurrection—she laid out the contrast between the two candidates' conception of inclusion and American national identity, drawing on themes she had emphasized throughout the campaign:

> Donald Trump has spent a decade trying to keep the American people divided and afraid of each other. That is who he is. But, America, I am here tonight to say that is not who we are. That is not who we are. That is not who we are. You see, what Donald Trump has never understood is that E pluribus unum, out of many, one, isn't just a phrase on a dollar bill. It is a living truth about the heart of our nation.
>
> [...] The fact that someone disagrees with us does not make them the enemy within (see Chapter 7). They are family, neighbors, classmates, coworkers. They are fellow Americans. And as Americans, we rise and fall together. America, for too long, we have been consumed with too much division, chaos, and mutual distrust, and it can be easy then to forget a simple truth: It doesn't have to be this way.
>
> [...] America, I know the vast majority of us have so much more in common than what separates us (Roll Call, 2024).

Through his language, the twice-elected president challenges the vision of an inclusive, pluralistic yet ultimately unified American nationhood put forth by Harris, Biden, and, most comprehensively over the decades, Obama (Reifowitz, 2012). Trump's heavy use of stereotypes exacerbates the tribalization of our society. It divides middle- and working-class Americans from others who share the same material interests and invokes a race-based alignment that undermines an understanding of people's need for cooperation with those who share a roughly similar socio-economic status, as well as the mutual benefits that flow therefrom.

We have discussed a great number of theories in this book. Is it likely that Trump read up on them and then decided to employ stereotype-laden rhetoric in a way that would maximize their impact? It is not. His rhetoric centers around stereotypes, hyperbole, misinformation, disinformation, and other lies simply because speaking that way has been second nature for him over many decades. There is no reason for him to change an approach that has served him well, bringing him to the pinnacle of power in 2016 and again in 2024. Change can only come from those who support Trump deciding they want to move in a different direction.

References

ABC News. (2006, August 16). The Macaca heard round the world. https://abcnews.go.com/Nightline/story?id=2322630&page=1 (accessed January 21, 2025).

ABC News. (2016a, September 16). How Donald Trump perpetuated the "Birther" movement for years. https://abcnews.go.com/Politics/donald-trump-perpetuated-birther-movement-years/story?id=42138176 (accessed January 21, 2025).

ABC News. (2016b, November 7). A timeline of Hillary Clinton's email saga. https://abcnews.go.com/Politics/timeline-hillary-clintons-email-saga/story?id=29442707 (accessed January 21, 2025).

ABC News. (2018, January 17). Obama undone: In first year, Trump unravels predecessor's signature achievements. https://abcnews.go.com/Politics/obama-undone-year-trump-unravels-predecessors-signature-achievements/story?id=52234311 (accessed January 21, 2025).

ACLU. (2010, February 1). Issue brief: Criminalizing undocumented immigrants. *American Civil Liberties Union.* https://www.aclu.org/documents/issue-brief-criminalizing-undocumented-immigrants (accessed January 21, 2025).

ACLU. (2024, July 2). Trump's attacks on DEI reveal administration's agenda for second term. *American Civil Liberties Union.* https://www.aclu.org/news/racial-justice/trumps-attacks-on-dei-reveal-administrations-agenda-for-second-term (accessed January 21, 2025).

Adorno, T. W., Frenkel-Brunswik, E., Levinson, D. J., and Sanford, R. N. (1950). *The Authoritarian Personality.* Harper.

Agence France-Presse. (2023, June 10). Red airwave: America's conservative talk radio saturation. *France 24.* https://france24.com/en/live-news/20231006-red-airwave-america-s-conservative-talk-radio-saturation (accessed January 21, 2025).

Alba, M., and Terkel, A. (2024, October 29). Biden sets off a firestorm with his response to Trump rally comedian's Puerto Rico comments. *NBC News.* https://www.nbcnews.com/politics/2024-election/biden-republican-outrage-trump-rally-comedians-puerto-rico-rcna177926 (accessed January 21, 2025).

Aleaziz, H. (2024, August 24). Biden's asylum restrictions are working as predicted, and as warned. *The New York Times.* https://www.nytimes.com/2024/08/24/us/politics/biden-asylum-restrictions.html (accessed January 21, 2025).

Alfaro, M. (2024, June 2). Donald Trump claims he never called for Hillary Clinton to be locked up. *The Washington Post.* https://www.washingtonpost.com/politics/2024/06/02/trump-hillary-clinton-lock-her-up/ (accessed January 21, 2025).

Alfonseca, K. (2023, December 6). AP African American Studies course finalized for next school year. *ABC News.* https://abcnews.go.com/US/ap-african-american-studies-course-finalized-next-school-year/story?id=105418166 (accessed January 21, 2025).

Alfonseca, K. (2024, August 1). Trump's comments on Jewish Democrats, second gentleman Doug Emhoff spark criticism. *ABC News.* https://abcnews.go.com/Politics/trumps-comments-jewish-democrats-gentleman-doug-emhoff-spark/story?id=112473802 (accessed January 21, 2025).

Alfonseca, K. (2025, January 30). Trump's missing the point on DEI and meritocracy, experts say. *ABC News.* https://abcnews.go.com/Politics/trumps-missing-point-dei-meritocracy-experts/story?id=117975699 (accessed January 30, 2025).

Allen, J., Dixon, M., and Doyle, K. (2024, September 16). Trump dispenses with unity and blames Democrats after apparent second assassination attempt. *NBC News.* https://www.nbcnews.com/politics/donald-trump/trump-dispenses-unity-blames-democrats-apparent-second-assassination-rcna171218 (accessed January 21, 2025).

https://doi.org/10.1515/9783111426327-013

Allport, G. W. (1954/1979). *The nature of prejudice.* Addison-Wesley.

Allsop, J. (2019, May 13). The dangerous power of Trump's 'fairy tale' nicknames. *Columbia Journalism Review.* https://www.cjr.org/the_media_today/trump_buttigieg_neuman_nickname.php (accessed January 21, 2025).

Allyn, B. (2019, December 24). Trump campaign site offers help in winning arguments with "snowflake" relatives. *NPR.* https://www.npr.org/2019/12/24/791125357/trump-campaign-site-offers-help-in-winning-arguments-with-snowflake-relatives (accessed January 21, 2025).

Almond, K. (2024, January 27). Just two northern white rhinos are left on Earth. A new breakthrough offers hope. *CNN.* https://edition.cnn.com/interactive/2024/01/world/rhino-ivf-pregnancy-scn-cnnphotos/ (accessed January 21, 2025).

Alonso, J. (2024, November 8). Education-level voting gaps are highest among men, white people. *Inside Higher Ed.* https://www.inside (highered.com/news/government/politics-elections/2024/11/08/men-and-white-people-vote-differently-based-education (accessed January 21, 2025).

Amiri, F. (2024, November 22). Matt Gaetz says he won't return to Congress after withdrawing from Trump's AG nomination. PBS. https://www.pbs.org/newshour/politics/matt-gaetz-says-he-wont-return-to-congress-after-withdrawing-from-trumps-ag-nomination (accessed January 21, 2025).

Anastasio, J. (2024, September 11). Trump claimed cities like Aurora are seeing "the highest level of criminality." here's what the data shows. Denver 7 Colorado News (KMGH). https://www.denver7.com/news/local-news/trump-claimed-cities-like-aurora-are-seeing-the-highest-level-of-criminality-heres-what-the-data-shows (accessed January 21, 2025).

Anbinder, T. (2019, November 7). Trump has spread more hatred of immigrants than any American in history. *The Washington Post.* https://www.washingtonpost.com/outlook/trump-has-spread-more-hatred-of-immigrants-than-any-american-in-history/2019/11/07/7e253236-ff54-11e9-8bab-0fc209e065a8_story.html (accessed January 21, 2025).

Anti-Defamation League. (n.d.). Myth: Jews are greedy. *ADL.* https://antisemitism.adl.org/greed/ (accessed January 21, 2025).

Arango, T. (2024, September 23). Murder in U.S. continues steep decline, F.B.I. Reports. *The New York Times.* https://www.nytimes.com/2024/09/23/us/murder-crime-rate-fbi.html?smid=nytcore-ios-shareandreferringSource=articleShareandsgrp=c-cb (accessed January 21, 2025).

Aries, E. (1996). *Men and women in interaction.* Oxford University Press.

Arkin, D., Alcindor, Y., and Lavietes, M. (2025, January 20). Trump signs executive orders proclaiming there are only two biological sexes, halting diversity programs. *NBC News.* https://www.nbcnews.com/news/amp/rcna188388 (accessed February 10, 2025).

Ashford, G. (2024, October 14). In heated house race, a moderate Republican goes full Trump. *The New York Times.* https://www.nytimes.com/2024/10/14/nyregion/marc-molinaro-josh-riley.html (accessed January 21, 2025).

Ashmore, R. D., and Del Boca, F. K. (1981). Conceptual approaches to stereotypes and stereotyping. In D. L. Hamilton, (Ed.), *Cognitive processes in stereotyping and intergroup behavior* (pp. 1–35). Erlbaum.

Associated Press. (2023, October 17). Trump vows to expand Muslim ban and bar Gaza refugees if he wins presidency. *The Guardian.* https://www.theguardian.com/us-news/2023/oct/17/trump-muslim-ban-gaza-refugees (accessed January 21, 2025).

Associated Press. (2024a, March 11). Florida teachers can discuss LGBTQ topics under "don't say gay" law, settlement says. *NPR.* https://www.npr.org/2024/03/11/1237730819/florida-dont-say-gay-law-settlement-lgbtq (accessed January 21, 2025).

Associated Press. (2024b, September 28). The latest: Harris heads to US-Mexico border and Trump meets with Zelenskyy. *Associated Press.* https://apnews.com/article/harris-trump-walz-vance-elec tion-46c9bf1c35975f4a181c3585dd41c0d8 (accessed January 21, 2025).

Associated Press. (2024c, October 13). Trump suggests a protester may get "the hell knocked out of her" by her parents. *AP News.* https://apnews.com/article/trump-election-protester-violence-cal ifornia-d7d68895390b6b289d146b7377bc1c18 (accessed January 21, 2025).

AP-NORC. (2022, May). Immigration attitudes and conspiratorial thinkers. The Associated Press – NORC Center for Public Affairs Research. https://apnorc.org/wp-content/uploads/2022/05/Immi gration-Report_V15.pdf (accessed January 21, 2025).

Astor, M. (2024a, September 15). Vance sticks by pet-eating claims and says he's willing to "create stories." *The New York Times.* https://www.nytimes.com/2024/09/15/us/politics/jd-vance-spring field-pets.html (accessed January 21, 2025).

Astor, M. (2024b, October 20). Confronted with facts on Fox News, Trump claims ignorance. *The New York Times.* https://www.nytimes.com/2024/10/20/us/politics/trump-fox-news-jan-6-haitians.html? smid=url-share (accessed January 21, 2025).

Astor, M., and Levien, S. J. (2024, September 10). "Flip-flop" or evolution: Trump and Harris and their reversals on issues. *The New York Times.* https://www.nytimes.com/2024/09/10/us/politics/harris-trump-flip-flops.html (accessed January 21, 2025).

Bach, A. (1995, December 11). Nolo contendere. *New York Magazine,* pp. 49 – 55.

Bacon, Jr., P (2016). Trump and other conservatives embrace "Blue Lives Matter" movement. NBC News. https://www.nbcnews.com/politics/2016-election/trump-other-conservatives-embrace-blue-lives-matter-movement-n615156 (accessed January 21, 2025).

Bailey P. (1966). Hysteria: The history of a disease. *Arch Gen Psychiatry, 14*(3): 332 – 333. doi:10.1001/archpsyc.1966.01730090108024 (accessed January 21, 2025).

Baker, M., and Graham, R. (2024, December 5). Pete Hegseth and his "battle cry" for a new Christian crusade. *The New York Times.* https://www.nytimes.com/2024/12/05/us/hegseth-church-crusades.html (accessed January 21, 2025).

Baker, P. (2018, December 4). Bush made Willie Horton an issue in 1988, and the racial scars are still fresh. *The New York Times.* https://www.nytimes.com/2018/12/03/us/politics/bush-willie-horton. html (accessed January 21, 2025).

Baker, P. (2024a, September 16). Trump, outrage and the modern era of political violence. *The New York Times.* https://www.nytimes.com/2024/09/16/us/politics/trump-violence-assassination-at tempt.html (accessed January 21, 2025).

Baker, P. (2024b, November 3). Trump's wild claims, conspiracies and falsehoods redefine presidential bounds. *The New York Times.* https://www.nytimes.com/2024/11/03/us/politics/trump-falsehoods-claims-election.html (accessed January 21, 2025).

Baker, P. (2024c, November 6). "Trump's America": Comeback victory signals a different kind of country. *The New York Times.* https://www.nytimes.com/2024/11/06/us/politics/trump-america-election-victory.html (accessed January 21, 2025).

Baker, P. (2024d, November 17). Trump signals a "seismic shift," shocking the Washington Establishment. *The New York Times.* https://www.nytimes.com/2024/11/17/us/politics/trump-sig nals-a-seismic-shift-shocking-the-washington-establishment.html (accessed January 21, 2025).

Baker, P. (2025). From anguish to aggression: Trump goes on offense after midair collision. *The New York Times.* https://www.nytimes.com/2025/01/31/us/politics/trump-washington-plane-crash.html (accessed February 1, 2025).

Balk, T. (2024a, September 20). Timeline: What Donald Trump has said about Mark Robinson. *The New York Times.* https://www.nytimes.com/2024/09/20/us/politics/trump-mark-robinson-relationship.html (accessed January 21, 2025).

Balk, T. (2024b, October 5). Aides say Trump resisted sending federal funds after California wildfires. *The New York Times.* https://www.nytimes.com/2024/10/04/us/politics/trump-wildfire-aid-california.html (accessed January 21, 2025).

Ballentine, S. (2024, July 31). Black and other minority farmers are getting $2 billion from USDA after years of discrimination. *Associated Press.* https://apnews.com/article/black-minority-farmers-discrimination-usda-payments-4471b3f3cdccd9050408a43208114638 (accessed January 21, 2025).

Balz, D. (2024, September 14). Trump can't accept his poor debate. So he's spiraled into conspiracy theories. *The Washington Post.* https://www.washingtonpost.com/politics/2024/09/14/trump-conspiracies-lies-analysis/ (accessed January 21, 2025).

Bandura, A. (1963). *Social learning and personality development.* Holt, Rinehart, and Winston.

Banerji, O. (2024, April 17). History group finds little evidence of K-12 "indoctrination." *Education Week.* https://www.edweek.org/teaching-learning/history-group-finds-little-evidence-of-k-12-indoctrination/2024/03 (accessed January 21, 2025).

Baron, R. M. (1995). An ecological view of stereotype accuracy. In Y.-T. Lee, L. J. Jussim, and C. R. McCauley (Eds.), *Stereotype accuracy: Toward appreciating group differences* (pp. 115–140). American Psychological Association. https://doi.org/10.1037/10495-005 (accessed January 21, 2025).

Bar-Tal, D., Graumann, C. F., Kruglanski, A. W., Stroebe, W. (1989). *Stereotyping and prejudice: Changing conceptions.* Springer-Verlag.

Bassin, I., and Potter, M. (2024, October 8). On anticipatory obedience and the media. *Columbia Journalism Review.* https://www.cjr.org/analysis/anticipatory-obedience-bassin-potter-scheppele-orban-trump-hungary-media-punish.php (accessed January 21, 2025).

Bateson, G. (1991) *Steps to an ecology of mind.* Chandler Publishing.

BBC News. (2016, October 10). US presidential debate: Trump launches ferocious attack on Clintons. https://www.bbc.com/news/election-us-2016-37604151 (accessed January 21, 2025).

BBC News. (2018, August 26). John McCain: Five times he clashed with Trump. https://www.bbc.com/news/world-us-canada-45313845 (accessed January 21, 2025).

Beaumont, T., and Colvin, J. (2024, October 23). Trump hurls a string of insults at Harris including "lazy," a racist trope against black people. *Associated Press.* https://apnews.com/article/trump-kamala-lazy-trope-stereotype-4c2ded1046e492c5d24c7382245d0f7b (accessed January 21, 2025).

Bedi, N., Gamio, L., Jhaveri, I., Lum, D., Willis, H., and Yourish, K. (2024, October 29). Inside Trump's Truth Social Conspiracy Theory Machine. *The New York Times.* https://www.nytimes.com/interactive/2024/10/29/us/politics/trump-truth-social-conspiracy-theories.html (accessed January 21, 2025).

Bellware, K., and Menn, J. (2024, November 18). FBI investigating post-election text threats sent to Latino, LGBTQ people. *The Washington Post.* https://www.washingtonpost.com/nation/2024/11/18/election-texts-fbi-investigation/ (accessed January 21, 2025).

Bem, S. L. (1993). *The lenses of gender: Transforming the debate on sexual inequality.* Yale University Press.

Bender, M. C. (2024a, September 22). On the trail, Trump and Vance sharpen a nativist, anti-immigrant tone. *The New York Times.* https://www.nytimes.com/2024/09/22/us/politics/trump-vance-nativist.html (accessed January 21, 2025).

Bender, M. C. (2024b, September 25). Inside a Trump ad ridiculing Harris over taxpayer-paid gender transition surgery. *The New York Times.* https://www.nytimes.com/2024/09/25/us/politics/trump-ad-anti-trans-harris.html (accessed January 21, 2025).

Bensinger, K. (2024, September 13). Laura Loomer, a social-media instigator, is back at Trump's side. *The New York Times.* https://www.nytimes.com/2024/09/12/us/politics/trump-laura-loomer.html (accessed January 21, 2025).

Bensinger, K., and Fausset, R. (2024, September 7). Heritage foundation spreads deceptive videos about noncitizen voters. *The New York Times.* https://www.nytimes.com/2024/09/07/us/politics/heritage-foundation-2024-campaign-immigration.html (accessed January 21, 2025).

Bensinger, K., Yourish, K., and Gold, M. (2024, August 29). Trump keeps turning up the dial on vulgarity. Will he alienate the voters he needs? *The New York Times.* https://www.nytimes.com/2024/08/29/us/politics/trump-crass-imagery.html (accessed January 21, 2025).

Berzon, A. (2024, September 5). Republicans seize on false theories about immigrant voting. *The New York Times.* https://www.nytimes.com/2024/09/05/us/politics/immigrant-noncitizen-voting-republicans.html (accessed January 21, 2025).

Biernat, M. (1995). The shifting standards model: Implications of stereotype accuracy for social judgment. In Y. T. Lee, L. Jussim, and C. McCauley (Eds.), *Stereotype accuracy: Toward appreciating group differences* (pp. 87–114). American Psychological Association.

Biernat, M., and Manis, M. (1994). Shifting standards and stereotype-based judgments. *Journal of Personality and Social Psychology, 66*(1): 5–20. https://doi.org/10.1037/0022-3514.66.1.5 (accessed January 21, 2025).

Bickerton, J. (2024, July 28). Donald Trump issues World War III warning if he isn't president. *Newsweek.* https://www.newsweek.com/donald-trump-issues-world-war-iii-warning-isnt-president-1931064 (accessed January 21, 2025).

Bidgood, J. (2024a, September 9). How Trump has used debates to belittle women. *The New York Times.* https://www.nytimes.com/2024/09/09/us/politics/trump-debate-women.html (accessed January 21, 2025).

Bidgood, J. (2024b, October 7). Trump's ugly closing argument. *The New York Times.* https://www.nytimes.com/2024/10/07/us/politics/trump-harris-fema-funding.html (accessed January 21, 2025).

Binkley, C. (2025, February 18). Trump administration gives schools a deadline to end DEI programs or risk losing federal money. *Associated Press.* https://apnews.com/article/dei-critical-race-theory-colleges-diversity-db8317ad37931558dd5a396cf5ab3d42 (accessed March 18, 2025).

Blackburn, M. (2021, July 12). Why is critical race theory dangerous for our kids? *U.S. Senator Marsha Blackburn of Tennessee.* https://www.blackburn.senate.gov/2021/7/why-is-critical-race-theory-dangerous-for-our-kids (accessed January 21, 2025).

Blake, A. (2024a, June 3). Trump's many dog whistles about unrest and violence. *The Washington Post.* https://www.washingtonpost.com/politics/2024/06/03/trumps-many-dog-whistles-about-unrest-violence/ (accessed January 21, 2025).

Blake, A. (2024b, August 26). Trump predicts a hellscape under Harris. His predictions about Biden were often wrong. *The Washington Post.* https://www.washingtonpost.com/politics/2024/08/26/trump-predictions-kamala-harris-biden/ (accessed January 21, 2025).

Blake, A. (2024c, September 9). Trump reiterates: There will be blood. *The Washington Post.* https://www.washingtonpost.com/politics/2024/09/09/trump-reiterates-there-will-be-blood/ (accessed January 21, 2025).

Blake, A. (2024d, September 25). The nativists have taken over the GOP. *The Washington Post.* https://www.washingtonpost.com/politics/2024/09/25/republican-nativist-immigrant-threat/ (accessed January 21, 2025).

Blake, A. (2024e, October 14). How reported militia threats in N.C. Trace to trump-fueled misinformation. *The Washington Post.* https://www.washingtonpost.com/politics/2024/10/14/militia-threats-trace-to-trump-conspiracies/ (accessed January 21, 2025).

Blanchar, J. C., and Norris, C. J. (2024, December 11). Trump, Twitter, and truth judgments: The effects of "disputed" tags and political knowledge on the judged truthfulness of election misinformation. *HKS Misinformation Review.* https://misinforeview.hks.harvard.edu/article/trump-twitter-and-truth-judgments-the-effects-of-disputed-tags-and-political-knowledge-on-the-judged-truthfulness-of-election-misinformation (accessed January 21, 2025).

Bloom, L. B. (2024, March 6). America's 15 safest (and most dangerous) cities for 2023, according to a report. *Forbes.* https://www.forbes.com/sites/laurabegleybloom/2023/01/31/report-ranks-americas-15-safest-and-most-dangerous-cities-for-2023/ (accessed January 21, 2025).

Boak, J. (2019, February 8). AP FACT CHECK: Trump taps false stereotypes about immigrants. *Associated Press.* https://apnews.com/article/immigration-north-america-donald-trump-ap-top-news-politics-7eb07814117f46a098bed1f3466f4775 (accessed January 21, 2025).

Boak, J., Price, M., and Colvin, J. (2024, March 10). Trump blasts Biden over Laken Riley's death after Biden says he regrets using term "illegal." *Associated Press.* https://apnews.com/article/biden-illegal-riley-marjorie-taylor-greene-trump-04924ffb3be76d60e1b6e8796a968051 (accessed January 21, 2025).

Bodenhausen, G. V., and Macrae, C. N. (1996). The self-regulation of intergroup perception: Mechanisms and consequences of stereotype suppression. In M. Hewstone, C. N. Macrae, and C. Stangor (Eds.), *Stereotypes and Stereotyping.* Guilford Press.

Bohannan, L. (1966). Shakespeare in the Bush. *Natural History, 75:* 28 – 33.

Borisoff, D., and Victor, D. A. (1989). *Conflict management: A communication skills approach.* Prentice Hall.

Boss, G. P. (1979). The stereotype and its correspondence in discourse to the enthymeme. *Communication Quarterly, 27*(2): 22 – 27. https://doi.org/10.1080/01463377909369329 (accessed January 21, 2025).

Bouie, J. (2024a, September 18). Trump knows what he's doing in Springfield. So does Vance. *The New York Times.* https://www.nytimes.com/2024/09/18/opinion/trump-vance-springfield-charlottesville-haitians.html (accessed January 21, 2025).

Bouie, J. (2024b, September 20). The Trump Guide to Civil Discourse. *The New York Times.* https://www.nytimes.com/2024/09/20/opinion/trump-political-violence-rhetoric.html (accessed January 21, 2025).

Bowdler, J., and Harris, B. (2022, July 21). Racial inequality in the United States. *U.S. Department of the Treasury.* https://home.treasury.gov/news/featured-stories/racial-inequality-in-the-united-states (accessed January 21, 2025).

Bowman, B. (2023, April 25). Trump's "MAGA movement" widely unpopular, new poll finds. *NBC News.* https://www.nbcnews.com/meet-the-press/meetthepressblog/maga-movement-widely-unpopular-new-poll-finds-rcna81200 (accessed January 21, 2025).

Bradner, E. (2024, September 28). Harris tries to turn the tables on Trump by embracing the border as a key issue. *CNN.* https://www.cnn.com/2024/09/28/politics/harris-trump-border/index.html (accessed January 21, 2025).

Bradner, E., and Sullivan, K. (2024, November 5). Trump describes us as an occupied country in dark closing message focused on immigration. *CNN.* https://www.cnn.com/2024/11/04/politics/donald-trump-closing-message/index.html (accessed January 21, 2025).

Brauer, M., Judd, C. M., and Jacquelin, V. (2001). The communication of social stereotypes: The effects of group discussion and information distribution on stereotypic appraisals. *Journal of Personality and Social Psychology, 81:* 463–475.

Bredemeier, K. (2021, February 2). Biden signs executive orders reversing trump immigration policies. *Voice of America.* https://www.voanews.com/a/usa_biden-signs-executive-orders-reversing-trump-immigration-policies/6201520.html (accessed January 21, 2025).

Brenan, M. (2024, November 18). Smaller majorities say crime in U.S. is serious, increasing. *Gallup.com.* https://news.gallup.com/poll/652763/smaller-majorities-say-crime-serious-increasing.aspx (accessed January 21, 2025).

Brennan, C. (2024, August 25). Trump Stokes fear about migrants driving up crime rate, despite data debunking that. *USA Today.* https://www.usatoday.com/story/opinion/columnist/2024/08/25/trump-campaign-lies-migrant-crime/74905797007/ (accessed January 21, 2025).

Brennan, D. (2024, November 5). Trump campaign doubles down in final hours of election dash. *ABC News.* https://abcnews.go.com/US/trump-campaign-doubles-final-hours-election-dash/story?id=115509852 (accessed January 21, 2025).

Breuninger, K., and Rozelle, J. (2024, September 16). Ohio GOP gov. DeWine says "at least 33" bomb threats prompt Springfield to begin daily school sweeps. *CNBC.* https://www.cnbc.com/2024/09/16/springfield-bomb-threats-ohio-republican.html (accessed January 21, 2025).

Brewer, M. B. (1996). When stereotypes lead to stereotyping: the use of stereotypes in person perception. In M. Hewstone, C. N. Macrae, and C. Stangor (Eds.), *Stereotypes and stereotyping* (pp. 193–226). Guilford Press.

Bridges, K. M. (2022). Language on the move: "Cancel Culture," "Critical Race Theory," and the Digital Public Sphere, *Yale Law Journal.* https://www.yalelawjournal.org/forum/language-on-the-move (accessed January 26, 2025).

Bridgland, V. M. E., Jones, P. J., and Bellet, B. W. (2024). A meta-analysis of the efficacy of trigger warnings, content warnings, and content notes. *Clinical Psychological Science, 12*(4): 751–771. https://doi.org/10.1177/21677026231186625 (accessed January 21, 2025).

Bond, P. (2016, February 29). Leslie Moonves on Donald Trump: "It may not be good for America, but it's damn good for CBS". *The Hollywood Reporter.* https://www.hollywoodreporter.com/news/general-news/leslie-moonves-donald-trump-may-871464/ (accessed January 21, 2025).

Brockell, G. (2016, July 1). "They don't look like Indians to me": Donald Trump on Native American casinos in 1993 [Video]. *The Washington Post.* https://www.washingtonpost.com/video/politics/they-dont-look-like-indians-to-me-donald-trump-on-native-american-casinos-in-1993/2016/07/01/20736038-3fd4-11e6-9e16-4cf01a41decb_video.html (accessed January 21, 2025).

Brown, M. (2024, June 29). Trump's debate references to "Black jobs" and "Hispanic jobs" stir Democratic anger. *Associated Press.* https://apnews.com/article/trumpblackjobsdebatebiden-7c520492a34fa902028ed4537d48cdb0 (accessed January 21, 2025).

Brown, T.C., Menon, T., Oyolola, F. (2024, March 13). Four things to know about noncitizen voting. *Bipartisan Policy.* https://bipartisanpolicy.org/blog/four-things-to-know-about-noncitizen-voting/ (accessed January 21, 2025)

Brown, T. K., Ayoola, T., and Matza, M. (2016, November 9). Election 2016: Trump voters on why they backed him. *BBC News.* https://www.bbc.com/news/election-us-2016-36253275 (accessed January 21, 2025)

Browning, K., and Medina, J. (2024, November 20). Why are Latinos fleeing Democrats? Arizona's new senator offers answers. *The New York Times.* https://www.nytimes.com/2024/11/20/us/poli tics/ruben-gallego-arizona-latino-voters-democrats.html (accessed January 21, 2025).

Bruner, J. S., and Tagiuri, R. (1954). Person perception. *Handbook of Social Psychology, 2:* 634–654.

Buettner, R., and Craig, S. (2024). *Lucky loser: How Donald Trump squandered his father's fortune and created the illusion of success.* Penguin Press.

Bullock, P. (2016, October 8). Transcript: Donald Trump's taped comments about women. *The New York Times.* https://www.nytimes.com/2016/10/08/us/donald-trump-tape-transcript.html (accessed January 21, 2025).

Bumiller, E. (2016, January 31). What caused a crash into the Potomac? For Trump it was diversity. *The New York Times.* https://www.nytimes.com/2025/01/30/us/politics/plane-crash-trump-diversity. html (accessed January 31, 2025).

Bump, P. (2021, October 8). In disparaging Haitian migrants, Trump is done with pretending he isn't who he is. *The Washington Post.* https://www.washingtonpost.com/politics/2021/10/08/trump-hai tian-migrants/ (accessed January 21, 2025).

Bump, P. (2024a, January 15). Half of Americans agree with Trump's 'poisoning the blood' immigration rhetoric. *The Washington Post.* https://www.washingtonpost.com/politics/2024/01/15/ trump-poisoning-blood-immigration-polling/ (accessed January 21, 2025).

Bump, P. (2024b, August 21). Trump's claims about violent crime increasingly diverge from reality. *The Washington Post.* https://www.washingtonpost.com/politics/2024/08/21/trump-crime-fear/ (accessed January 21, 2025).

Bump, P. (2024c, October 9). Fox News quietly reports on a fact sheet correcting Fox News misinformation. *The Washington Post.* https://www.washingtonpost.com/politics/2024/10/09/fox-news-quietly-reports-fact-sheet-correcting-fox-news-misinformation/ (accessed January 21, 2025).

Bump, P. (2024d, October 16). Trump clarifies that his "enemy within" comment was about evil Democrats. *The Washington Post.* https://www.washingtonpost.com/politics/2024/10/16/trump-clarifies-that-his-enemy-within-comment-was-about-evil-democrats/ (accessed January 21, 2025).

Bureau of Labor Statistics. (2022, May 18). Foreign-born workers: labor force characteristics—2021. *U.S. Department of Labor.* https://www.bls.gov/news.release/archives/forbrn_05182022.pdf (accessed January 21, 2025).

Bureau of Labor Statistics. (n.d.). 12-month percentage change, *Consumer Price Index.* https://www. bls.gov/charts/consumer-price-index/consumer-price-index-by-category-line-chart.htm (accessed January 21, 2025).

Burke, K. (1969). *A rhetoric of motives.* University of California Press.

Burke, G., and Kinnard, M. (2024, June 7). A new account rekindles allegations that Trump disrespected black people on "the Apprentice." Associated Press. https://apnews.com/article/ donald-trump-apprentice-racism-nbc-election-2024-d962dfce1220920681ede63b90058f5d (accessed January 21, 2025).

Bushard, B. (2023, September 23). Trump calls Howard Stern a "broken weirdo" after radio host's increasing jabs. *Forbes.* https://www.forbes.com/sites/brianbushard/2023/09/23/trump-calls-ho ward-stern-a-broken-weirdo-after-radio-hosts-increasing-jabs/ (accessed January 21, 2025).

Byrne, D. and Przybyla, D. P. J. (1980). Authoritarianism and political preferences in 1980. *Bulletin of the Psychonomic Society, 16:* 471–472.

Caldwell, L. A. (2016, September 16). Donald Trump finally admits President Obama born in U.S. *NBC News.* https://www.nbcnews.com/politics/2016-election/donald-trump-obama-was-born-united-states-n649501 (accessed January 21, 2025).

Cameron, C. (2024, March 18). *Trump says Jews who support Democrats "hate Israel" and "their religion." The New York Times.* https://www.nytimes.com/2024/03/18/us/politics/trump-israel-jewish-voters.html (accessed January 21, 2025).

Cameron, C., and Gold, M. (2024, September 20). Trump says that if he loses, "the Jewish people would have a lot to do" with it. *The New York Times.* https://www.nytimes.com/2024/09/19/us/politics/trump-jews-antisemitism-israel.html (accessed January 21, 2025).

Cameron, C., Levien, S. J., and Vigdor, N. (2024, November 1). Vance tells Rogan: Teens become trans to get into Ivy League. *The New York Times.* https://www.nytimes.com/2024/10/31/us/politics/jd-vance-joe-rogan.html (accessed January 21, 2025).

Canary, D. J., Emmers-Sommer, T. M. and Faulkner, S. (1997). *Sex and gender differences in personal relationships.* Guilford Press.

Carbaugh, D. (1990). Toward a perspective on cultural communication and intercultural contact. *Semiotica, 80*(1/2): 15 – 35.

Carlson, M., Robinson, S., and Lewis, S. C. (2021). *News after Trump: Journalism's crisis of relevance in a changed media culture.* Oxford University Press.

Carmon, I. (2015, August 10). Donald Trump draws on long history of period stigma. *NBC News.* https://www.msnbc.com/msnbc/donald-trump-draws-long-history-period-stigma-msna658411 (accessed January 21, 2025).

Chambers, S. (2021, January 21). Islamophobia in western media is based on false premises. *The Conversation.* https://theconversation.com/islamophobia-in-western-media-is-based-on-false-premises-151443 (accessed March 17, 2025).

Chetty, R., Dobbie, W., Goldman, B., Porter, S. R., and Yang, C. S. (2024, July 31). Changing opportunity: Sociological mechanisms underlying growing class gaps and shrinking race gaps in economic mobility. *Opportunity Insights.* https://opportunityinsights.org/paper/changingopportunity/ (accessed January 21, 2025).

Chodorow, N. (1979). *The reproduction of mothering: Psychoanalysis and the sociology of gender.* University of California.

Chotiner, I. (2019, April 30). A political scientist defends white identity politics. *The New Yorker.* https://www.newyorker.com/news/q-and-a/a-political-scientist-defends-white-identity-politics-eric-kaufmann-whiteshift-book (accessed January 21, 2025).

Cialdini, R. (1984). *Influence: The Psychology of Persuasion.* Collins.

Cillizza, C. (2019, March 19). The awful reality that Donald Trump's attacks on John McCain prove. *CNN.* https://www.cnn.com/2019/03/19/politics/donald-trump-john-mccain-dead/index.html (accessed January 21, 2025).

Clark, S. (2024, October 31). Clip of Trump calling Harris allies "scum" and "garbage" resurfaces. *Newsweek.* https://www.newsweek.com/donald-trump-comments-garbage-kamala-harris-1977791 (accessed January 21, 2025).

Clemens, D. (2018, August 26). "He's a decent family man": Watch the moment John McCain defended Barack Obama on 2008 campaign trail. *ABC7 Chicago.* https://abc7chicago.com/mccain-defends-obama-arab-2008-campaign-john/4058948/ (accessed January 21, 2025).

CNN. (2024a, Oct 14). Tapper presses Youngkin on Trump's authoritarian rhetoric [Video]. *YouTube.* https://www.youtube.com/watch?v=24YZmMdJKmU (accessed January 21, 2025).

CNN. (2024b, Oct 23). "He gets to be lawless. She has to be flawless.": Van Jones on Trump and Harris [Video]. https://www.cnn.com/2024/10/23/politics/video/van-jones-trump-kamala-harris-town-hall-digvid (accessed January 21, 2025).

Cochrane, E., Flavelle, C., Shear, M. D., and Hsu, T. (2024, October 6). Another hurdle in recovery from Helene: Misinformation is getting in the way. *The New York Times*. https://www.nytimes.com/2024/10/06/us/hurricane-helene-north-carolina-misinformation.html (accessed January 21, 2025).

Coffey, A. and Atkinson, P. (1996). *Making sense of qualitative data: Complementary research strategies*. Sage.

Coghill, A. (2023, January 19). Florida colleges will no longer "fund or support" critical race theory. *Mother Jones*. https://www.motherjones.com/politics/2023/01/florida-state-colleges-will-no-longer-fund-or-support-critical-race-theory/ (accessed January 21, 2025).

Cohen, J. (2001, March 25). Pitching softballs. FAIR. https://fair.org/article/pitching-softballs/ (accessed January 21, 2025).

Cohn, N. (2021, September 8). How educational differences are widening America's political rift. *The New York Times*. https://www.nytimes.com/2021/09/08/us/politics/how-college-graduates-vote.html (accessed January 21, 2025).

Collinson, S. (2024, October 21). Analysis: Trump's wild and lewd rhetoric reaches a new extreme. *CNN*. https://www.cnn.com/2024/10/21/politics/trump-wild-lewd-rhetoric-analysis/index.html (accessed January 21, 2025).

Condor, S. (2006). Public prejudice as collaborative accomplishment: Towards a dialogic social psychology of racism. *Journal of Community and Applied Social Psychology, 16:* 1–18.

Confessore, N. (2024, October 16). The University of Michigan doubled down on D.E.I. What went wrong? *The New York Times*. https://www.nytimes.com/2024/10/16/magazine/dei-university-michigan.html (accessed January 21, 2025).

Contorno, S. (2024, October 20). Trump thrusts McDonald's into the political arena in final days of campaign. *CNN*. https://www.cnn.com/2024/10/20/politics/mcdonalds-donald-trump-pennsylvania/index.html (accessed January 21, 2025).

Contreras, R. (2024, August 14). New data show homicides down in Biden's last year vs. Trump's. *Axios*. https://www.axios.com/2024/08/14/homicides-biden-trump-violent-crime-drop (accessed January 21, 2025).

Cooper, J. J. (2024, November 5). Trump called Megyn Kelly "nasty" 9 years ago. She just helped deliver his closing message. *Associated Press*. https://apnews.com/article/donald-trump-megyn-kelly-rally-closing-message-11f88728b4ee24f8bfed59e68200805b (accessed January 21, 2025).

Corasaniti, N., and Haberman, M. (2016, August 9). Donald Trump suggests "second amendment people" could act against Hillary Clinton. *The New York Times*. https://www.nytimes.com/2016/08/10/us/politics/donald-trump-hillary-clinton.html (accessed January 21, 2025).

Corkery, M., Taft, I., and Hubler, S. (2024, November 16). Trump's cabinet picks, panned in Washington, thrill many of his voters. *The New York Times*. https://www.nytimes.com/2024/11/16/us/trump-cabinet-picks-voter-reactions.html (accessed January 21, 2025).

Corn, D. (2024, October 8). Trump is not running a political campaign. He's running a disinformation campaign. *Mother Jones*. https://www.motherjones.com/politics/2024/10/donald-trump-is-running-a-disinformation-campaign/ (accessed January 21, 2025).

Cortellessa, E. (2017, September 28). Jewish aide who helped launch Trump's campaign sees him dropping early positions. *The Times of Israel*. https://www.timesofisrael.com/jewish-aide-who-helped-launch-trumps-campaign-sees-him-dropping-early-positions/ (accessed January 21, 2025).

Costa, R. (2018, March 6). The Beatles had Pete Best. Donald Trump had Sam Nunberg. *The Washington Post.* https://www.washingtonpost.com/politics/the-beatles-had-pete-best-trump-had-sam-nunberg/2018/03/06/6e778ae4-2159-11e8-94da-ebf9d112159c_story.html (accessed January 21, 2025).

Coster, H., Ulmer, A., and Morgan, D. (2024, July 27). As racist and sexist attacks fly, Republicans grapple with how to take on Harris. *Reuters.* https://www.reuters.com/world/us/racist-sexist-at tacks-fly-republicans-grapple-with-how-take-harris-2024-07-27/ (accessed January 21, 2025).

Covert, B. (2018, May 23). The not-so-subtle racism of trump-era "welfare reform." *The New York Times.* https://www.nytimes.com/2018/05/23/opinion/trump-welfare-reform-racism.html (accessed January 21, 2025).

Crandall, C. S., Eshleman, A., and O'Brien, L. (2002). Social norms and the expression and suppression of prejudice: The struggle for internalization. *Journal of Personality and Social Psychology, 82:* 359 – 378.

Crenshaw, K. W. (1989). Demarginalizing the intersection of race and sex: A black feminist critique of antidiscrimination doctrine, feminist theory and antiracist politics. *University of Chicago Legal Forum*, 1989(1): 139 – 167.

Crowley, M., and Schuessler, J. (2021, January 19). Trump's 1776 commission critiques liberalism in report derided by historians. *The New York Times.* https://www.nytimes.com/2021/01/18/us/poli tics/trump-1776-commission-report.html (accessed January 21, 2025).

C-SPAN. (2020, December 2). President Trump Statement on 2020 election results. https://www.c-span.org/video/cc/?progid=585847 (accessed January 21, 2025).

C-SPAN. (2024, September 26). Former president Trump speaks to reporters in New York City. https://www.c-span.org/program/campaign-2024/former-president-trump-speaks-to-reporters-in-new-york-city/649567 (accessed January 21, 2025).

Dahlkamp, O. (2024, July 5). Donald Trump's secret weapon to dismantle American education. *The Nation.* https://www.thenation.com/article/politics/donald-trump-second-term-education-accred itation/ (accessed January 21, 2025).

Dale, D. (2020, September 2). Fact check: A guide to 9 conspiracy theories Trump is currently pushing. *CNN.* https://edition.cnn.com/2020/09/02/politics/fact-check-trump-conspiracy-theories-biden-covid-thugs-plane/index.html (accessed January 21, 2025).

Dale, D. (2024a, August 16). Fact check: Debunking trump attack on Walz, Minnesota schools say they don't provide tampons in boys' bathrooms. *CNN.* https://www.cnn.com/2024/08/16/politics/fact-check-trump-walz-minnesota-schools-tampons/index.html (accessed January 21, 2025).

Dale, D. (2024b, September 19). Fact check: 12 completely fictional stories Trump has told in the last month. *CNN.* https://www.cnn.com/2024/09/19/politics/fact-check-donald-trump-fictional-stories/index.html (accessed January 21, 2025).

Dale, D. (2024c, September 29). Fact check: To attack Harris, Trump falsely describes new stats on immigrants and homicide. *CNN.* https://www.cnn.com/2024/09/29/politics/fact-check-trump-har ris-immigrants-homicide/index.html (accessed January 21, 2025).

Dale, D. (2024d, October 3). Fact check: Amid bipartisan praise for Biden hurricane response, Trump falsely claims reviews are "universally" negative. *CNN.* https://www.cnn.com/2024/10/03/politics/fact-check-trump-biden-hurricane-response/index.html (accessed January 21, 2025).

Dale, D. (2024e, October 8). Fact check: No evidence for Trump's claim he has been to Gaza. *CNN.* https://www.cnn.com/2024/10/08/politics/trump-gaza-fact-check/index.html (accessed January 21, 2025).

Dale, D. (2024f, October 16). Fact check: John Deere says Trump's story about how he saved US jobs with a tariff threat is fictional. *CNN.* https://www.cnn.com/2024/10/16/politics/trump-fact-check-john-deere-economy/index.html (accessed January 21, 2025).

Damiano, M., and Burns, H. (2024, July 17). "Attack the universities." Trump's VP pick JD Vance has harsh words for higher education. *The Boston Globe.* https://www.bostonglobe.com/2024/07/16/metro/vance-trump-rnc-universities/ (accessed January 21, 2025).

Darcy, O. (2018, November 6). Sean Hannity said he wouldn't campaign on stage at Trump's rally. Hours later, he did exactly that. *CNN.* https://www.cnn.com/2018/11/06/media/trump-rally-missouri-hannity/index.html (accessed January 21, 2025).

Dawsey, J., Helderman, R. S., and Fahrenthold, D. A. (2020, October 24). How Trump abandoned his pledge to "drain the swamp." *The Washington Post.* https://www.washingtonpost.com/politics/trump-drain-the-swamp/2020/10/24/52c7682c-0a5a-11eb-9be6-cf25fb429f1a_story.html (accessed January 21, 2025).

Davis, J. H. (2019, August 20). Trump accuses Jewish Democrats of "great disloyalty." *The New York Times.* https://www.nytimes.com/2019/08/20/us/politics/trump-jewish-voters.html (accessed January 21, 2025).

Deetz, S. A. (1994). Future of the Discipline: The Challenges, the Research, and the Social Contribution. *Annals of the International Communication Association, 17*(1): 565–600. https://doi.org/10.1080/23808985.1994.11678904 (accessed January 21, 2025).

de Longhe, B., and Fernbach, P. (2019). The dangers of categorical thinking. *Harvard Business Review.* https://hbr.org/2019/09/the-dangers-of-categorical-thinking (accessed January 21, 2025).

DelReal, J.A. (2015, December 20). Jeb Bush said he "hated" being the front-runner. *The Washington Post.* https://www.washingtonpost.com/news/post-politics/wp/2015/12/20/jeb-bush-says-he-hated-being-the-front-runner/ (accessed January 21, 2025).

Demissie, H. (2024, July 15). The rise of JD Vance: From "never-Trump" guy to VP Pick. *ABC News.* https://abcnews.go.com/Politics/rise-jd-vance-trump-guy-potential-vp-pick/story?id=111310334 (accessed January 21, 2025).

Detrow, S. (2024, September 7). The downfall of DEI. *NPR.* https://www.npr.org/2024/09/07/nx-s1-5100700/the-downfall-of-dei (accessed January 21, 2025).

Devine, P.G. (1989). Stereotypes and prejudice: Their automatic and controlled components. *Journal of Personality and Social Psychology, 56*: 5–18.

Diamond, J. (2016, August 6). Trump escalates attacks on Clinton's character. *CNN.* https://www.cnn.com/2016/08/05/politics/donald-trump-hillary-clinton-unhinged-lock-her-up/index.html (accessed January 21, 2025).

Dias, E. (2020, August 9). "Christianity will have power." *The New York Times.* https://www.nytimes.com/2020/08/09/us/evangelicals-trump-christianity.html (accessed January 21, 2025).

Dias, E. (2024, November 3). Trump promises to bring about a new era of Christian power. *The New York Times.* https://www.nytimes.com/2024/11/03/us/trump-christian-religion.html (accessed January 21, 2025).

Dickinson, T., and Suebsaeng, A. (2024, July 20). Inside the MAGA asylum: Four days of worship with the cult of Trump. *Rolling Stone.* https://www.rollingstone.com/politics/politics-features/trump-rnc-cult-maga-asylum-1235064421/ (accessed January 21, 2025).

Dillon, S. (2005, January 18). Harvard chief defends his talk on women. *The New York Times.* https://www.nytimes.com/2005/01/18/us/harvard-chief-defends-his-talk-on-women.html (accessed January 21, 2025).

Dilulio, J. J. (2024, April 14). Biden, Trump, and the 4 categories of white votes. *Brookings*. https://www.brookings.edu/articles/biden-trump-and-the-4-categories-of-white-votes/ (accessed January 21, 2025).

Dixon, M., Edelman, A., and Lebowitz, M. (2024, September 30). Trump falsely says Georgia's governor was unable to talk to Biden about storm damage. *NBC News*. https://www.nbcnews.com/politics/2024-election/trump-georgia-governor-brian-kemp-unable-talk-biden-hurricane-helene-rcna173236 (accessed January 21, 2025).

Dooley, B. (2014, March 31). Why are Newsweek's new owners so anxious to hide their ties to an enigmatic religious figure? *Mother Jones*. https://www.motherjones.com/media/2014/03/newsweek-ibt-olivet-david-jang/ (accessed January 21, 2025).

Dovidio, J. F., Brigham, J. C., Johnson, B. T., and Gaertner, S. L. (1996). Stereotyping, prejudice, and discrimination: Another look. In C. N. Macrae, C. Stangor, and M. Hewstone (Eds.), *Stereotypes and stereotyping* (pp. 276–319). Guilford Press.

Dovidio, J. F., Major, B. and Crocker, J. (2000). Stigma: introduction and overview. In T. F. Heatherton, R. E. Kleck, and M. R. Hebl, (Eds.), *The social psychology of stigma* (pp. 1–30). Guilford Press.

Dowd, M. (2024a, October 5). JD smirks his way into the future. *The New York Times*. https://www.nytimes.com/2024/10/05/opinion/jd-vance-kamala-harris.html?smid=nytcore-ios-share andreferringSource=articleShareandsgrp=c-cb (accessed January 21, 2025).

Dowd, M. (2024b, October 26). How bad do you want it, ladies? *The New York Times*. https://www.nytimes.com/2024/10/26/opinion/donald-trump-gender-election.html (accessed January 21, 2025).

Dreisbach, T. (2024, October 21). Trump has made more than 100 threats to prosecute or punish perceived enemies. *NPR*. https://www.npr.org/2024/10/21/nx-s1-5134924/trump-election-2024-kamala-harris-elizabeth-cheney-threat-civil-liberties (accessed January 21, 2025).

Duffy, C. (2024, November 13). "Your body, my choice" and other attacks on women surge on social media following electio*n. CNN*. https://www.cnn.com/2024/11/11/business/your-body-my-choice-movement-election/index.html (accessed January 21, 2025).

Duke, A. (2012, September 21). Paris Hilton apologizes for calling gay men "disgusting." *CNN*. https://www.cnn.com/2012/09/21/showbiz/paris-hilton-gays/index.html (accessed January 21, 2025).

Ebbert, S., and Fernandes, D. (2024, March 21). Larry Summers was ousted as Harvard president. He has a lot to say about what's wrong with the university now. *The Boston Globe*. https://www.bostonglobe.com/2024/03/21/metro/larry-summers-vocal-critic-of-harvard-successors/ (accessed January 21, 2025).

The Economist/YouGov. (n.d.). December 2–5, 2023—The Economist/YouGov poll. https://d3nkl3psvxxpe9.cloudfront.net/documents/econTabReport_tT4jyzG.pdf (accessed January 21, 2025).

Ede-Osifo, U. (2024, April 3). The Trump campaign's big lie about anti-white racism has reached a new low. *Slate*. https://slate.com/news-and-politics/2024/04/dei-trump-campaign-racism-white-backlash-diversity.html (accessed January 21, 2025).

Eder, S. (2018, December 26). Did a Queens podiatrist help Donald Trump avoid Vietnam? *The New York Times*. https://www.nytimes.com/2018/12/26/us/politics/trump-vietnam-draft-exemption.html (accessed January 21, 2025).

Edsall, T. B. (2019, June 19). Trump is changing the shape of the Democratic Party, too. *The New York Times*. https://www.nytimes.com/2019/06/19/opinion/trump-racial-resentment.html (accessed January 21, 2025).

Edsall, T. B. (2024, October 30). Let me ask a question we never had to ask before. *The New York Times.* https://www.nytimes.com/2024/10/30/opinion/trump-harris-election-day-aftermath.html (accessed January 21, 2025).

Frank, M. and Ekman, P. (1993). Not all smiles are created equal: The differences between enjoyment and non-enjoyment smiles. *Humor, 6*(1): 9 – 26. https://doi.org/10.1515/humr.1993.6.1.9 (accessed January 21, 2025).

Elliott, D. (2003, June 11). Wallace in the schoolhouse door. *NPR.* https://www.npr.org/2003/06/11/1294680/wallace-in-the-schoolhouse-door (accessed January 21, 2025).

Enoch, J., McDonald, L., Jones, L., Jones, P. R., and Crabb, D. P. (2019). Evaluating whether sight is the most valued sense. *JAMA Ophthalmology, 137*(11: 1317 – 1320. doi: 10.1001/jamaophthalmol.2019.3537 (accessed January 21, 2025).

Enns, P. K., and Jardina, A. (2021). Complicating the role of white racial attitudes and anti-immigrant sentiment in the 2016 US presidential election. *Public Opinion Quarterly, 85*(2), 539 – 570. https://doi.org/10.1093/poq/nfab040 (accessed January 21, 2025).

Fahrenthold, D. A. (2024, October 28). Musk repeatedly raises the idea that Harris, or he, could be assassinated. *The New York Times.* https://www.nytimes.com/2024/10/28/us/politics/musk-harris-assassination-attempts.html (accessed January 21, 2025).

Falcon, R. (2023, September 2). 'Latinx': Why do many Hispanics hate the term? *KTLA.* https://ktla.com/news/nationworld/latinx-why-do-many-hispanics-hate-the-term/ (accessed January 21, 2025).

Faludi, S. (2024, October 6). Kamala Harris is turning a Trump tactic on its head. *The New York Times.* https://www.nytimes.com/2024/10/06/opinion/kamala-harris-donald-trump-security.html (accessed January 21, 2025).

Fausto-Sterling, A. (1985/1992), *Myths of gender: Biological theories about women and men.* Basic Books.

FEMA. (2024, October 4). FEMA launches web page to respond to rumors and confirm the facts related to Hurricane Helene Response and recovery. https://www.fema.gov/press-release/20241004/fema-launches-web-page-respond-rumors-and-confirm-facts-related-hurricane (accessed January 21, 2025).

Federal Reserve History. (2023, June 2). Redlining. https://www.federalreservehistory.org/essays/redlining (accessed January 21, 2025).

Ferré-Sadurní, L. (2019, November 18). What happens when black people search for suburban homes. *The New York Times.* https://www.nytimes.com/2019/11/18/nyregion/fair-housing-discrimination-long-island.html (accessed January 21, 2025).

Fetters, A. (2019, June 3). Men aren't quite sure how to be abortion-rights activists. *The Atlantic.* https://www.theatlantic.com/family/archive/2019/06/men-abortion-debate/591259/ (accessed January 21, 2025).

Fialk, A. (2021, November 1). Why teaching critical race theory matters for mental health. *Psychology Today.* https://www.psychologytoday.com/us/blog/our-youth-today/202111/why-teaching-critical-race-theory-matters-mental-health (accessed January 21, 2025).

Fiske, S. T. (1998). Stereotyping, prejudice, and discrimination. In D. T. Gilbert, S. T. Fiske, and G. Lindzey, (Eds.), *The handbook of social psychology* (pp. 357 – 411). McGraw-Hill.

Fiske, S. T., and Taylor, S. E. (1984). *Social cognition.* Addison-Wesley.

Forbes Breaking News. (2024, August 3). Trump gets personal in attacks on Kamala Harris, bringing up Willie Brown during Georgia rally [Video]. *YouTube.* https://www.youtube.com/watch?v=mhGJIc1HyiQ (accessed January 21, 2025).

Ford, T. E., Wentzel, E. R., and Lorion, J. (2001). Effects of exposure to sexist humor on perceptions of normative tolerance of sexism. *European Journal of Social Psychology, 31:* 677–691.

Fox, J. (2022, June 7). Is New York City more dangerous than rural America? *Bloomberg.com.* https://www.bloomberg.com/opinion/articles/2022-06-07/is-new-york-city-more-dangerous-than-rural-america (accessed January 21, 2025).

Fram, A., and Lemire, J. (2021, May 1). Trump: Why allow immigrants from "shithole countries"? *Associated Press.* https://apnews.com/article/immigration-north-america-donald-trump-ap-top-news-international-news-fdda2ff0b877416c8ae1c1a77a3cc425# (accessed January 21, 2025).

Frances-Wright, I., and Ayad, M. (2024, November 8). "Your body, my choice:" hate and harassment towards women spreads online. *ISD Global.* https://www.isdglobal.org/digital_dispatches/your-body-my-choice-hate-and-harassment-towards-women-spreads-online/ (accessed January 21, 2025).

French, D. (2024, October 27). Four lessons from nine years of being "never Trump." *The New York Times.* https://www.nytimes.com/2024/10/27/opinion/never-trump-maga-evangelicals.html (accessed January 21, 2025).

Funder, D. C. (1995). Stereotypes, base rates, and the fundamental attribution mistake: A content-based approach to judgmental accuracy. In Y. Lee, L. Jussim, and C. McCauley (Eds.) *Stereotype accuracy: Toward appreciating group differences* (pp. 141–156). American Psychological Association.

Funder, D.C. (1996). Base rates, stereotypes, and judgmental accuracy. *Behavioral and Brain Sciences, 19:* 22–23.

Gabbatt, A. (2024, March 18). Trump calls for Liz Cheney to be jailed for investigating him over Capitol attack. *The Guardian.* https://www.theguardian.com/us-news/2024/mar/18/trump-liz-cheney-prison-jan-6-investigation (accessed January 21, 2025).

Galanes, G. J., and Leeds-Hurwitz, W. (2009). *Socially constructing communication.* Hampton Press.

Gamio, L., and Clement, S. (2016, February 20). South Carolina Republican exit poll results. *The Washington Post.* https://www.washingtonpost.com/graphics/politics/2016-election/primaries/south-carolina-exit-poll/ (accessed January 21, 2025).

Ganesh, Z. (2007). Outsourcing as symptomatic: Class visibility and ethnic scapegoating in the US IT sector. *Journal of Communication Management, 11:* 71–83.

Garcia, M. (2016, November 7). How the Trumps tried – and failed – to keep black families like mine out of their neighborhood. *Vox.* https://www.vox.com/policy-and-politics/2016/11/7/13508914/trumps-jamaica-estates-queens-segregated (accessed January 21, 2025).

Garsd, J. (2024, March 9). Immigrants are less likely to commit crimes than U.S.-born Americans, studies find. *NPR.* https://www.npr.org/2024/03/08/1237103158/immigrants-are-less-likely-to-commit-crimes-than-us-born-americans-studies-find (accessed January 21, 2025).

Gergen, K. (1992). *The saturated self: Dilemmas of identity in contemporary life.* Basic Books.

Gjelten, T. (2020, November 8). 2020 faith vote reflects 2016 patterns. *NPR.* https://www.npr.org/2020/11/08/932263516/2020-faith-vote-reflects-2016-patterns (accessed January 21, 2025)

Gibson, G. (2023, December 17). Trump says immigrants are "poisoning the blood of our country." Biden campaign likens comments to Hitler. *NBC News.* https://www.nbcnews.com/politics/2024-election/trump-says-immigrants-are-poisoning-blood-country-biden-campaign-liken-rcna130141 (accessed January 21, 2025).

Gilbert, S. (2024, July 29). Kamala Harris and the threat of a woman's laugh. *The Atlantic.* https://www.theatlantic.com/culture/archive/2024/07/kamala-harris-laugh-trump-sexism/679215/ (accessed January 21, 2025).

Gilbert, D. T., and Hixon, J. G. (1991). The trouble of thinking: Activation and application of stereotypic beliefs. *Journal of Personality and Social Psychology, 60*(4): 509–517. https://doi.org/10.1037/0022-3514.60.4.509 (accessed January 21, 2025).

Gilens, M. (1999). *Why Americans hate welfare: Race, media, and the politics of antipoverty policy.* University of Chicago Press.

Giles, H. (1978). Linguistic differentiation in ethnic groups. In H. Tajfel (Ed.), *Differentiation between social groups: Studies in the social psychology of intergroup relations* (pp. 361–394). London: Academic Press.

Gilovich, T. (1991). *How we know what isn't so: The fallibility of human reason in everyday life.* The Free Press.

Goffman, E. (1963a). *Behavior in public places.* Free Press.

Goffman, E. (1963b). *Stigma: Notes on the management of spoiled identity.* Simon and Schuster.

Gold, H., and Reilly, L. (2024, October 16). Fox News did not disclose its all-women Town Hall with Trump was packed with his supporters. *CNN.* https://amp.cnn.com/cnn/2024/10/16/media/fox-news-women-town-hall-supporters (accessed January 21, 2025).

Gold, M. (2023, November 12). In Veterans Day speech, Trump promises to "root out" the left. *The New York Times.* https://www.nytimes.com/2023/11/11/us/politics/trump-new-hampshire-veterans.html (accessed January 21, 2025).

Gold, M. (2024a, July 27). Trump, honing attacks on Harris, casts her as a far-left threat. *The New York Times.* https://www.nytimes.com/2024/07/26/us/politics/trump-harris-turning-point-action.html (accessed January 21, 2025).

Gold, M. (2024b, August 28). Trump reposts crude sexual remark about Harris on Truth Social. *The New York Times.* https://www.nytimes.com/2024/08/28/us/politics/trump-truth-social-posts.html (accessed January 21, 2025).

Gold, M. (2024c, October 1). Trump's consistent message online and onstage: Be afraid. *The New York Times.* https://www.nytimes.com/2024/10/01/us/politics/trump-fear-speeches.html (accessed January 21, 2025).

Gold, M. (2024d, October 9). Trump's remarks on migrants illustrate his obsession with genes. *The New York Times.* https://www.nytimes.com/2024/10/09/us/politics/trump-migrants-genes.html (accessed January 21, 2025).

Gold, M. (2024e, October 19). At a Pennsylvania rally, Trump descends to new levels of vulgarity. *The New York Times.* https://www.nytimes.com/2024/10/19/us/politics/trump-vulgarity-pennsylvania-rally.html (accessed January 21, 2025).

Gold, M., Haberman, M., and Goldmacher, S. (2024, November 3). Trump, in increasingly dark and dour tones, says he "shouldn't have left" The White House. *The New York Times.* https://www.nytimes.com/2024/11/03/us/politics/trump-pa-rally-election.html (accessed January 21, 2025).

Gold, M., and Nagourney, A. (2024, November 6). Trump assails Liz Cheney and imagines guns "shooting at her." *The New York Times.* https://www.nytimes.com/2024/11/01/us/politics/trump-liz-cheney-tucker-carlson.html (accessed January 21, 2025).

Goldberg, M. (2024, October 28). MAGA unchained in Madison Square Garden. *The New York Times.* https://www.nytimes.com/2024/10/28/opinion/trump-rally-msg-racism.html (accessed January 21, 2025).

Goldberg, M. (2025, February 14). Trump wants to destroy all academia, not just the woke parts. *The New York Times.* https://www.nytimes.com/2025/02/14/opinion/trump-college-academia-woke.html (accessed March 18, 2025).

Golden, H. (2024, January 1). History of DEI: The evolution of diversity training programs. *Notre Dame de Namur University.* https://www.ndnu.edu/history-of-dei-the-evolution-of-diversity-train ing-programs/ (accessed January 21, 2025).

Goldmacher, S., Haberman, M., and Gold, M. (2024, October 27). Trump at the garden: A closing carnival of grievances, misogyny and racism. *The New York Times.* https://www.nytimes.com/ 2024/10/27/us/trump-msg-rally.html (accessed January 21, 2025).

Goldmacher, S., Haberman, M., and Swan, J. (2024, November 7). How Trump won, and how Harris lost. *The New York Times.* https://www.nytimes.com/2024/11/07/us/politics/trump-win-election-har ris.html (accessed January 21, 2025).

Gonyea, D. (2017, October 24). Majority of white Americans say they believe whites face discrimination. *NPR.* https://www.npr.org/2017/10/24/559604836/majority-of-white-americans-think-theyre-discriminated-against (accessed January 21, 2025).

Gonzalez, X. (2024, September 9). Trump called Harris "beautiful." Now he has a problem. *The Atlantic.* https://www.theatlantic.com/politics/archive/2024/09/trump-hot-or-not-approach-to-women-harris-debate/679755/ (accessed January 21, 2025).

Goodman, J. D., Sandoval, E., and Gebeloff, R. (2024, November 8). "An earthquake" along the border: Trump flipped Hispanic south Texas. *The New York Times.* https://www.nytimes.com/ 2024/11/08/us/texas-border-latinos-election.html (accessed January 21, 2025).

Graham, C. (2024, September 4). Donald Trump thinks schools make kids trans: Do you need this fact-checked? *Augusta Free Press.* https://augustafreepress.com/news/donald-trump-thinks-schools-make-kids-trans-do-you-need-this-fact-checked/ (accessed January 21, 2025).

Graham, D. A. (2024, September 9). An article the likes of which nobody has ever seen before. *The Atlantic.* https://www.theatlantic.com/ideas/archive/2024/09/article-likes-which-nobody-has-ever-seen/679703/ (accessed January 21, 2025).

Gramlich, J. (2020, March 2). How border apprehensions, ice arrests and deportations have changed under Trump. *Pew Research Center.* https://www.pewresearch.org/short-reads/2020/03/02/how-border-apprehensions-ice-arrests-and-deportations-have-changed-under-trump/ (accessed January 21, 2025).

Granderson, L. (2024, May 7). Granderson: Trump's racist "welfare" dog whistle is nonsense just like Reagan's. *Los Angeles Times.* https://www.latimes.com/opinion/story/2024-05-07/trump-welfare-fundraiser (accessed January 21, 2025).

Grayer, A., Rimmer, M., and Gainor, D. (2024, September 25). GOP rep. Clay Higgins deletes post calling Haitian migrants "thugs," telling them to "get… their a** out of our country". *CNN.* https://www.cnn.com/2024/09/25/politics/clay-higgins-deletes-post-haitian-migrants/index.html (accessed January 21, 2025).

Green, E. L. (2024, October 31). They want to ensure that, this time, white women vote for a woman. *The New York Times.* https://www.nytimes.com/2024/10/31/us/politics/white-women-har ris-trump-2024-election.html (accessed January 21, 2025).

Grynbaum, M. M. (2017, February 17). Trump calls the news media the "enemy of the American people." *The New York Times.* https://www.nytimes.com/2017/02/17/business/trump-calls-the-news-media-the-enemy-of-the-people.html (accessed January 21, 2025).

Gudykunst, W. (2003). *Cross-cultural and intercultural communication.* Sage.

Guerin, B. (2003). Combating prejudice and racism: New interventions from a functional analysis. *Journal of Community and Applied Social* Psychology, 13: 29–45.

Gunn, E. (2024, September 10). A one-time Trump voter turns her back on the former president. *Wisconsin Examiner.* https://wisconsinexaminer.com/2024/09/10/a-one-time-trump-voter-turns-her-back-on-the-former-president/ (accessed January 21, 2025).

Gunter, J. (2018, March 2). What is the Einstein Visa? and how did Melania Trump get one? *BBC News.* https://www.bbc.com/news/world-us-canada-43256318 (accessed January 21, 2025).

Guralnik, O. (2024, November 27). As a couples therapist, I see the same destructive patterns in our political discourse. *The New York Times.* https://www.nytimes.com/2024/11/27/opinion/couples-therapy-political-divide.html (accessed January 21, 2025).

Guynn, J. (2023, December 20). DEI under siege: why more businesses are being accused of "reverse discrimination." *USA Today.* https://www.usatoday.com/story/money/careers/2023/12/20/dei-reverse-discrimination-lawsuits-increase-woke/71923487007/ (accessed January 21, 2025).

Haberman, M., and Burns, A. (2020, May 29). Trump's looting and "shooting" remarks escalate crisis in Minneapolis. *The New York Times.* https://www.nytimes.com/2020/05/29/us/politics/trump-looting-shooting.html (accessed January 21, 2025).

Haberman, M., and Feuer, A. (2022, November 25). Trump's latest dinner guest: Nick Fuentes, White Supremacist. *The New York Times.* https://www.nytimes.com/2022/11/25/us/politics/trump-nick-fuentes-dinner.html (accessed January 21, 2025).

Haberman, M., and Swan, J. (2024, July 23). Trump accuses Biden-Harris administration of failing to "properly protect me." *The New York Times.* https://www.nytimes.com/2024/07/23/us/politics/trump-biden-harris-security.html (accessed January 21, 2025).

Haberman, M., Gold, M., and Igielnik, R. (2024, October 18). Trump tries to rewrite history of Jan. 6 in campaign's final stretch. *The New York Times.* https://www.nytimes.com/2024/10/18/us/politics/trump-jan-6.html (accessed January 21, 2025).

Hackman, R. (2015, May 13). What will happen when Harlem becomes white? *The Guardian.* https://www.theguardian.com/us-news/2015/may/13/harlem-gentrification-new-york-race-black-white (accessed January 21, 2025).

Hamilton, D. L., and Sherman, J. W. (1994). Stereotypes. In R. S. Wyer, Jr. and T. K. Srull (Eds.), *Handbook of social cognition: Basic processes* (2nd ed., pp. 1–68). Lawrence Erlbaum Associates, Inc.

Hamilton, D. L., Sherman, S. J., and Ruvolo, C. M. (1990). Stereotype-based expectancies: Effects on information processing and social behavior. *Journal of Social Issues, 46*(2), 35–60. https://doi.org/10.1111/j.1540-4560.1990.tb01922.x (accessed January 21, 2025).

Hannah-Jones, N. (2024, August 4). The willful amnesia behind Trump's attacks on Harris's identity. *The New York Times.* https://www.nytimes.com/2024/08/04/magazine/kamala-harris-black-identity-history.html (accessed January 21, 2025).

Hart, W., Albarracín, D., Eagly, A. H., Brechan, I., Lindberg, M. J., Merrill, L. (2009). Feeling validated versus being correct: A meta-analysis of selective exposure to information. *Psychological Bulletin, 135* (4): 555–588. doi:10.1037/a0015701 (accessed January 21, 2025).

Harwood, J., Giles, H., and Bourhis, R. Y. (1994). The genesis of vitality theory: Historical patterns and discoursal dimensions. *International Journal of the Sociology of Language, 108*(1): 167–206. doi:10.1515/ijsl.1994.108.167 (accessed January 21, 2025).

Haskins, C. (2024, November 7). Rogan, Musk and an emboldened manosphere salute Trump's win: "let that sink in." *The Guardian.* https://www.theguardian.com/us-news/2024/nov/07/joe-rogan-elon-musk-heterodoxy-trump-win-reaction (accessed January 21, 2025).

Haslam, N. (2024, November 18). The trouble with "microaggressions." *The Conversation.* https://theconversation.com/the-trouble-with-microaggressions-71364 (accessed January 21, 2025).

Haslam, S. A., Turner, J. C., Oakes, P. J., Reynolds, K. J., and Doosje, B. (2002). From personal pictures in the head to collective tools in the world: How shared stereotypes allow groups to represent and change social reality. In C. McGarty, V. Y. Yzerbyt, and R. Spears, (Eds.), *Stereotypes as explanations: The formation of meaningful beliefs about social groups* (pp. 157–185). Cambridge University Press.

Haste, H. (1994). *The sexual metaphor.* Harvard University Press.

Heider, F. (1958). *The psychology of interpersonal relations.* John Wiley and Sons Inc. https://doi.org/10.1037/10628-000 (accessed January 21, 2025).

Herbert, B. (2006, September 28). A platform of bigotry. *The New York Times.* https://www.nytimes.com/2006/09/28/opinion/28herbert.html (accessed January 21, 2025).

Herchenroeder, K. (2024, August 31). Trump calls journalists "enemy of the people" during Pennsylvania rally minutes before man storms into media section. *Vanity Fair.* https://www.vanityfair.com/news/story/trump-rally-man-attacks-journalists (accessed January 21, 2025).

Hilton, J. L., and von Hippel, W. (1996). Stereotypes. *Annual review of psychology, 47,* 237–271. https://doi.org/10.1146/annurev.psych.47.1.237 (accessed January 21, 2025).

Hilton, P. (2023). *Paris: The memoir.* HarperCollins.

Hinton, P. R. (2000). *Stereotypes, culture, and cognition (psychology focus).* Psychology Press.

Hobbs, A. V. (2016). *A chosen exile: A history of racial passing in American Life.* Harvard University Press.

Hoffman, J. (2020, September 16). Trump turns Rosh Hashanah call into campaign pitch and tells Jewish leaders "we love your country". *CNN.* https://www.cnn.com/2020/09/16/politics/trump-rosh-hashanah-campaign/index.html (accessed January 21, 2025).

Hoffman, R. (2024, September 10). READ: Harris-Trump presidential debate transcript. *ABC News.* https://abcnews.go.com/Politics/harris-trump-presidential-debate-transcript/story?id=113560542 (accessed January 21, 2025).

Hopper, R. (2003). *Gendering talk.* Michigan State University Press.

Horowitz, J. (2015, September 22). Donald Trump's old Queens neighborhood contrasts with the diverse area around it. *The New York Times.* https://www.nytimes.com/2015/09/23/us/politics/donald-trumps-old-queens-neighborhood-now-a-melting-pot-was-seen-as-a-cloister.html (accessed January 21, 2025).

Houghtaling, E. Q. (2024). The bizarre way Trump's allies are showing loyalty to him. *Y! Entertainment.* https://www.yahoo.com/entertainment/bizarre-way-trump-allies-showing-181124092.html (accessed January 21, 2025).

Hubbard, K., Rosen, J., and Huey-Burns, C. (2024, October 14). Trump's anti-immigrant, domestic "enemy" rhetoric in focus in final stretch to Election Day. *CBS News.* https://www.cbsnews.com/news/donald-trump-rhetoric-enemy-anti-immigrant/ (accessed January 21, 2025).

Igielnik, R., Keeter, S., and Hartig, H. (2021, June 30). Behind Biden's 2020 victory. *Pew Research Center.* https://www.pewresearch.org/politics/2021/06/30/behind-bidens-2020-victory/ (accessed January 21, 2025).

Ingber, S. (2018, June 30). Protesters across the country rally against Trump's immigration policies. *NPR.* https://www.npr.org/2018/06/30/624950726/protesters-across-the-country-rally-against-trumps-immigration-policies (accessed January 21, 2025).

Ingraham, C. (2020, October 12). New research explores authoritarian mind-set of Trump's core supporters. *The Washington Post.* https://www.washingtonpost.com/business/2020/10/12/trump-voter-authoritarian-research/ (accessed January 21, 2025).

Insights. (2014). Advertising and audiences: Making ad dollars make sense. *Nielsen.* https://www.niel sen.com/insights/2014/advertising-and-audiences-making-ad-dollars-make-sense/ (accessed January 21, 2025).

Isaac, C., Kaatz, A., and Carnes, M., (2012). Deconstructing the glass ceiling. *Scientific Research/ Sociology Mind, 2*(1): 80–86.

Itkowitz, C. (2024, October 30). Trump alleges fraud in Pennsylvania, but officials say the election is secure. *The Washington Post.* https://www.washingtonpost.com/politics/2024/10/30/democracy-trump-pennsylvania-voter-fraud/ (accessed January 21, 2025).

Irwin, L. (2024, September 7). Trump slams Dick Cheney as "irrelevant" after he backed Harris. *The Hill.* https://thehill.com/homenews/campaign/4867243-donald-trump-dick-cheney-liz-cheney-kama la-harris-2024-election/ (accessed January 21, 2025).

Iyengar, S. (2022). *Media politics: A citizen's guide.* W. W. Norton.

Iyer, K. (2023, August 5). Trump calls Mike Pence "delusional" in sharpest attack yet on his former vice president. *CNN.* https://www.cnn.com/2023/08/05/politics/trump-mike-pence-delusional-*truth*-social/index.html (accessed January 21, 2025).

Jackson, D. (2016, July 21). Donald Trump accepts GOP nomination, says "I alone can fix" system. *USA Today.* https://www.usatoday.com/story/news/politics/elections/2016/07/21/donald-trump-re publican-convention-acceptance-speech/87385658/ (accessed January 21, 2025).

Jacobson, L. (2023, September 1). Is U.S. inflation lower than in other leading economic powers? *PolitiFact.* https://www.politifact.com/factchecks/2023/sep/01/joe-biden/does-the-us-have-less-in flation-than-other-leading/ (accessed January 21, 2025).

James, F. (2012, September 10). Political pro with race-baiting past doesn't see it in Romney's welfare charge. *NPR.* https://www.npr.org/sections/itsallpolitics/2012/09/10/160885683/political-pro-with-race-baiting-past-doesnt-see-it-in-romneys-welfare-charge (accessed January 21, 2025).

Jamieson, A. (2016, May 25). Trump calls Clinton "Crooked Hillary" – should she ignore it or fight back? *The Guardian.* https://www.theguardian.com/us-news/2016/may/25/donald-trump-crooked-hillary-clinton-nickname-ignore-fight (accessed January 21, 2025).

Jardina, A. (2019). *White identity politics.* Cambridge University Press.

Jardina, A., and Piston, S. (2023). Trickle-down racism: Trump's effect on whites' racist dehumanizing attitudes. *Current Research in Ecological and Social Psychology, 5,* 100158. https://doi.org/10.1016/j. cresp.2023.100158 (accessed January 21, 2025).

Jennings, R. (2024). Why the most powerful men in America are the worst dressed. *Vox.* https://www.vox.com/culture/355026/trump-red-tie-menswear-guy-republican-style (accessed January 21, 2025).

Johnson, C. (2016, June 21). Clinton scandals: A guide from whitewater to the Clinton Foundation. *NPR.* https://www.npr.org/2016/06/12/481718785/clinton-scandals-a-guide-from-whitewater-to-the-clinton-foundation (accessed January 21, 2025).

Johnson, J., and Hauslohner, A. (2017, May 20). "I think Islam hates us": A timeline of Trump's comments about Islam and Muslims. *The Washington Post.* https://www.washingtonpost.com/news/post-politics/wp/2017/05/20/i-think-islam-hates-us-a-timeline-of-trumps-comments-about-islam-and-muslims/ (accessed January 21, 2025).

Johnson, S. R. (2024, April 15). Study: Deaths of despair move higher among blacks than whites. *US News.* https://www.usnews.com/news/health-news/articles/2024-04-15/study-deaths-of-despair-move-higher-among-blacks-than-whites (accessed January 21, 2025).

Johnson, T. (2023, September 14). Megyn Kelly gives Donald Trump praise for infamous 2015 Republican debate moment with her: "you handled it well." *Deadline.* https://deadline.com/2023/09/donald-trump-megyn-kelly-interview-1235547001/ (accessed January 21, 2025).

Jones, J.M. (2016, November 17). Trump favorability up, but trails other presidents-elect. *Gallup.* https://news.gallup.com/poll/197576/trump-favorability-trails-presidents-elect.aspx (accessed January 21, 2025).

Jones, J. M. (2021, January 18). Last trump job approval 34%; average is record-low 41%. *Gallup.* https://news.gallup.com/poll/328637/last-trump-job-approval-average-record-low.aspx (accessed January 21, 2025).

Jordan, M. (2024, September 18). Far from Ohio, Haitian Americans feel the sting of threats in Springfield. *The New York Times.* https://www.nytimes.com/2024/09/18/us/haitian-americans-springfield-ohio-reaction.html (accessed January 21, 2025).

Judd, C. M., and Park, B. (1993). Definition and assessment of accuracy in social stereotypes. *Psychological Review, 100:* 109–128.

Judd, C. M., Ryan, C. S., and Park, B. (1991). Accuracy in the judgment of ingroup and outgroup variability. *Journal of Personality and Social Psychology, 61*(3): 366–379. https://doi.org/10.1037/0022-3514.61.3.366 (accessed January 21, 2025).

Jussim, L. J., McCauley, C. R., and Lee, Y. (1995). Why study stereotype accuracy and inaccuracy? In Y. Lee, L. Jussim, and C. McCauley (Eds.), *Stereotype accuracy: Toward appreciating group differences* (pp. 3–27). American Psychological Association.

Kaczynski, A., and Steck, E. (2024, September 19). Mark Robinson, NC GOP nominee for governor, called himself a "Black Nazi," supported slavery in past comments made on Porn Forum. *CNN.* https://www.cnn.com/2024/09/19/politics/kfile-mark-robinson-Black-nazi-pro-slavery-porn-forum/index.html (accessed January 21, 2025).

Kane, J. V., Mason, L., and Wronski, J. (2021). Who's at the party? Group sentiments, knowledge, and partisan identity. *The Journal of Politics, 83*(4): 1783–1799. https://doi.org/10.1086/715072 (accessed January 21, 2025).

Kapur, S., and Thorp, F. (2024, February 7). Republicans kill border bill in a sign of Trump's strength and McConnell's waning influence. *NBCNews.com.* https://www.nbcnews.com/politics/congress/republicans-kill-border-bill-sign-trumps-strength-mcconnells-waning-in-rcna137477 (accessed January 21, 2025).

Karlins, M., Coffman, T. L., and Walters, G. (1969). On the fading of social stereotypes: Studies in three generations of college students. *Journal of Personality and Social Psychology, 13:* 1–16.

Karma, R. (2020, February 18). How Democrats can talk about race and win. Vox. https://www.vox.com/2020/2/18/21116867/ian-haney-lopez-merge-left-race-class-project-trump-racism-dog-whistles-2020-democrats (accessed January 21, 2025).

Karni, A., Haberman, M., and Ember, S. (2020, July 29). Trump plays on racist fears of terrorized suburbs to court white voters. *The New York Times.* https://www.nytimes.com/2020/07/29/us/politics/trump-suburbs-housing-white-voters.html (accessed January 21, 2025).

Kashima, Y. (2000). Maintaining cultural stereotypes in the serial reproduction of narratives. *Personality and Social Psychology Bulletin, 26:* 594–604.

Katz, D., and Braly, K. (1933) Racial stereotypes of one hundred college students. *Journal of Abnormal and Social Psychology, 28:* 280–290.

Katz, D., and Braly, K. (1935). Racial prejudice and racial stereotypes. *Journal of Abnormal and Social Psychology, 30:* 175–193.

Kaufmann, E. (2019). *Whiteshift: Populism, immigration, and the future of white majorities.* Abrams Press.

Kaye, M. (1995). Organisational Myths and Storytelling as Communication Management: A Conceptual Framework for Learning an Organization's Culture. *Journal of Management and Organization, 1*(2): 1–13. https://doi.org/10.5172/jmo.1995.1.2.1 (accessed January 21, 2025).

Kelkar, K. (2017, September 16). How a shifting definition of 'white' helped shape U.S. immigration policy. *PBS.* https://www.pbs.org/newshour/nation/white-u-s-immigration-policy (accessed January 21, 2025).

Kellman, L. (2024, October 16). Trump emphasizes hypermasculinity as he and Harris pursue male voters. *Associated Press.* https://apnews.com/article/men-trump-harris-vote-election-hyper masculinity-97aab19f115ece7057c6ab049bcfed97 (accessed January 21, 2025).

Kelley, H. H., and Thibaut, J. W. (1978). *Interpersonal relations: A theory of interdependence.* Wiley.

Kelly, A. (2015, December 3). Trump to Jewish Republicans: "I'm a negotiator like you folks." *NPR.* https://www.npr.org/2015/12/03/458329895/trump-to-jewish-republicans-im-a-negotiator-like-you-folks (accessed January 21, 2025).

Kemper, S., and Thissen, D. (1981). Memory dimensions of requests. *Journal of Verbal Learning and Verbal Behavior, 20*(5): 552–563.

Kendi, I. (2019). *How to be an antiracist.* One World.

Kenrick, D. T., Maner, J. K., Butner, J., Li, N. P., Becherk, D. V., and Schaller, M. (2002). Dynamical evolutionary psychology: Mapping the domains of the New Interactionist Paradigm. *Personality and Social Psychology Review, 6*: 347–356.

Kent, A.H., Ricketts, L.R. (2024, October 22). The state of U.S. wealth inequality. *Federal Reserve Bank of St. Louis.* https://www.stlouisfed.org/community-development-research/the-state-of-us-wealth-inequality#:~:text=White%20households%20continue%20to%20own,in%20the%20U.S.%20might%20predict. (accessed January 21, 2025).

Kessler, G. (2016, October 19). Fact check: Trump's claim that he built his company with $1 million loan. *The Washington Pos*t. https://www.washingtonpost.com/politics/2016/live-updates/general-election/real-time-fact-checking-and-analysis-of-the-final-2016-presidential-debate/fact-check-trumps-claim-that-he-built-his-company-with-1-million-loan/ (accessed January 21, 2025).

Kessler, G. (2024, October 4). No, Biden didn't take FEMA relief money to use on migrants—but Trump did. *The Washington Post.* https://www.washingtonpost.com/politics/2024/10/04/no-biden-didnt-take-fema-relief-money-use-migrants-trump-did/ (accessed January 21, 2025).

Kessler, G., and Clement, S. (2018, December 14). Trump Fact Checker Poll: Few Americans believe his falsehoods. *The Washington Post.* https://www.washingtonpost.com/graphics/2018/politics/po litical-knowledge-poll-trump-falsehoods/ (accessed January 21, 2025).

Kessler, G., Clement, S., and Guskin, E. (2024, April 9). Which Trump lies stick? Republicans believe some falsehoods more than they did six years ago, our poll finds. *The Washington Post.* https://www.washingtonpost.com/politics/2024/04/09/some-trump-falsehoods-stick-more-than-others-fact-checker-poll-finds/ (accessed January 21, 2025).

Kessler, G., Rizzo, S., and Kelly, M. (2021, January 24). Analysis: Tracking all of President Trump's false or misleading claims. *The Washington Post.* https://www.washingtonpost.com/politics/2021/01/24/trumps-false-or-misleading-claims-total-30573-over-four-years/ (accessed January 21, 2025).

Kim, J. (2008, October 14). Arab or Decent? *Columbia Journalism Review.* https://www.cjr.org/campaign_desk/arab_or_decent.php (accessed January 21, 2025).

Kim., S. R., Ibssa, L., Walsh, K. (2024, October 25). ABC News. How Trump has undermined public trust in election system leading up to 2024 race. *ABC News.* https://abcnews.go.com/Politics/

trump-undermined-public-trust-election-system-leading-2024/story?id=115102966 (accessed January 21, 2025).

King, M. D. (2022, May 24). New Interactive data tool shows characteristics of those who receive assistance from government programs. *Census.gov*. https://www.census.gov/library/stories/2022/05/who-is-receiving-social-safety-net-benefits.html (accessed January 21, 2025).

Kirtley, M. D. and Weaver III, J. B. (1999). Exploring the impact of gender role self-perception on communication style. *Women's Studies in Communication, 22*(2):190–209.

Kitzinger, C. (2000). Doing feminist conversation analysis. *Feminism and Psychology, 10:* 163–193.

Kivovitz, E., and Kung, E. UCLA study tracks former President Donald Trump's weaponization of words. *UCLA Newsroom*. https://newsroom.ucla.edu/releases/ucla-study-tracks-former-president-donald-trumps-weaponization-of-words (accessed January 21, 2025).

Klaas, B. (2023, January 16). Schemas and the political brain. *The Garden of Forking Paths*. https://www.forkingpaths.co/p/schemas-and-the-political-brain?utm_campaign=postandutm_medium=emailandtriedRedirect=true (accessed January 21, 2025).

Klein, E. (2024, October 22). What's wrong with Donald Trump? *The New York Times*. https://www.nytimes.com/2024/10/22/opinion/donald-trump-ezra-klein-podcast.html (accessed January 21, 2025).

Klein, O., Jacobs, A., Gemoets, S., Licata, L., and Lambert, S. M. (2003). Hidden profiles and the consensualization of social stereotypes: How information distribution affects stereotype content and sharedness. *European Journal of Social Psychology, 33:* 755–777.

Klineberg, O. (1954). *Social psychology*. Henry Holt and Company.

Kochhar, R., and Moslimani, M. (2023, December 4). 2. Wealth gaps across racial and ethnic groups. *Pew Research Center*. https://www.pewresearch.org/2023/12/04/wealth-gaps-across-racial-and-ethnic-groups/ (accessed January 21, 2025).

Konerman, J. (2017, January 24). "Fight Club" writer takes credit for 'Snowflake' term. *The Hollywood Reporter*. https://www.hollywoodreporter.com/movies/movie-news/fight-club-writer-takes-credit-snowflake-term-968267/ (accessed January 21, 2025).

Kornfield, M. (2024, July 25). Trump botches Kamala Harris's first name, again and again and again. *The Washington Post*. https://www.washingtonpost.com/politics/2024/07/25/trump-mispronounces-kamala-harris-name/ (accessed January 21, 2025).

Kornfield, M. and Iati, M. (2024, October 24). Trump compares undocumented migrants to trash at insult-fueled rallies. *The Washington Post*. https://www.washingtonpost.com/politics/2024/10/24/trump-arizona-immigrants-garbage-can-trash-rally/ (accessed January 21, 2025).

Krieg, G. (2016, September 9). 14 of Trump's most outrageous "birther" claims – half from after 2011. *CNN*. https://www.cnn.com/2016/09/09/politics/donald-trump-birther/index.html (accessed January 21, 2025).

Krieg, G., and Sullivan, K. (2024, November 3). Trump says he "shouldn't have left" the White House as he closes campaign with increasingly dark message. *CNN*. https://www.cnn.com/2024/11/03/politics/trump-dark-closing-message/index.html (accessed January 21, 2025).

Krugman, P. (2024a, August 22). Trump's made-up "Kamala crime wave." *The New York Times*. https://www.nytimes.com/2024/08/22/opinion/kamala-harris-trump-crime.html (accessed January 21, 2025).

Krugman, P. (2024b, August 26). Inflation is fading, statistically and politically. *The New York Times*. https://www.nytimes.com/2024/08/26/opinion/inflation-trump-harris-powell.html (accessed January 21, 2025).

Kruse, M. (2015, August 14). The 199 most Donald Trump things Donald Trump has ever said. *Politico*. https://www.politico.com/magazine/story/2015/08/the-absolute-trumpest-121328/ (accessed January 21, 2025).

Kurtzleben, D. (2024, September 24). How Trump and Vance's tour of dude influencers might help them win. *NPR*. https://www.npr.org/2024/09/20/g-s1-23911/how-trump-and-vances-tour-of-dude-influencers-might-help-them-win (accessed January 21, 2025).

Kurylo, A. (2004). Understanding the stereotype as a complex communication tool. *Communication Teacher, 18:* 74–77.

Kurylo, A. (2013). *The communicated stereotype: from celebrity vilification to everyday talk.* Lexington Books.

Kurylo, A. (2018). American people vs. politicians: Group vitality achieved through the construction and realignment of political cultural identity in online comments about "Obamacare". In Bilge, N. and Marino, M. I. (Eds.), *Reconceptualizing new media and intercultural communication in a networked society* (pp. 251–279). IGI Global.

Kurylo, A. (2021). *Building your social world: Constructing reality through interpersonal communication.* Dubuque, IA: Kendall Hunt.

Kurylo, A., and Robles, J. S. (2015). How should I respond to them? An emergent categorization of responses to interpersonally communicated stereotypes. *Journal of Intercultural Communication Research, 44*(1): 64–91. https://doi.org/10.1080/17475759.2014.1001994 (accessed January 21, 2025).

Kurylo, A., and Hu, Y. (2024). *Communicated stereotypes at work.* Lexington Books.

Kurylo, A., and Veeramani, K. (2024). Calling in and calling out: Human Resource DEI strategies and interpersonally communicated stereotypes in academic settings. In Kurylo, A. and Hu, Y. *Communicated stereotypes at work* (pp. 15–29). Lexington Books.

Landler, M., and Lichtblau, E. (2016, July 5). FBI director James Comey recommends no charges for Hillary Clinton on email. *The New York Times*. https://www.nytimes.com/2016/07/06/us/politics/hillary-clinton-fbi-email-comey.html (accessed January 21, 2025).

Langer, E., Blank, A., and Chanowitz, B. (1978). The mindlessness of ostensibly thoughtful action: The role of placebic information in interpersonal interaction. *Journal of Personality and Social Psychology, 36:* 635–642.

Lapiere, R. T. (1936). Type-rationalizations of group antipathy. *Social Forces, 15*(2), 232–237. https://doi.org/10.2307/2570963 (accessed January 21, 2025).

Lau, I. Y.-M., Chiu, C., and Lee, S. (2001). Communication and shared reality: Implications for the psychological foundations of culture. *Social Cognition, 19:* 350–371.

Leake, L. (2024). 17 years of your adult life may be spent online. These expert tips may help curb your screen time. *Fortune*. https://fortune.com/well/article/screen-time-over-lifespan/ (accessed January 21, 2025).

Leary, A. (2024, November 2). Trump says suburban women have to be 'protected when they are home.' *Wall Street Journal*. https://www.wsj.com/livecoverage/harris-trump-election-11-01-24/card/trump-says-suburban-women-have-to-be-protected-when-they-are-home-MM07aVMyHQbjsU5o4mW2 (accessed January 21, 2025).

Lee, S. J. (1996). *Unraveling the "model minority" stereotype: Listening to Asian American youth.* Teachers College Press.

Lee, Y.-T. and Duenas, G. (1995). Stereotype accuracy in multicultural business. In Y. T. Lee, L. Jussim, and C. McCauley (Eds.), *Stereotype accuracy: Toward appreciating group differences.* The American Psychological Association.

Lee, Y., Jussim, L., and McCauley, C. (1995). *Stereotype accuracy: Toward appreciating group differences.* Washington, DC: American Psychological Association.

Leibovich, M. (2022). *Thank you for your servitude: Donald Trump's Washington and the price of submission.* Penguin Press.

Lerer, L., and Gold, M. (2024, October 15). Trump escalates threats to political opponents he deems the "enemy." *The New York Times.* https://www.nytimes.com/2024/10/15/us/politics/trump-opponents-enemy-within.html (accessed January 21, 2025).

Lerer, L., and King, M. (2024, July 31). Trump remarks on Harris evoke a haunting and unsettling history. *The New York Times.* https://www.nytimes.com/2024/07/31/us/politics/trump-harris-race.html (accessed January 21, 2025).

Levenson, M. (2021, June 23). Judge blocks $4 billion U.S. debt relief program for minority farmers. *The New York Times.* https://www.nytimes.com/2021/06/23/us/politics/biden-debt-relief-Black-farmers.html (accessed January 21, 2025).

Levien, S. J. (2024, September 25). Rep. Clay Higgins posts, then deletes, racist comments about Haitians. *The New York Times.* https://www.nytimes.com/2024/09/25/us/politics/clay-higgins-haitians-springfield-ohio.html (accessed January 21, 2025).

Levin, B. (2024, August 20). Trump "disgusts me to my core": Ex-MAGA supporters tell the world why they're voting for Kamala Harris. *Vanity Fair.* https://www.vanityfair.com/news/story/ex-trump-supporters-explain-why-theyre-voting-for-kamala-harris?srsltid=AfmBOooCGPcVjMil4Xsc WymDm4jTENnh0dnf0x_7KbvYKUS8qZjvCVFL (accessed January 21, 2025).

Levine, M. (2020, May 30). "No Blame?" ABC News finds 54 cases invoking "Trump" in connection with violence, threats, alleged assaults. *ABC News.* https://abcnews.go.com/Politics/blame-abc-news-finds-17-cases-invoking-trump/story?id=58912889 (accessed January 21, 2025).

LeVine, M., and Arnsdorf, I. (2024, October 21). Trump declines to condemn threats to FEMA workers, repeats false claims. *The Washington Post.* https://www.washingtonpost.com/politics/2024/10/21/trump-fema-threats-misinformation-hurricane-helene/ (accessed January 21, 2025).

LeVine, M., and Knowles, H. (2024, September 25). Donald Trump says he will 'protect' women. Many don't see it that way. *The Washington Post.* https://www.washingtonpost.com/elections/2024/09/25/trump-women-voters-harris/ (accessed January 21, 2025).

LeVine, M., Stein, J., Cheeseman, A., and Arnsdorf, I. (2024, August 19). Trump portrays Harris as foreign, echoing past attacks on Democrats of color. *The Washington Post.* https://www.washingtonpost.com/politics/2024/08/19/trump-speech-pa-event-dnc/ (accessed January 21, 2025).

Lewis, K. (2023). Republicans' Identical Outfits at Debate Spark Flood of Memes, Jokes. *Newsweek.* https://www.newsweek.com/republicans-identical-outfits-debate-sparks-flood-memes-jokes-1822082 (accessed January 21, 2025).

Leyens, J. P., Yzerbyt, V., and Schadron, G. (1994). *Stereotypes and social cognition.* Sage Publications.

Liberman, A., Newman, L. S., and Chaiken, S. (1998). Rethinking the role of facilitation and inhibition in stereotyping. In R. S. Wyer, Jr. (Ed.), *Stereotype activation and inhibition* (pp. 145–162). Lawrence Erlbaum Associates.

Licon, A. G. (2024a, July 23). Clip resurfaces of Vance criticizing Harris for being "childless," testing Trump's new running mate. *Associated Press.* https://apnews.com/article/jd-vance-kamala-harris-childless-trump-0a37e991097b66c52bff5bf7ecf8de7b (accessed January 21, 2025).

Licon, A. G. (2024b, August 16). Praise for Hungary and people having more children: Takeaways from Vance's statements on birth rates. *Associated Press.* https://apnews.com/article/jd-vance-birth-rates-hungary-day-care-c0344da9335c7c4c816ea42cdaf3caf6 (accessed January 21, 2025).

Licon, A. G., Fernando, C., and Amy, J. (2024, September 30). Trump makes false claims about federal response as he campaigns in area ravaged by Hurricane Helene. *Associated Press.* https://apnews.com/article/kamala-harris-donald-trump-hurricane-helene-3097f1706455929ad f5a4eb67f9cdf0f (accessed January 21, 2025).

Lind, D. (2016, September 8). Nobody ever tells Donald Trump to smile. *Vox.* https://www.vox.com/2016/9/8/12847456/clinton-trump-sexism (accessed January 21, 2025).

Lippmann, W. (1922/1965). *Public opinion.* Free Press.

LoBianco, T. (2015, November 23). Trump video shows Clinton laughing over Benghazi wreckage. *CNN.* https://www.cnn.com/2015/11/23/politics/donald-trump-hillary-clinton-laughing-benghazi/index.html (accessed January 21, 2025).

LoBianco, T., and Killough, A. (2016, August 19). Trump pitches black voters: "What the hell do you have to lose?". *CNN.* https://www.cnn.com/2016/08/19/politics/donald-trump-african-american-voters/index.html (accessed January 21, 2025).

Lopez, G. (2020, August 13). Donald Trump's long history of racism, from the 1970s to 2020. *Vox.* https://www.vox.com/2016/7/25/12270880/donald-trump-racist-racism-history (accessed January 21, 2025).

López, I. H. (2014). *Dog whistle politics: How coded racial appeals have reinvented racism and wrecked the middle class.* Oxford University Press.

López, I. H. (2019). *Merge left: Fusing race and class, winning elections, and saving America.* The New Press.

Lozada, C. (2021, November 19). The 1619 project started as history. Now it's also a political program. *The Washington Post.* https://www.washingtonpost.com/outlook/2021/11/19/1619-project-book-history/ (accessed January 21, 2025).

Luciano, M. (2024, November 1). Trump boasts he has "beautiful white skin" right after slamming Kamala Harris. *Mediaite.* https://www.mediaite.com/trump/trump-boasts-he-has-beautiful-white-skin-right-after-slamming-kamala-harris/ (accessed January 21, 2025).

Lussenhop, J. (2016, September 27). Presidential debate 2016: Four ways gender played a role. *BBC News.* https://www.bbc.com/news/election-us-2016-37481754 (accessed January 21, 2025).

Lynch, F. R. (2002). *The diversity machine: The drive to change the white male workplace.* Routledge.

Lyons, A., and Kashima, Y. (2001). The reproduction of culture: Communication processes tend to maintain cultural stereotypes. *Social Cognition, 19:* 372–394.

Lyons, A., and Kashima, Y. (2003). How are stereotypes maintained through communication? The influence of stereotype sharedness. *Journal of Personality and Social Psychology, 85:* 989–1005.

Maass, A., and Arcuri, L. (1996). Language and stereotyping. In C. N. Macrae, C. Stangor, and M. Hewstone (Eds.), *Stereotypes and stereotyping* (pp. 193–226). Guilford Press.

Mackie, D. M., Hamilton, D. L., Susskind, J., and Rosseli, F. (1996). Social psychological foundations of stereotype formation. In C. N. Macrae, C. Stangor, and M. Hewstone (Eds.), *Stereotypes and stereotyping* (pp. 41–78). Guilford Press.

Macrae, C. N., and Bodenhausen, G. V. (2001). Social cognition: Categorical person perception. *British Journal of Psychology, 92*(1): 239–255. https://doi.org/10.1348/000712601162059 (accessed January 21, 2025).

Macrae, C. N., Milne, A. B., and Bodenhausen, G. V. (1994). Stereotypes as energy-saving devices: A peek inside the cognitive toolbox. *Journal of Personality and Social Psychology, 66*(1): 37–47. https://doi.org/10.1037/0022-3514.66.1.37 (accessed January 21, 2025).

MacWilliams, M. C. (2020, September 23). Trump is an authoritarian. So are millions of Americans. *Politico.* https://www.politico.com/news/magazine/2020/09/23/trump-america-authoritarianism-420681 (accessed January 21, 2025).

Maher, K., Bauerlein, V., and Hobbes, T. D. (2024, September 18). How the Trump campaign ran with rumors about pet-eating migrants—after being told they weren't true. *Wall Street Journal.* https://www.wsj.com/us-news/springfield-ohio-pet-eating-claims-haitian-migrants-04598d48 (accessed January 21, 2025).

Maher, K., and Krieg, G. (2024, October 27). Vance insists Trump's "enemy from within" comments weren't directed at political rivals. *CNN.* https://www.cnn.com/2024/10/27/politics/jd-vance-state-of-the-union/index.html (accessed January 21, 2025).

Mahler, J., Mac, R., and Schleifer, T. (2024, October 18). How tech billionaires became the G.O.P.'s new donor class. *The New York Times.* https://www.nytimes.com/2024/10/18/magazine/trump-donors-silicon-valley.html (accessed January 21, 2025).

Main, A. (2024, October 11). Trump picks a fight with Detroit. *CNN.* https://www.cnn.com/2024/10/10/politics/trump-detroit/index.html (accessed January 21, 2025).

Major, B., Blodorn, A., and Major Blascovich, G. (2018). The threat of increasing diversity: Why many white Americans support Trump in the 2016 presidential election. *Group Processes and Intergroup Relations, 21*(6): 931–940. https://doi.org/10.1177/1368430216677304 (accessed January 21, 2025).

Mancini, J. (2023, September 18). Donald Trump made billions in real estate, but his dad was the one who built a billion-dollar empire from scratch – learn their strategies and start investing with just $100. *Yahoo! Finance.* https://finance.yahoo.com/news/donald-trump-made-billions-real-162840688.html (accessed January 21, 2025).

Markovits, E. (2016, March 4). Trump "tells it like it is."That's not necessarily a good thing for democracy. *The Washington Post.* https://www.washingtonpost.com/news/monkey-cage/wp/2016/03/04/trump-tells-it-like-it-is-thats-not-necessarily-a-good-thing-for-democracy/ (accessed January 21, 2025).

Marsden, E. (2024, September 15). Donald Trump faces backlash for Springfield bomb threat response. *Newsweek.* https://www.newsweek.com/donald-trump-faces-backlash-springfield-bomb-threat-response-1954022 (accessed January 21, 2025).

Martin, E. (2024, October 7). Trump on immigrants: "we got a lot of bad genes in our country right now." *Politico.* https://www.politico.com/news/2024/10/07/trump-immigrants-crime-00182702 (accessed January 21, 2025).

Martin, M., Ermyas, T. (2022, May 9). Former Pentagon chief Esper says Trump asked about shooting protesters. *NPR.* https://www.npr.org/2022/05/09/1097517470/trump-esper-book-defense-secretary (accessed January 21, 2025).

Mathias, C. (2024, September 20). Trump used an alarming word––and most people missed it. *HuffPost.* https://www.huffpost.com/entry/trump-remigration-fascist-martin-sellner-europe_n_66ed912be4b07a173e51416d?ruf (accessed January 21, 2025).

Matthews, D. (2018, April 3). Sinclair, the pro-Trump, conservative company taking over local news, explained. *Vox.* https://www.vox.com/2018/4/3/17180020/sinclair-broadcast-group-conservative-trump-david-smith-local-news-tv-affiliate (accessed January 21, 2025).

Mauger, C. (2024, August 20). Trump returns to Michigan to talk crime, but data shows rates dropped after he left office. *The Detroit News.* https://www.detroitnews.com/story/news/politics/2024/08/20/donald-trump-howell-michigan-crime-campaign-speech-kamala-harris-illegal-immigration/74844154007/ (accessed January 21, 2025).

Mayer, J. (2019, March 4). The making of the Fox News White House. *The New Yorker.* https://www.newyorker.com/magazine/2019/03/11/the-making-of-the-fox-news-white-house (accessed January 21, 2025).

Mayorquín, O., and Morales, C. (2024, November 25). In California's heartland, some Latino immigrants back Trump's border stance. *The New York Times.* https://www.nytimes.com/2024/11/25/us/latino-immigrants-trump-fresno-california.html (accessed January 21, 2025).

Mazza, E. (2024, September 24). Trump's unsettling new message for women is creeping people out. *HuffPost.* https://www.huffpost.com/entry/donald-trump-protect-women_n_66f25f8de4b02f84278be7c8 (accessed January 21, 2025).

McAdams, D. P. (2020). *The strange case of Donald J. Trump: A psychological reckoning.* Oxford University Press.

McCammon, S. (2016, June 22). Donald Trump delivers speech attacking Hillary Clinton as corrupt. *NPR.* https://www.npr.org/2016/06/22/483129527/donald-trump-delivers-speech-attacking-crooked-hillary (accessed January 21, 2025).

McCammon, S. (2024, September 10). Trump repeats the false claim that Democrats support abortion 'after birth' in debate. *NPR.* https://www.npr.org/2024/09/10/nx-s1-5107942/abortion-roe-wade-ivf-donald-trump-kamala-harris-debate-2024 (accessed January 21, 2025).

McCarthy, M. (2024, October 6). Speaker Johnson won't condemn Eric Trump comments blaming Dems for assassination attempts. *Politico.* https://www.politico.com/news/2024/10/06/johnson-trump-democrats-assassination-attempts-00182619 (accessed January 21, 2025).

McCauley, C. (1995). Are stereotypes exaggerated? A sampling of racial, gender, academic, occupational and political stereotypes. In Y. Lee, L. Jussim, and C. McCauley (Eds.), *Stereotype accuracy: Toward appreciating group differences* (pp. 215–243). American Psychological Association.

McCreesh, S. (2024a, August 31). Conservative moms, charmed by Trump, would rather avoid his misogyny. *The New York Times.* https://www.nytimes.com/2024/08/31/us/elections/conservative-moms-for-liberty-trump.html (accessed January 21, 2025).

McCreesh, S. (2024b, October 14). The Trump voters who don't believe trump. *The New York Times.* https://www.nytimes.com/2024/10/14/us/elections/trump-promises-extreme-rhetoric.html (accessed January 21, 2025).

McCreesh, S. (2024c, October 31). "I'm not supposed to say this," Trump says. But then he does. *The New York Times.* https://www.nytimes.com/2024/10/31/us/elections/trump-blaming-staff.html (accessed January 21, 2025).

McCreesh, S. (2024d, November 6). How Trump connected with so many Americans. *The New York Times.* https://www.nytimes.com/2024/11/06/us/elections/donald-trump-supporters.html (accessed January 21, 2025).

McDaniel, J. (2024, October 31). Harris rebukes Trump for saying he will protect women whether they "like it or not". *The Washington Post.* https://www.washingtonpost.com/politics/2024/10/31/trump-women-protector-harris/ (accessed January 21, 2025).

McGarty, C. (2002). Stereotype formation as category formation. In C. McGarty, V. Y.Yzerbyt, and R. Spears (Eds.) *Stereotypes as explanations: The formation of meaningful beliefs about social groups* (pp. 16–37). Cambridge University Press.

McGarty, C., Yzerbyt, V. Y., and Spears, R. (2002). Social, cultural and cognitive factors in stereotype formation. In C. McGarty, V. Y.Yzerbyt, and R. Spears (Eds.) *Stereotypes as explanations: The formation of meaningful beliefs about social groups* (pp. 1–15). Cambridge: Cambridge University Press.

McGhee, H. (2021). *The sum of us: What racism costs everyone and how we can prosper together.* One World.

McIntosh, J. (2020). Crybabies and snowflakes. *Language in the Trump era:* 74–88. https://doi.org/10.1017/9781108887410.005 (accessed January 21, 2025).

McLeary, P., and O'Brien, C. (2024, August 29). "Unfairly attacked": Army defends employee involved in Trump campaign incident at Arlington. *Politico.* https://www.politico.com/news/2024/08/29/donald-trump-arlington-cemetery-army-employee-00176729 (accessed January 21, 2025).

Meckler, L. (2024, September 2). With his 1776 Commission on patriotism, Trump helped sparked a culture war. *The Washington Post.* https://www.washingtonpost.com/politics/2024/09/02/trump-1776-commission-education/ (accessed January 21, 2025).

Medina, J. (2024, October 29). How Trump exploits divisions among Black and Latino voters. *The New York Times.* https://www.nytimes.com/2024/10/29/us/politics/trump-Black-latino-voters.html (accessed January 21, 2025).

Mehrara, M. (2024, August 9). Trump claims MAGA base is 75% of country. *Newsweek.* https://www.newsweek.com/trump-claims-maga-base-kamala-harris-polls-1936903 (accessed January 21, 2025).

Mendelberg, T. (2001). *The race card: Campaign strategy, implicit messages, and the norm of equality.* Princeton University Press.

Mercieca, J. R. (2020). *Demagogue for president: The rhetorical genius of Donald Trump.* Texas A&M University Press.

Merriam-Webster. (n.d.). Microaggression––words we're watching. https://www.merriam-webster.com/wordplay/microaggression-words-were-watching (accessed January 21, 2025).

Metzl, J. (2019). *Dying of whiteness: How the politics of racial resentment is killing America's heartland.* Basic Books.

Miller, G. (2020, September 23). Allegations of racism have marked Trump's presidency and become key issue as election nears. *The Washington Post.* https://www.washingtonpost.com/national-security/trump-race-record/2020/09/23/332b0b68-f10f-11ea-b796-2dd09962649c_story.html (accessed January 21, 2025).

Miner, H. (1956). Body Ritual among the Nacirema. *American Anthropologist, 58*(3): 503–507.

Mokros, H. B. (2003). *Identity matters: Communication-based explorations and explanations.* Hampton Press.

Monmouth University. (2015, July 13). Bush, Trump get bumps. *Monmouth University Polling Institute.* https://www.monmouth.edu/polling-institute/reports/monmouthpoll_us_071315/ (accessed January 21, 2025).

Montanaro, D. (2024, August 11). 162 lies and distortions in a news conference. NPR fact-checks former president Trump. *NPR.* https://www.npr.org/2024/08/11/nx-s1-5070566/trump-news-conference (accessed January 21, 2025).

Moody, C. (2016, March 3). Gay conservatives who helped Kickstart Trump's GOP career have serious regrets. *CNN.* https://www.cnn.com/2016/03/03/politics/donald-trump-first-speech-to-cpac/ (accessed January 21, 2025).

Moody, C., and Holmes, K. (2015, September 18). Donald Trump's history of suggesting Obama is a Muslim. *CNN.* https://www.cnn.com/2015/09/18/politics/trump-obama-muslim-birther/index.html (accessed January 21, 2025).

Morrison, C. N., Ukert, B., Palumbo, A., Dong, B., Jacoby, S. F., and Wiebe, D. J. (2018). Assaults on days of campaign rallies during the 2016 U.S. presidential election. *Epidemiology, 29*(4): 490–493. https://doi.org/10.1097/ede.0000000000000821 (accessed January 21, 2025).

Moyer, J. M. (2015, June 12). "Are you an African American?" Why an NAACP official isn't saying. *The Washington Post*. https://www.washingtonpost.com/news/morning-mix/wp/2015/06/12/spokane-naacp-president-rachel-dolezal-may-be-white/ (accessed January 21, 2025).

Moyers, B. D. (1988, November 12). What a real president was like. *The Washington Post*. https://www.washingtonpost.com/archive/opinions/1988/11/13/what-a-real-president-was-like/d483c1be-d0da-43b7-bde6-04e10106ff6c/ (accessed January 21, 2025).

MSNBC. (2024a, February 9). Mika: Donald Trump is the "wizard of MAGA Oz" [Video]. *YouTube*. https://www.youtube.com/watch?v=MtfR4-byGmk (accessed January 21, 2025).

MSNBC. (2024b, October 8). "Double standard": Trump LIES freely about fake Gaza trip, Walz slammed for Tiananmen Square gaffe [Video]. *YouTube*. https://www.youtube.com/watch?v=kwZz9HyINq4 (accessed January 21, 2025).

Mutz, D. C. (2018). Status threat, not economic hardship, explains the 2016 Presidential Vote. *Proceedings of the National Academy of Sciences, 115*(19). https://doi.org/10.1073/pnas.1718155115 (accessed January 21, 2025).

Nagourney, A. (2024, August 2). Not one of us: Trump uses old tactic to sow suspicion about Harris. *The New York Times*. https://www.nytimes.com/2024/08/02/us/trump-tactic-suspicion-harris.html (accessed January 21, 2025).

Nagourney, A., and Nehamas, N. (2024, November 20). Harris loss has Democrats fighting over how to talk about transgender rights. *The New York Times*. https://www.nytimes.com/2024/11/20/us/politics/presidential-campaign-transgender-rights.html (accessed January 21, 2025).

Naishadham, S. (2021, January 8). U.S. judge Blocks Trump administration's sweeping asylum rules. *Associated Press*. https://apnews.com/article/donald-trump-immigration-courts-local-governments-3d6ab9e79153e67d974cee1bf592862f (accessed January 21, 2025).

Natanson, H. and Meckler, L. (2024, June 13). Red states strike deals to show controversial conservative videos in schools. *The Washington Post*. https://www.washingtonpost.com/education/2024/06/13/prageru-conservative-education-videos/ (accessed January 21, 2025).

National Conference of State Legislatures. (2023, April 12). Legislatures at a glance. https://www.ncsl.org/about-state-legislatures/legislatures-at-a-glance (accessed January 21, 2025).

Naylor, B. (2021, February 10). Read trump's Jan. 6 speech, a key part of impeachment trial. *NPR*. https://www.npr.org/2021/02/10/966396848/read-trumps-jan-6-speech-a-key-part-of-impeachment-trial (accessed January 21, 2025).

Network Contagion Research Institute. (2024, November 25). Instructing animosity: How DEI pedagogy produces the hostile attribution bias. https://networkcontagion.us/reports/instructing-animosity-how-dei-pedagogy-produces-the-hostile-attribution-bias/ (accessed January 21, 2025).

NBC News. (2024, December 2). National exit polls: Election 2024 results. https://www.nbcnews.com/politics/2024-elections/exit-polls (accessed January 21, 2025).

Newport, F. (2024, January 7). Controversy over the term "latinx": Public opinion context. *Gallup.com*. https://news.gallup.com/opinion/polling-matters/388532/controversy-term-latinx-public-opinion-context.aspx (accessed January 21, 2025).

Nguyen, T. (2021, January 19). A big chunk of Trump's 1776 report appears lifted from an author's prior work. *Politico*. https://www.politico.com/news/2021/01/19/trump-1776-report-plagiarism-460464?nid=00000170-c000-da87-af78-e185fa700000andnlid=2670445nlid%3D2670445andnname=politico-nightlyandnrid=0000016c-a5de-d088-a3ef-b7df92720000 (accessed January 21, 2025).

Nicholls, F. (2024, September 30). Donald Trump's call for "really violent day" compared to 'The Purge.' *Newsweek*. https://www.newsweek.com/donald-trump-call-really-violent-day-compared-purge-1961090 (accessed January 21, 2025).

Nichols, T. (2024, October 16). Donald Trump's fascist romp. *The Atlantic*. https://www.theatlantic.com/politics/archive/2024/10/donald-trumps-fascist-romp/680252/ (accessed January 21, 2025).

Nilsson, J., Humes, E., Eubanks, C., and Cypher, C. (2024, March 19). The case of the falling crime rate. *The Saturday Evening Post*. https://www.saturdayeveningpost.com/2024/03/the-case-of-the-falling-crime-rate/ (accessed January 21, 2025).

Nisbett, R., and Ross, L. (1980). *Human inference: Strategies and shortcomings of social judgment*. Prentice Hall.

Nisbett, E., and Wilson, T. D. (1977). Telling more than we know: Verbal reports on mental processes. *Psychological Review, 84*(3): 231–259.

Noah, T. (2002, December 16). The legend of Strom's remorse. *Slate*. https://slate.com/news-and-politics/2002/12/the-legend-of-strom-s-remorse.html (accessed January 21, 2025).

Noe-Bustamante, L., Martinez, G., and Lopez, M. H. (2024, September 12). Latinx awareness has doubled among U.S. Hispanics since 2019, but only 4% use it. *Pew Research Center*. https://www.pewresearch.org/race-and-ethnicity/2024/09/12/latinx-awareness-has-doubled-among-u-s-hispanics-since-2019-but-only-4-percent-use-it/ (accessed January 21, 2025).

Noor, N., Beram, S., Huat, F. K. C., Gengatharan, K, and Rasidi, M. S. M. (2023). Bias, Halo Effect and Horn Effect: A systematic literature review. *International Journal of Academic Research in Business and Social Sciences, 13*(3): 1117–1140.

NPR Staff. (2016, September 29). Decades-old housing discrimination case plagues Donald Trump. *NPR*. https://www.npr.org/2016/09/29/495955920/donald-trump-plagued-by-decades-old-housing-discrimination-case (accessed January 21, 2025).

NPR Staff. (2019, February 5). Fact check: Trump's State of the Union Address. *NPR*. https://www.npr.org/2019/02/05/690345256/fact-check-trumps-state-of-the-union-address (accessed January 21, 2025).

Oakes, P. J., Haslam, S. A., and Turner, J. C. (1994). *Stereotyping and social reality*. Blackwell.

O'Hara, M. E. (2017, January 24). Trump administration removes LGBTQ content from federal websites. *NBC News*. https://www.nbcnews.com/feature/nbc-out/trump-administration-removes-lgbtq-content-federal-websites-n711416 (accessed January 21, 2025).

Olmsted, E. (2024, September 4). Trump says gangs overran an apartment complex. Here's the truth. *The New Republic*. https://newrepublic.com/post/185593/donald-trump-gangs-apartment-complex-truth?utm_source=Twitterandutm_medium=socialandutm_campaign=SF_TNR (accessed January 21, 2025).

Ottati, V., and Lee, Y. (1995). Accuracy: A neglected component of stereotype research. In Y. Lee, L. Jussim, and C. McCauley (Eds.) *Stereotype accuracy: Toward appreciating group differences* (pp. 29–59). American Psychological Association.

Owen, P. (2018, August 2). Here's a montage of Trump saying "it's true," courtesy of "Jimmy Kimmel Live" (video). *The Wrap*. https://www.thewrap.com/heres-montage-trump-saying-true-courtesy-jimmy-kimmel-live-video/ (accessed January 21, 2025).

P2016. (2015, June 16). Donald Trump Announcement of Candidacy. https://www.p2016.org/trump/trump061615sp.html (accessed January 21, 2025).

Pais, J. F., South, S. J. and Crowder, K. White Flight Revisited: A Multiethnic Perspective on Neighborhood Out-Migration. *Population Research and Policy Review, 28:* 321–346 (2009). https://doi.org/10.1007/s11113-008-9101-x (accessed January 21, 2025).

Pamer, M., Wynter, K., and Hawkins, K. (2015, July 10). Slain football player Jamiel Shaw's father: Donald Trump 'is telling the truth' on immigration. *KTLA.* https://ktla.com/news/local-news/family-of-jamiel-shaw-jr-teen-fatally-shot-by-undocumented-gang-member-to-meet-with-donald-trump/ (accessed January 21, 2025).

Pappas, S. (2023, July 1). More than 20 % of teens have seriously considered suicide. Psychologists and communities can help tackle the problem. *American Psychological Association.* https://www.apa.org/monitor/2023/07/psychologists-preventing-teen-suicide (accessed January 21, 2025).

Paquette, D. (2024, October 30). They're coming after you, Trump says. But who are 'they'? *The Washington Post.* https://www.washingtonpost.com/politics/2024/10/30/trump-maga-blame-immigrants-democrats/ (accessed January 21, 2025).

Parker, A. (2020, August 21). The permanent outsider. *The Washington Post.* https://www.washingtonpost.com/outlook/2020/08/21/trump-outsider-incumbent-campaign/ (accessed January 21, 2025).

Parker, A. (2024a, July 26). A Trump shark's tale: Whether to be eaten or electrocuted. *The Washington Post.* https://www.washingtonpost.com/politics/2024/07/26/trump-shark-ev-boat-electrocution/ (accessed January 21, 2025).

Parker, A. (2024b, October 21). Trump keeps calling Harris "stupid," offending many voters. *The Washington Post.* https://www.washingtonpost.com/politics/2024/10/21/trump-harris-dumb-stupid-low-iq/ (accessed January 21, 2025).

Parker, A. and Dawsey, J. (2024, November 5). Trump's last day on the trail in his third run: "It's ours to lose". *The Washington Post.* https://www.washingtonpost.com/politics/2024/11/05/trump-final-days-2024-campaign/ (accessed January 21, 2025).

Parker, K., Morin, R., and Horowitz, J. M. (2019, March 21). Looking to the future, public sees an America in decline on many fronts. *Pew Research Center.* https://www.pewresearch.org/social-trends/2019/03/21/public-sees-an-america-in-decline-on-many-fronts/ (accessed January 21, 2025).

Passantino, J., and Reilly, L. (2024, September 24). Did you know violent crime is down? Not if you're watching right-wing media. *CNN.* https://www.cnn.com/2024/09/24/media/violent-crime-report-fbi-right-wing-media-fox/index.html (accessed January 21, 2025).

Pearlman, J. (2014, April 4). A reporter's tale: The John Rocker story 15 years later. *Bleacher Report.* https://bleacherreport.com/articles/2009128-a-reporters-tale-the-john-rocker-story-15-years-later (accessed January 21, 2025).

Peñaloza, M. (2021, January 6). Trump supporters storm U.S. Capitol, clash with police. *NPR.* https://www.npr.org/sections/congress-electoral-college-tally-live-updates/2021/01/06/953616207/diehard-trump-supporters-gather-in-the-nations-capital-to-protest-election-resul (accessed January 21, 2025).

Pengelly, M. (2023, October 27). "Ha, ha, ha": Mitt Romney laughs off Trump's "total loser" attack. *The Guardian.* https://www.theguardian.com/us-news/2023/oct/27/mitt-romney-book-trump-comment-reckoning (accessed January 21, 2025).

Peoples, S., Farrington, B., and Stafford, K. (2023, July 27). DeSantis is defending new slavery teachings. civil rights leaders see a pattern of "policy violence." *Associated Press.* https://apnews.com/article/desantis-slavery-election-2024-1fb51d663e6051051aa23b71421b9479 (accessed January 21, 2025).

Pérez, J., Wilkes, M. (2025, January 29). Trump issues orders on K-12 "indoctrination," school choice and campus protests. *Politico.* https://www.politico.com/news/2025/01/29/trump-k12-indoctrination-school-choice-campus-protests-education-00201235 (accessed January 29, 2025).

Peters, G., and Woolley, J. T. (2020, September 17). Remarks at a White House conference on American history. *The American Presidency Project.* https://www.presidency.ucsb.edu/documents/remarks-white-house-conference-american-history (accessed January 21, 2025).

Pettigrew, T. F. (1979). The ultimate attribution error: Extending Allport's cognitive analysis of prejudice. *Personality and Social Psychology Bulletin, 5:* 461–476.

Petty, R. E., and Cacioppo, J. T. (1986b). The elaboration likelihood model of persuasion. In L. Berkowitz, (Ed.), *Advances in experimental social psychology, 19:* 123–205.

Pew Research Center. (2019, May 16). Trump's staunch GOP supporters have roots in the Tea Party. https://www.pewresearch.org/politics/2019/05/16/trumps-staunch-gop-supporters-have-roots-in-the-tea-party/ (accessed January 21, 2025).

Philipsen, G. (1992). *Speaking culturally: Explorations in social communication.* SUNY Press.

Picoult, J. (2005). *Vanishing Acts.* Atria/Emily Bestler.

Pillai, R. M., Kim, E., and Fazio, L. K. (2023). All the president's lies: Repeated false claims and public opinion. *Public Opinion Quarterly, 87*(3): 764–802. https://doi.org/10.1093/poq/nfad032 (accessed January 21, 2025).

Pinchin, K. (2019, October 22). "The snake": What Trump's use of metaphors reveals. *PBS.* https://www.pbs.org/wgbh/frontline/article/insects-floods-and-the-snake-what-trumps-use-of-metaphors-reveals/ (accessed January 21, 2025).

Poerksen, B. (2024, September 2). Meinung: Der Spiegel's coverage of Donald Trump: We have failed to tame the Media Monster. *Der Speigel.* https://www.spiegel.de/international/zeitgeist/der-spiegels-coverage-of-donald-trump-we-have-failed-to-tame-the-media-monster-a-f46ce63b-f71e-4469-ac7a-8a7ed3010e01 (accessed January 21, 2025).

Politico. (2016, June 22). Full transcript: Donald Trump NYC speech on stakes of the election. https://www.politico.com/story/2016/06/transcript-trump-speech-on-the-stakes-of-the-election-224654 (accessed January 21, 2025).

Pomerantz, A. (1986). Extreme case formulations: A way of legitimizing claims. *Human Studies, 9*(2/3): 219–229

Poniewozik, J. (2024, July 19). Donald Trump promised a softer image. He delivered Hulkamania. *The New York Times.* https://www.nytimes.com/2024/07/19/arts/television/donald-trump-rnc.html (accessed January 21, 2025).

Press Release. (2022, September 29). Justice Department announces actions to resolve lending discrimination claims against Evolve Bank and Trust. *Office of Public Affairs.* https://www.justice.gov/opa/pr/justice-department-announces-actions-resolve-lending-discrimination-claims-against-evolve (accessed January 21, 2025).

Price, M. L. (2024, August 30). Trump says he'll vote to uphold Florida abortion ban after seeming to signal he'd support repeal. *Associated Press.* https://apnews.com/article/trump-abortion-florida-six-weeks-ae0ce47cb2af82a6586fa19235ea2226 (accessed January 21, 2025).

Pryor, J. B., Reeder, G. D., Yeadon, C., and Hesson-McInnis, M. (2004). A dual-process model of reactions to perceived stigma. *Journal of Personality and Social Psychology, 87:* 436–452.

Public Religion Research Institute. (2024, October 11). Challenges to democracy: The 2024 election in focus. https://www.prri.org/research/challenges-to-democracy-the-2024-election-in-focus-findings-from-the-2024-american-values-survey/ (accessed January 21, 2025).

Qin, A. (2024, November 1). Xenophobia and hate speech are spiking heading into the election. *The New York Times.* https://www.nytimes.com/2024/11/01/us/xenophobia-hate-speech-increase-election.html (accessed January 21, 2025).

Qiu, L. (2024a, October 18). Trump's claims that blame migrants: False or misleading. *The New York Times*. https://www.nytimes.com/2024/10/18/us/politics/trump-immigration-fact-check.html (accessed January 21, 2025).

Qiu, L. (2024b, November 4). Trump keeps decrying rampant crime. Here's how his misleading claim has shifted. *The New York Times*. https://www.nytimes.com/interactive/2024/11/04/us/trump-crime-fact-check.html (accessed January 21, 2025).

Qiu, L., and Shao, E. (2024, September 21). Every falsehood, exaggeration and untruth in Trump's and Harris's stump speeches. *The New York Times*. https://www.nytimes.com/interactive/2024/09/21/us/politics/trump-harris-2024-election-speech.html (accessed January 21, 2025).

Ramirez, N.M. (2025, January 8). Fox News insider leaked Town Hall questions to Trump's team: Book. *Rolling Stone*. https://www.rollingstone.com/politics/politics-news/fox-news-leaked-town-hall-questions-trump-1235228924/ (accessed January 21, 2025).

Rashid, H. (2024a, August 28). Trump goes on crazed, violent rant calling for death of his enemies. *The New Republic*. https://newrepublic.com/post/185393/trump-fascist-violent-posts-truth-social-death-enemies (accessed January 21, 2025).

Rashid, H. (2024b, September 18). JD Vance's fascist threat against all immigrants-"illegal" or not. *The New Republic*. https://newrepublic.com/post/186129/jd-vance-fascist-threat-immigrants-illegal-haiti-tps-deport (accessed January 21, 2025).

RealClearPolling. (n.d.). 2016 Republican presidential nomination polls. https://www.realclearpolling.com/polls/president/republican-primary/2016/national (accessed January 21, 2025).

Recht, H., Lau, E., and Cadenhead, M. (2024, July 19). All the RNC speakers who got Kamala Harris's name wrong. *The Washington Post*. https://www.washingtonpost.com/politics/2024/07/18/all-rnc-speakers-who-got-kamala-harriss-name-wrong-so-far/ (accessed January 21, 2025).

Reifowitz, I. (2012). *Obama's America: A transformative vision of our national identity*. Potomac Books.

Reifowitz, I. (2019). *The tribalization of politics: How Rush Limbaugh's race-baiting rhetoric on the Obama presidency paved the way for Trump*. Ig Publishing.

Reilly, K. (2016a, August 31). Donald Trump: All the times he's insulted Mexico. *Time*. https://time.com/4473972/donald-trump-mexico-meeting-insult/ (accessed January 21, 2025).

Reilly, K. (2016b, September 10). Hillary Clinton transcript: "basket of deplorables" comment. *Time*. https://time.com/4486502/hillary-clinton-basket-of-deplorables-transcript/ (accessed January 21, 2025).

Reilly, L. (2024, October 10). FCC chair denounces trump's calls for CBS to "lose its license" over Harris' "60 Minutes" interview. *CNN*. https://www.cnn.com/2024/10/10/media/fcc-rosenworcel-trump-cbs-license-60-minutes/index.html (accessed January 21, 2025).

Reja, M. (2021, March 18). *Trump's* "Chinese Virus" tweet helped lead to rise in racist anti-Asian Twitter content: Study. *ABC News*. https://abcnews.go.com/Health/trumps-chinese-virus-tweet-helped-lead-rise-racist/story?id=76530148 (accessed January 21, 2025).

Resnick, B. (2017, July 10). Trump supporters know Trump lies. They just don't care. *Vox*. https://www.vox.com/2017/7/10/15928438/fact-checks-political-psychology (accessed January 21, 2025).

Reston, M. (2015, August 7). No one eclipses Donald Trump at GOP debate. *CNN*. https://www.cnn.com/2015/08/07/politics/donald-trump-republican-debate/index.html (accessed January 21, 2025).

Reston, M. (2024, October 18). Harris calls out Trump for 'gaslighting' Americans about Jan. 6 attack. *The Washington Post*. https://www.washingtonpost.com/politics/2024/10/17/harris-trump-jan-6-day-of-love-gaslighting/ (accessed January 21, 2025).

Riccardi, N. (2024, September 9). Trump's rhetoric on elections turns ominous as voting nears in the presidential race. *Associated Press.* https://apnews.com/article/trump-voting-elections-prosecute-dangerous-rhetoric-2ed9908e82075705f4b00ecfc93fa3fa (accessed January 21, 2025).

Richardson, H. C. (2024a, June 28). June 27, 2024. https://heathercoxrichardson.substack.com/p/june-27-2024 (accessed January 21, 2025).

Richardson, H. C. (2024b, September 8). September 7, 2024. https://heathercoxrichardson.substack.com/p/september-7-2024 (accessed January 21, 2025).

Richardson, H. C. (2024c, October 6). October 6, 2024. https://heathercoxrichardson.substack.com/p/october-6-2024 (accessed January 21, 2025).

Richardson, H. C. (2024d, October 13). October 13, 2024. https://heathercoxrichardson.substack.com/p/october-13-2024 (accessed January 21, 2025).

Roberts, D., and Felton, R. (2016, August 20). Trump and Clinton's free trade retreat: A pivotal moment for the world's economic future. *The Guardian.* https://www.theguardian.com/us-news/2016/aug/20/trump-clinton-free-trade-policies-tpp (accessed January 21, 2025).

Roberts, J. (2004, September 29). Kerry's top ten flip-flops. *CBS News.* https://www.cbsnews.com/news/kerrys-top-ten-flip-flops/ (accessed January 21, 2025).

Robertson, D. (2021, March 21). How "owning the libs" became the GOP's core belief. *Politico.* https://www.politico.com/news/magazine/2021/03/21/owning-the-libs-history-trump-politics-pop-culture-477203 (accessed January 21, 2025).

Robillard, K. (2024, September 10). How Dick Cheney's groundbreaking endorsement of Kamala Harris could actually matter. *Yahoo! News.* https://www.yahoo.com/news/dick-cheney-ground breaking-endorsement-kamala-100011201.html (accessed January 21, 2025).

Robinson, E. (2024, October 24). The double standard for Harris and Trump has reached a breaking point. *The Washington Post.* https://www.washingtonpost.com/opinions/2024/10/24/harris-trump-cnn-town-hall/ (accessed January 21, 2025).

Rocheleau, J. (2019, August 21). A former slur is reclaimed, and listeners have mixed feelings. *NPR.* https://www.npr.org/sections/publiceditor/2019/08/21/752330316/a-former-slur-is-reclaimed-and-listeners-have-mixed-feelings (accessed January 21, 2025).

Rodriguez, S. (2021, January 12). Trump's partially built "big, beautiful wall." *Politico.* https://www.politico.com/news/2021/01/12/trump-border-wall-partially-built-458255 (accessed January 21, 2025).

Rogers, K. (2020, August 13). Trump encourages racist conspiracy theory about Kamala Harris. *The New York Times.* https://www.nytimes.com/2020/08/13/us/politics/trump-kamala-harris.html (accessed January 21, 2025).

Rogers, K., Epstein, R. J., and Kolata, G. (2024, October 12). Daring Trump, Harris's campaign releases medical information. *The New York Times.* https://www.nytimes.com/2024/10/12/us/politics/harris-medical-records-trump.html (accessed January 21, 2025).

Rogers, K., Gold, M., and Nehamas, N. (2024, November 2). Trump and Harris offer night-and-day views of the economy. *The New York Times.* https://www.nytimes.com/2024/11/02/us/politics/harris-trump-georgia-north-carolina-virginia.html (accessed January 21, 2025).

Roll Call. (2024a, October 29). Speech: Donald Trump Holds a Campaign Rally in Macon, Georgia–– October 16, 2020. https://rollcall.com/factbase/trump/transcript/donald-trump-speech-campaign-rally-macon-georgia-october-16-2020/ (accessed January 21, 2025).

Roll Call. (2024b, October 29). Remarks: Kamala Harris holds a campaign rally on the Ellipse in Washington––October 29, 2024. https://rollcall.com/factbase/harris/transcript/kamala-harris-re marks-campaign-rally-ellipse-washington-october-29-2024/ (accessed January 21, 2025).

Rosenberg, Y. (2017, August 14). "Jews will not replace us": Why white supremacists go after Jews. *The Washington Post.* https://www.washingtonpost.com/news/acts-of-faith/wp/2017/08/14/jews-will-not-replace-us-why-white-supremacists-go-after-jews/ (accessed January 21, 2025).

Rouhandeh, A. J., and Jamali, N. (2023, June 29). Newsweek shareholders end legal dispute, co-owner Davis leaves Olivet sect. *Newsweek.* https://www.newsweek.com/newsweek-shareholders-end-legal-dispute-co-owner-davis-leaves-olivet-sect-1810029 (accessed January 21, 2025).

Roy, J. (2016, November 15). Analysis: "cuck," "snowflake," "masculinist": A guide to the language of the "alt-right." *Los Angeles Times.* https://www.latimes.com/nation/la-na-pol-alt-right-terminology-20161115-story.html (accessed January 21, 2025).

Rubin, R. B., Perse, E. M., and Barbato, C. A. (1988). Conceptualization and measurement of interpersonal communication motives. *Human Communication Research, 14*(4): 602–628.

Rucker, P. (2015a, August 7). Trump says Fox's Megyn Kelly had "blood coming out of her wherever". *The Washington Post.* https://www.washingtonpost.com/news/post-politics/wp/2015/08/07/trump-says-foxs-megyn-kelly-had-blood-coming-out-of-her-wherever/ (accessed January 21, 2025).

Rucker, P. (2015b, August 31). Chilling Trump video attacks Bush for calling illegal immigration "act of love'. *The Washington Post.* https://www.washingtonpost.com/news/post-politics/wp/2015/08/31/chilling-trump-video-attacks-bush-for-calling-illegal-immigration-act-of-love/ (accessed January 21, 2025).

Rupar, A. (2024, July 31). Trump self-immolates at NABJ: a supercut [Video]. *YouTube.*https://www.youtube.com/watch?v=kJFmvXQp6F8 (accessed January 21, 2025).

Rupar, A. [@atrupar]. (2024, September 23). NEWSMAX: What's your most important issue as a Pennsylvania voter? TRUMP FAN: The illegal immigration into this country NEWSMAX: How is... [Tweet; thumbnail link to video]. *X.* https://x.com/atrupar/status/1838264429055442960?mx=2 (accessed January 21, 2025).

Ryan, E., Dorning, C., and Shapiro, A. (2024, July 24). Powerful women tend to be called by their first name. It's not an accident. *NPR.* https://www.npr.org/2024/07/24/nx-s1-5049773/powerful-women-tend-to-be-called-by-their-first-name-its-not-an-accident (accessed January 21, 2025).

Ryan, C. S., Park, B., and Judd, C. M. (1996). Assessing stereotype accuracy: Implications for understanding the stereotyping process. In C. N. Macrae, C. Stangor, and M. Hewstone (Eds.) *Stereotypes and stereotyping* (pp. 121–157). Guilford Press.

Sacks, H. (1972). On the analyzability of stories by children. In John J. Gumperz and Dell Hymes (Eds.), *Directions in sociolinguistics: The ethnography of communication* (pp. 329–345). Holt, Rinehart and Winston.

Sacks, H. (1992). *Lectures on conversation* (edited by G. Jefferson). Basil Blackwell.

Salvanto, A., Backus, F., De Pinto, J., and Khanna, K. (2024, September 22). Harris shows some gains and economic views brighten a bit – CBS News Poll. *CBS News.* https://www.cbsnews.com/news/trump-harris-poll-debate-economy-09-22-2024/ (accessed January 21, 2025).

Samuels, B. (2024a, October 29). Trump calls Madison Square Garden rally a "Love fest." *The Hill.* https://thehill.com/homenews/4959432-trump-ny-msg-rally-love-fest/ (accessed January 21, 2025).

Samuels, B. (2024b, November 4). Trump caps Pennsylvania campaign: "The only way we can blow it is if you blow it". *The Hill.* https://thehill.com/homenews/campaign/4971704-trump-pennsylvania-campaign-night-before-election/ (accessed January 21, 2025).

Sanchez, M., and Rosenberg, M. (2024, November 26). Immigrants' resentment over new arrivals helped boost Trump's popularity with Latino voters. *ProPublica.* https://www.propublica.org/article/immigration-latino-trump-election-resentment-asylum (accessed January 21, 2025).

Sargent, G. (2024a, September 13). Trump's ugly rants about Haitians suddenly take on a more sinister hue. *The New Republic*. https://newrepublic.com/article/185953/trump-vance-haitians-springfield-ohio (accessed January 21, 2025).

Sargent, G. (2024b, September 25). Trump's hateful new rants at rally are harshly debunked by Town leader. *The New Republic*. https://newrepublic.com/article/186331/trump-hateful-rally-pennsylvania-debunked-town-leader (accessed January 21, 2025).

Sargent, G. (2024c, November 1). Transcript: Brutal new ad nukes Trump-with his own ugly words on women. *The New Republic*. https://newrepublic.com/article/187786/transcript-brutal-new-ad-nukes-trumpwith-ugly-words-women (accessed January 21, 2025).

Sawchuk, S. (2021, May 18). What is critical race theory, and why is it under attack? *Education Week*. https://www.edweek.org/leadership/what-is-critical-race-theory-and-why-is-it-under-attack/2021/05 (accessed January 21, 2025).

Schaeffer, K. (2023, January 9). U.S. Congress continues to grow in racial, ethnic diversity. *Pew Research Center*. https://www.pewresearch.org/short-reads/2023/01/09/u-s-congress-continues-to-grow-in-racial-ethnic-diversity/ (accessed January 21, 2025).

Schaffner, B. F., Macwilliams, M., and Nteta, T. (2018). Understanding white polarization in the 2016 vote for president: The sobering role of racism and sexism. *Political Science Quarterly, 133*(1): 9–34. https://doi.org/10.1002/polq.12737 (accessed January 21, 2025).

Schaller, M., and Conway, L. G. (1999). Influence of impression-management goals on the emerging contents of group stereotypes: Support for a social-evolutionary process. *Personality and Social Psychology Bulletin, 25*(7): 819–833. https://doi.org/10.1177/0146167299025007005 (accessed January 21, 2025).

Schaller, M., and Latané, B. (1996). Dynamic Social Impact and the evolution of Social Representations: A natural history of stereotypes. *Journal of Communication, 46*(4): 64–77. https://doi.org/10.1111/j.1460-2466.1996.tb01506.x (accessed January 21, 2025).

Schaller, M., Conway, L. G., and Tanchuk, T. L. (2002). Selective pressures on the once and future contents of ethnic stereotypes: Effects of the communicability of traits. *Journal of Personality and Social Psychology, 82*(6): 861–877. https://doi.org/10.1037//0022-3514.82.6.861 (accessed January 21, 2025).

Schermerhorn, C. (2023, December 4). History explains the U.S. racial wealth gap. *Time*. https://time.com/6334291/racial-wealth-gap-reagan-history/ (accessed January 21, 2025).

Schertzer, R., and Woods, E. (2020). #Nationalism: the ethno-nationalist populism of Donald Trump's Twitter communication. *Ethnic and Racial Studies, 44*(7): 1154–1173. https://doi.org/10.1080/01419870.2020.1713390 (accessed January 21, 2025).

Schmidt, M. S. (2018, July 13). Trump invited the Russians to hack Clinton. were they listening? *The New York Times*. https://www.nytimes.com/2018/07/13/us/politics/trump-russia-clinton-emails.html (accessed January 21, 2025).

Schmidt, M. S. (2024, October 22). As election nears, Kelly warns Trump would rule like a dictator. *The New York Times*. https://www.nytimes.com/2024/10/22/us/politics/john-kelly-trump-fitness-character.html (accessed January 21, 2025).

Schneider, D. J. (1996). Research: Unfinished business. In C. N. Macrae, C. Stangor, and M. Hewstone (Eds.), *Stereotypes and stereotyping* (pp. 419_453). Guilford Press.

Schoenfeld, G. (2024, July 14). The truth about political violence. *The Bulwark*. https://www.thebulwark.com/p/truth-about-political-violence-trump-shooting (accessed January 21, 2025).

Schwartz, D. (2017, February 1). Why Trump supporters love calling people "snowflakes." *GQ*. https://www.gq.com/story/why-trump-supporters-love-calling-people-snowflakes (accessed January 21, 2025).

Schwartz, S. (2021, June 11). Map: Where critical race theory is under attack. *Education Week*. https://www.edweek.org/policy-politics/map-where-critical-race-theory-is-under-attack/2021/06 (accessed January 21, 2025).

Scott, E. (2018, October 8). President Trump, "angry mobs" and "very fine people". *The Washington Post*. https://www.washingtonpost.com/politics/2018/10/08/president-trump-angry-mobs-very-fine-people/ (accessed January 21, 2025).

Searcey, D. (2024, August 30). Will Walz's rural upbringing lure small-town swing voters? *The New York Times*. https://www.nytimes.com/2024/08/30/us/elections/tim-walz-wisconsin-swing-state-voters.html (accessed January 21, 2025).

Searcey, D., and Alban, V. (2024, October 14). In rural Wisconsin, race is an undercurrent of the presidential election. *The New York Times*. https://www.nytimes.com/2024/10/14/us/elections/election-race-issues-baraboo-wisconsin.html (accessed January 21, 2025).

Seitz-Wald, A. (2020, January 31). Hillary Clinton isn't running, but she hasn't gone away (even if some might like her to). *NBC News*. https://www.nbcnews.com/politics/2020-election/hillary-clinton-isn-t-running-she-hasn-t-gone-away-n1127166 (accessed January 21, 2025).

Semin, G. R. (2000). Agenda 2000-Communication: Language as an implementational device for cognition. *European Journal of Social Psychology, 30:* 595 – 612.

Sentner, I. (2024, August 13). Trump calls Harris "a beautiful woman." He didn't mean it as a compliment. *Politico*. https://www.politico.com/news/2024/08/13/trump-beautiful-kamala-harris-00173840 (accessed January 21, 2025).

Serwer, A. (2024a, September 18). The real reason Trump and Vance are spreading lies about Haitians. *The Atlantic*. https://www.theatlantic.com/ideas/archive/2024/09/trumps-campaign-immigrants-springfield-ohio-haiti/679913/ (accessed January 21, 2025).

Serwer, A. (2024b, December 5). Trump's fans are suffering from Tony Soprano syndrome. *The Atlantic*. https://www.theatlantic.com/ideas/archive/2024/12/elon-musk-judge-dredd-autocrat/680881/ (accessed January 21, 2025).

Shalvey, K. (2024, September 18). Sarah Huckabee Sanders swipes at Kamala Harris for not having biological children. *ABC News*. https://abcnews.go.com/amp/US/huckabee-sanders-harris-lacks-humility-raising-biological-children/story?id=113800656 (accessed January 21, 2025).

Shear, M. D. (2020, August 26). Border officials weighed deploying migrant "heat ray" ahead of midterms. *The New York Times*. https://www.nytimes.com/2020/08/26/us/politics/trump-campaign-immigration.html (accessed January 21, 2025).

Shear, M. D. (2024, September 18). Trump's derision of Haitians goes back years. *The New York Times*. https://www.nytimes.com/2024/09/18/us/politics/trump-haitians.html (accessed January 21, 2025).

Shear, M. D., and Davis, J. H. (2019, October 1). Shoot migrants' legs, build alligator moat: Behind Trump's ideas for border. *The New York Times*. https://www.nytimes.com/2019/10/01/us/politics/trump-border-wars.html (accessed January 21, 2025).

Shear, M. D., and Sullivan, E. (2018, October 16). "Horseface," "lowlife," "fat, ugly": how the president demeans women. *The New York Times*. https://www.nytimes.com/2018/10/16/us/politics/trump-women-insults.html (accessed January 21, 2025).

Sheffey, A. (2025, February 2). Trump rolls out his vision to reshape America's schools. *Business Insider.* https://www.businessinsider.com/trump-school-choice-vouchers-education-policy-ex euctive-orders-anti-woke-2025-2 (accessed March 17, 2025).

Sherif, M. (1956). Experiments in group conflict. *Scientific American, 195:* 54–58.

Sherif, M., Harvey, O. J., White, B. J., Hood, W. E., and Sherif, C. W. (1961). *Intergroup conflict and cooperation: The Robbers Cave experiment.* Institute of Group Relations.

Sherman, G. (2016, April 3). Inside Operation Trump, the most unorthodox campaign in political history. *New York Magazine.* https://nymag.com/intelligencer/2016/04/inside-the-donald-trump-presidential-campaign.html (accessed January 21, 2025).

Shutt, J. (2015, August 16). Trump leads in first post-debate Fox poll. *Politico.* https://www.politico.com/story/2015/08/donald-trump-debate-fox-news-2016-poll-121412 (accessed January 21, 2025).

Sides, J., Tesler, M., and Vavreck, L. (2019). *Identity crisis: The 2016 presidential campaign and the battle for the meaning of America.* Princeton University Press.

Slotkin, R. (2024). *A great disorder: National myth and the Battle for America.* Harvard University Press.

Smith, P. (2024a, May 18). Jesus is their savior, Trump is their candidate. Ex-president's backers say he shares faith, values. *Associated Press.* https://apnews.com/article/trump-christian-evangelicals-conservatives-2024-election-43f25118c133170c77786daf316821c3 (accessed January 21, 2025).

Smith, P. (2024b, November 7). White evangelical voters show steadfast support for Donald Trump's presidency. *Associated Press.* https://apnews.com/article/white-evangelical-voters-support-donald-trump-president-dbfd2b4fe5b2ea27968876f19ee20c84 (accessed January 21, 2025).

So, L. (2021, June 11). Trump-inspired death threats are terrorizing election workers. *Reuters.* https://www.reuters.com/investigates/special-report/usa-trump-georgia-threats/ (accessed January 21, 2025).

Sourcestaff. (2024, October 21). Charlamagne Tha God hits Trump with cease and desist over manipulated anti Harris campaign ad. *The Source.* https://thesource.com/2024/10/21/charla magne-tha-god-hits-trump-with-cease-and-desist-over-manipulated-anti-harris-campaign-ad/ (accessed January 21, 2025).

Stafford, L., and Daly, J. A. (1984). Conversational memory: The effects of recall mode and memory expectancies on remembrances of natural conversations. *Human Communication Research, 10*(3): 379–402.

Stangor, C. (1995). Content and application inaccuracy in social stereotyping. In Y. Lee, L. Jussim, and C. McCauley (Eds.), *Stereotype accuracy: Toward appreciating group differences* (pp. 275–292). American Psychological Association.

Stangor, C., and Schaller, M. (1996). Stereotypes as individual and collective representations. In C. N. Macrae, C. Stangor, and M. Hewstone (Eds.), *Stereotypes and stereotyping* (pp. 3–37). Guilford Press.

The Statue of Liberty—Ellis Island Foundation, Inc. (2022, November 1). *Ellis Island.* https://www.stat ueofliberty.org/ellis-island/ (accessed January 21, 2025).

Steinhauser, P. (2024, November 6). Trump White House victory called "the greatest political comeback in American history." *Fox News.* https://www.foxnews.com/politics/trump-white-house-victory-called-the-greatest-political-comeback-american-history (accessed January 21, 2025).

Steinhorn, L. (2022, July 26). The fundamental flaw in "Make America Great Again." *The Washington Post.* https://www.washingtonpost.com/made-by-history/2022/07/26/fundamental-flaw-make-america-great-again/ (accessed January 21, 2025).

Stelter, B. (2021, November 16). This infamous Steve Bannon quote is key to understanding America's crazy politics. *CNN*. https://www.cnn.com/2021/11/16/media/steve-bannon-reliable-sources/index.html (accessed January 21, 2025).

Stelter, B. (2024a, October 5). False claims about the federal response to Helene are an ominous sign for the coming election. *CNN*. https://www.cnn.com/2024/10/05/media/hurricane-helene-fema-false-claims-recovery/index.html (accessed January 21, 2025).

Stelter, B. (2024b, October 17). How Bret Baier's combative interview with Harris compared to his sitdown with Trump. *CNN*. https://www.cnn.com/2024/10/17/media/bret-baier-fox-harris-trump-interview/index.html (accessed January 21, 2025).

Stempel, J. (2007, August 9). *Countrywide sued for racial bias in mortgage loans. Reuters.* https://www.reuters.com/article/idUSN12313883/ (accessed January 21, 2025).

Stephens, B. (2024, November 6). A party of prigs and pontificators suffers a humiliating defeat. *The New York Times.* https://www.nytimes.com/2024/11/06/opinion/donald-trump-defeat-democrats.html (accessed January 21, 2025).

Stewart, E. (2016, November 20). Donald Trump rode $5 billion in free media to the White House. *TheStreet.* https://www.thestreet.com/politics/donald-trump-rode-5-billion-in-free-media-to-the-white-house-13896916 (accessed January 21, 2025).

Stewart, E. (2018, August 25). Watch John McCain defend Barack Obama against a racist voter in 2008. *Vox.* https://www.vox.com/policy-and-politics/2018/8/25/17782572/john-mccain-barack-obama-statement-2008-video (accessed January 21, 2025).

Stockett, M. K. (2005). On the importance of difference: Re-envisioning sex and gender in ancient Mesoamerica. *World Archaeology, 37*(4): 566 – 578. https://doi.org/10.1080/00438240500404375 (accessed January 21, 2025).

Stokols, E. (2016, May 20). Donald Trump scores NRA backing and attacks "Heartless Hillary". *Politico.* https://www.politico.com/story/2016/05/donald-trump-nra-guns-223426 (accessed January 21, 2025).

Stoller, G. (2018, February 20). So you thought travel guidebooks were dead? Guess again. *Forbes.* https://www.forbes.com/sites/garystoller/2018/02/20/so-you-thought-travel-guidebooks-were-dead-guess-again/ (accessed January 21, 2025).

Stracqualursi, V. (2019, March 15). Trump suggests that supporters may get "tough" against Democrats. *CNN.* https://www.cnn.com/2019/03/15/politics/trump-breitbart-interview-tough-supporters-democrats-violence/index.html (accessed January 21, 2025).

Stroebe, W., and Insko, C. A. (1989). Stereotype, prejudice, and discrimination: Changing conceptions in theory and research. *Stereotyping and Prejudice*, pp. 3 – 34. https://doi.org/10.1007/978-1-4612-3582-8_1 (accessed January 21, 2025).

Sullivan, K. (2024, October 18). Trump says "manhood is under attack". *CNN.* https://www.cnn.com/politics/live-news/trump-harris-election-10-18-24/index.html (accessed January 21, 2025).

Sullivan, K., and Forrest, J. (2024, September 8). Trump threatens prosecution of 2024 election officials who "cheated" if he wins presidency. *CNN.* https://www.cnn.com/2024/09/08/politics/trump-threatens-prosecution-2024-election-officials/index.html (accessed January 21, 2025).

Svitek, P. (2024a, September 24). "Get them the hell out": Trump continues attacks on legal immigrants in Ohio town. *The Washington Post.* https://www.washingtonpost.com/politics/2024/09/24/trump-springfield-continued-attacks/ (accessed January 21, 2025).

Svitek, P. (2024b, October 1). JD Vance's mic is muted during debate exchange on immigration. *The Washington Post.* https://www.washingtonpost.com/politics/2024/10/01/vp-debate-mic-muted-vance-cbs-fact check-immigration/ (accessed January 21, 2025).

Swan, J., Haberman, M., and Goldmacher, S. (2024, October 12). A frustrated Trump lashes out behind closed doors over money. *The New York Times*. https://www.nytimes.com/2024/10/12/us/politics/trump-gop-donors.html (accessed January 21, 2025).

Swan, J., Haberman, M., Rogers, K., and Epstein, R. J. (2024, September 7). Inside the Trump-Harris debate prep: Method acting, insults, tough questions. *The New York Times*. https://www.nytimes.com/2024/09/07/us/politics/trump-harris-debate-prep.html (accessed January 21, 2025).

Swenson, A., and Alexander, A. (2023, August 22). Trump's attacks on prosecutors echo long history of racist language. *PBS*. https://www.pbs.org/newshour/politics/trumps-attacks-on-prosecutors-echo-long-history-of-racist-language (accessed January 21, 2025).

Swim, J. K. (1994). Perceived versus meta-analytic effects sizes: An assessment of the accuracy of gender stereotypes. *Journal of Personality and Social Psychology, 66:* 21 – 36.

Tajfel, H. (1969). Cognitive aspects of prejudice. *Journal of Social Issues, 25:* 79 – 97.

Tajfel, H., and Wilkes, A. L. (1963). Classification and quantitative judgment. *British Journal of Psychology, 54:* 101 – 114.

Tatum, S., and Acosta, J. (2017, November 29). Report: Trump continues to question Obama's birth certificate. *CNN*. https://www.cnn.com/2017/11/28/politics/donald-trump-barack-obama-birth-certificate-nyt/index.html (accessed January 21, 2025).

Taylor, J. (2015, December 7). Trump calls for "total and complete shutdown of Muslims entering" U.S. *NPR*. https://www.npr.org/2015/12/07/458836388/trump-calls-for-total-and-complete-shutdown-of-muslims-entering-u-s (accessed January 21, 2025).

Taylor, K.-Y. (2023, October 21). Ibram X. Kendi's anti-racism. *The New Yorker*. https://www.newyorker.com/news/our-columnists/ibram-x-kendis-anti-racism (accessed January 21, 2025).

Taylor, R. (2024, September 27). The "queen" of Charleroi: Trump disparages immigrants in Washington County town, but Courier learns they are making a positive impact. *New Pittsburgh Courier*. https://newpittsburghcourier.com/2024/09/27/the-queen-of-charleroi-trump-disparages-immigrants-in-washington-county-town-but-courier-learns-they-are-making-a-positive-impact/ (accessed January 21, 2025).

Tehranian, J. (2000). Performing whiteness: naturalization litigation and the construction of racial identity in America. *The Yale Law Journal, 109*(4): 817 – 848. https://doi.org/10.2307/797505 (accessed January 21, 2025).

Tensley, B. (2021, February 16). Analysis: Academia's troubling trend: white people passing as people of color. *CNN*. https://www.cnn.com/2021/02/16/politics/race-academia-trnd/index.html (accessed January 21, 2025).

Terkel, A., and Lebowitz, M. (2024, September 19). From "rapists" to "eating the pets": Trump has long used degrading language toward immigrants. *NBC News*. https://www.nbcnews.com/politics/donald-trump/trump-degrading-language-immigrants-rcna171120 (accessed January 21, 2025).

The New York Times. (2019, August 14). The 1619 Project. *The New York Times*. https://www.nytimes.com/interactive/2019/08/14/magazine/1619-america-slavery.html (accessed January 21, 2025).

The New York Times. (2024, July 19). Read the transcript of Donald J. Trump's convention speech. *The New York Times*. https://www.nytimes.com/2024/07/19/us/politics/trump-rnc-speech-transcript.html (accessed January 21, 2025).

The New York Times' Editorial Board. (2024, October 25). Trump is telling us what he would do. Believe him. *The New York Times*. https://www.nytimes.com/interactive/2024/10/25/opinion/what-trump-says.html (accessed January 21, 2025).

The White House. (2020, July 4). Remarks by President Trump at South Dakota's 2020 Mount Rushmore Fireworks Celebration, Keystone, South Dakota. *Trump Whitehouse Archives*. https://trumpwhitehouse.archives.gov/briefings-statements/remarks-president-trump-south-dakotas-2020-mount-rushmore-fireworks-celebration-keystone-south-dakota/ (accessed January 21, 2025).

Thomas, A., and Nichols, H. (2024, August 27). Harris flip-flops on building the border wall. *Axios*. https://www.axios.com/2024/08/27/kamala-harris-flip-flops-border-wall (accessed January 21, 2025).

Thomas, Z. (2016, April 13). How did Donald Trump make his fortune? *BBC News*. https://www.bbc.com/news/business-35836623 (accessed January 21, 2025).

Thompson, A. (2024, April 1). Exclusive: Trump allies plot anti-racism protections—for white people. *Axios*. https://www.axios.com/2024/04/01/trump-reverse-racism-civil-rights (accessed January 21, 2025).

Thompson, M. S., Judd, C. M., and Park, B. (2000). The consequences of communicating social stereotypes. *Journal of Experimental Social Psychology, 36*: 567–599.

Thorndike, E. L. (1920). A constant error in psychological ratings. *Journal of Applied Psychology, 4*(1): 25–29.

Thibodaux, D. (1994). *Beyond political correctness: Are there limits to this lunacy?* Huntington House Publishers.

Thrush, G., and Haberman, M. (2017, August 15). Trump gives white supremacists an unequivocal boost. *The New York Times*. https://www.nytimes.com/2017/08/15/us/politics/trump-charlottesville-white-nationalists.html (accessed January 21, 2025).

Time Staff. (2017, August 23). Trump's 2017 Phoenix, Arizona rally full speech transcript. *Time*. https://time.com/4912055/donald-trump-phoenix-arizona-transcript/ (accessed January 21, 2025).

Time Staff. (2024, April 30). Donald Trump time interview on 2024 transcript: Read. *Time*. https://time.com/6972022/donald-trump-transcript-2024-election/ (accessed January 21, 2025).

Tracy, K. and Robles, J. (2013). *Everyday talk: Building and reflecting identities* (2nd ed). Guilford Press.

Trautmann, M. (2023, December 22). Why does Trump keep saying migrants are "poisoning" America? Many GOP caucusgoers like it. *Des Moines Register*. https://www.desmoinesregister.com/story/news/politics/iowa-poll/caucus/2023/12/22/iowa-poll-shows-depth-of-republicans-support-for-donald-trump-poisoning-the-blood-speech-gop/71998614007/ (accessed January 21, 2025).

Treisman, R. (2024, October 19). Trump is promising deportations under the Alien Enemies Act of 1798. what is it? *NPR*. https://www.npr.org/2024/10/19/nx-s1-5156027/alien-enemies-act-1798-trump-immigration (accessed January 21, 2025).

Treisman, R. (2025, March 18). 4 things to know about the Alien Enemies Act and Trump's efforts to use it. *NPR*. https://www.npr.org/2025/03/18/nx-s1-5331857/alien-enemies-act-trump-deportations (accessed March 18, 2025).

The Trevor Project. (2024, December 15). Facts about suicide among LGBTQ+ young people. https://www.thetrevorproject.org/resources/article/facts-about-lgbtq-youth-suicide/ (accessed January 21, 2025).

Trump, D. (2023a, February 1). President Trump's plan to protect children from left-wing gender insanity. *DonaldJTrump.com*. https://www.donaldjtrump.com/agenda47/president-trumps-plan-to-protect-children-from-left-wing-gender-insanity (accessed January 21, 2025).

Trump, D. (2023b, November 1). Agenda47: The American Academy. *DonaldJTrump.com*. https://www.donaldjtrump.com/agenda47/agenda47-the-american-academy (accessed January 21, 2025).

Trump, D. and Schwartz, D. (1987) *Trump: The art of the deal.* Random House.

Tucker, B. and Knowles, H. (2024, July 31). Trump attacks Harris's black identity. Harris says Americans "deserve better." *The Washington Post.* https://www.washingtonpost.com/politics/2024/07/31/trump-Black-voters-nabj-harris/ (accessed January 21, 2025).

Ulloa, J. (2024a, September 10). "They're eating the cats": Trump repeats false claim about immigrants. *The New York Times.* https://www.nytimes.com/2024/09/10/us/politics/trump-debate-immigrants-pets.html (accessed January 21, 2025).

Ulloa, J. (2024b, November 1). The deep roots of four of Donald Trump's nativist remarks. *The New York Times.* https://www.nytimes.com/2024/11/01/us/politics/trump-immigration-rhetoric-history.html (accessed January 21, 2025).

United States Department of Homeland Security. (2009, April 7). Rightwing Extremism: Current Economic and Political Climate Fueling Resurgence in Radicalization and Recruitment. *Federation of American Scientists – Intelligence Resource Program.* https://irp.fas.org/eprint/rightwing.pdf (accessed January 21, 2025).

United States Holocaust Memorial Museum. (2024, November 26). An antisemitic conspiracy: The Protocols of the Elders of Zion. *Holocaust Encyclopedia.* https://encyclopedia.ushmm.org/content/en/article/protocols-of-the-elders-of-zion (accessed January 21, 2025).

University of California San Francisco. (n.d.). Unconscious bias training. *Office of Diversity and Outreach at University of California, San Francisco.* https://diversity.ucsf.edu/programs-resources/training/unconscious-bias-training#item-89 (accessed January 21, 2025).

Urban Dictionary. Makaka. (n.d.). https://www.urbandictionary.com/define.php?term=makaka (accessed January 21, 2025).

Uribe, M. R. (2024, September 10). Communicable disease rates in Springfield, Ohio, have not 'skyrocketed,' despite JD Vance's claim. *Politifact.* https://www.politifact.com/factchecks/2024/sep/26/jd-vance/communicable-disease-rates-in-springfield-ohio-hav/ (accessed January 21, 2025).

Usborne, D. (2008, November 24). Summers' "sexism" costs him top Treasury job. *The Independent.* https://www.independent.co.uk/news/world/americas/summers-sexism-costs-him-top-treasury-job-1033373.html (accessed January 21, 2025).

Valencia, P., and Lillich, C. (2024, July 19). Fact-checking former president Donald Trump at the RNC. *Arizona's Family.* https://www.azfamily.com/2024/07/19/fact-checking-former-president-donald-trump-rnc/ (accessed January 21, 2025).

Valentino, N. A., Neuner, F. G., and Vandenbroek, L. M. (2018). The changing norms of racial political rhetoric and the end of racial priming. *The Journal of Politics, 80*(3): 757 – 771. https://doi.org/10.1086/694845 (accessed January 21, 2025).

Vance, JD. (2016, February 18). Trump speaks for those Bush betrayed. *USA Today.* https://www.usatoday.com/story/opinion/2016/02/18/donald-trump-white-working-class-rust-belt-voters-elections-2016-column/80422422/ (accessed January 21, 2025).

Vazquez, M. (2024, October 13). Trump urges using military to handle 'radical left lunatics' on Election Day. *The Washington Post.* https://www.washingtonpost.com/politics/2024/10/13/trump-military-enemies-within/ (accessed January 21, 2025).

Vazquez, M., and Carvajal, N. (2020, October 27). Trump appears to give a pass to the domestic kidnapping plot against Whitmer. *CNN.* https://www.cnn.com/2020/10/27/politics/trump-gretchen-whitmer-kidnapping-michigan/index.html (accessed January 21, 2025).

Vazquez, M. and Rodriguez, S. (2024, September 28). Trump falsely attacks Harris as "mentally impaired" and "mentally disabled," prompting criticism. *The Washington Post.* https://www.wash

ingtonpost.com/politics/2024/09/28/trump-harris-attacks-mentally-impaired-criticism/ (accessed January 21, 2025).

Vedantam, S. (2016, October 26). "Double bind" explains the dearth of women in top leadership positions. *NPR.* https://www.npr.org/2016/10/26/499409051/double-bind-explains-the-dearth-of-women-in-top-leadership-positions (accessed January 21, 2025).

Vinacke, W. E. (1956). Explorations in the dynamic processes of stereotyping. *The Journal of Social Psychology, 43*(1): 105 – 132. https://doi.org/10.1080/00224545.1956.9919205 (accessed January 21, 2025).

Vitali, A. (2015, December 21). Donald Trump launches vulgar attack against Hillary Clinton. *NBC News.* https://www.nbcnews.com/politics/2016-election/donald-trump-launches-vulgar-attack-against-hillary-clinton-n484226 (accessed January 21, 2025).

Vrugt, A. (1987). The meaning of non-verbal sex differences. *Semiotica, 64*(3/4): 371 – 380.

Wadhwani, A. (2024, October 9). Local disaster relief officials add one more task to a full plate: combating misinformation. *Tennessee Lookout.* https://tennesseelookout.com/2024/10/09/local-disaster-relief-officials-add-one-more-task-to-a-full-plate-combating-misinformation/ (accessed January 21, 2025).

Wang, C. (2024, September 14). "A very old political trope": the racist US history behind Trump's Haitian Pet Eater claim. *The Guardian.* https://www.theguardian.com/us-news/2024/sep/14/racist-history-trump-pet-eating-immigrant (accessed January 21, 2025).

Wang, H. L. (2024, March 28). Next U.S. Census will have new boxes for "Middle Eastern or North African," "Latino." *NPR.* https://www.npr.org/2024/03/28/1237218459/census-race-categories-eth nicity-middle-east-north-africa (accessed January 21, 2025).

Ward, I. (2024, September 18). JD Vance's scapegoating theory is playing out in real time in Springfield. *Politico.* https://www.politico.com/news/magazine/2024/09/18/jd-vance-springfield-scapegoating-00179401 (accessed January 21, 2025).

Ward, M. (2024, October 12). We watched 20 Trump rallies. his racist, anti-immigrant messaging is getting darker. *Politico.* https://www.politico.com/news/2024/10/12/trump-racist-rhetoric-immi grants-00183537 (accessed January 21, 2025).

The Washington Post Staff. (2015a, June 16). Full text: Donald Trump announces a presidential bid. *The Washington Post.* https://www.washingtonpost.com/news/post-politics/wp/2015/06/16/full-text-donald-trump-announces-a-presidential-bid/ (accessed January 21, 2025).

The Washington Post Staff. (2015b, August 6). Annotated transcript: The Aug. 6 GOP debate. *The Washington Post.* https://www.washingtonpost.com/news/post-politics/wp/2015/08/06/annotated-transcript-the-aug-6-gop-debate/ (accessed January 21, 2025).

The Washington Post. (2020, December 14). Exit poll results and analysis for the 2020 presidential election. *The Washington Post.* https://www.washingtonpost.com/elections/interactive/2020/exit-polls/presidential-election-exit-polls/ (accessed January 21, 2025).

The Washington Post. (2024, December 2). Exit polls from the 2024 presidential election. *The Washington Post.* https://www.washingtonpost.com/elections/interactive/2024/exit-polls-2024-elec tion/ (accessed January 21, 2025).

Watts, D. J., and Rothschild, D. M. (2017, December 5). Don't blame the election on fake news. Blame it on the media. *Columbia Journalism Review.* https://www.cjr.org/analysis/fake-news-media-election-trump.php (accessed January 21, 2025).

Watzlawick, P., Bavelas, J. B., and Jackson, D. D. (1967) *Pragmatics of human communication, A study of interactional patterns, pathologies, and paradoxes.* WW Norton and Company.

Weiland, N. (2024, September 21). Drug overdose deaths are dropping. The reasons are not perfectly clear. *The New York Times*. https://www.nytimes.com/2024/09/21/us/politics/drug-overdose-deaths-decrease.html (accessed January 21, 2025).

Weissert, W., and Price, M. L. (2024, August 12). Harris is pushing joy. Trump paints a darker picture. Will mismatched moods matter? *The Associated Press*. https://www.ap.org/news-highlights/elections/2024/harris-is-pushing-joy-trump-paints-a-darker-picture-will-mismatched-moods-matter/ (accessed January 21, 2025).

Wicks, R. H., Wicks, J. L., and Morimoto, S. A. (2014). Partisan Media Selective Exposure During the 2012 Presidential Election. *American Behavioral Scientist, 58*(9): 1131–1143. https://doi.org/10.1177/0002764213506208 (accessed January 21, 2025).

Wiggins, C. (2024, September 13). JD Vance now says Haitian immigrants are spreading HIV after bizarre pet-eating claim flops. *Advocate*. https://www.advocate.com/election/jd-vance-haitian-hiv-stigma (accessed January 21, 2025).

Williams, J. (1995). *PC wars: Politics and theory in the academy*. Routledge.

Williams, M. T., Skinta, M. D., and Martin-Willett, R. (2021). After Pierce and Sue: A Revised Racial Microaggressions Taxonomy. *Perspectives on Psychological Science, 16*(5): 991–1007. https://doi.org/10.1177/1745691621994247 (accessed January 21, 2025).

Willingham, A., Kessler, A., and Griggs, B. (2017, April 21). The two-word phrase president Trump relies on most. *CNN*. https://www.cnn.com/2017/04/21/politics/donald-trump-president-speeches-favorite-phrases-trnd/index.html (accessed January 21, 2025).

Wines, M. (2020, December 3). Here are the threats terrorizing election workers. *The New York Times*. https://www.nytimes.com/2020/12/03/us/election-officials-threats-trump.html (accessed January 21, 2025).

Wisconsin Politics (2024, October 2). Trump promises crackdown on illegal immigration, tax cuts during Dane County speech. *WisPolitics*. https://www.wispolitics.com/2024/trump-promises-crackdown-on-illegal-immigration-tax-cuts-during-dane-county-speech/ (accessed January 21, 2025).

Withers, R. (2018, December 1). George H.W. Bush's "Willie Horton" ad will always be the reference point for dog-whistle racism. *Vox*. https://www.vox.com/2018/12/1/18121221/george-hw-bush-willie-horton-dog-whistle-politics (accessed January 21, 2025).

Witte, G. (2019, August 13). After El Paso, the "send her back" chant echoes to some as a prelude to murder. *The Washington Post*. https://www.washingtonpost.com/national/after-el-paso-the-send-her-back-chant-echoes-to-some-as-a-prelude-to-murder/2019/08/13/6e6ed198-bd15-11e9-a5c6-1e74f7ec4a93_story.html (accessed January 21, 2025).

Wolf, J. D. (2024, August 19). Trump posts video implying Kamala Harris performed oral sex for political power. *MeidasTouch News*. https://meidasnews.com/news/trump-posts-video-implying-kamala-harris-performed-oral-sex-for-political-power (accessed January 21, 2025).

Wolf, Z.B., Merrill, C., and Mullery, W. (2024, November 6). Anatomy of three Trump elections: How Americans voted in 2024 vs. 2020 and 2016. *CNN*. https://www.cnn.com/interactive/2024/politics/2020-2016-exit-polls-2024-dg/ (accessed January 21, 2025).

Wong, A., Ma, A. (2025, January 31). Federal agencies begin removing DEI guidance from websites in Trump crackdown. *ABC News*. https://apnews.com/article/trump-dei-education-diversity-equity-inclusion-20cf8a2941f4f35e0b5b0e07c6347ebb (accessed January 31, 2025).

Woodall, C. (2024, August 13). 5 takeaways from Trump's interview with Elon Musk: staff commentary. *Baltimore Sun*. https://www.baltimoresun.com/2024/08/13/5-takeaways-from-trumps-Interview-with-elon-musk-staff-commentary/ (accessed January 21, 2025).

Woods, E. T., and Schertzer, R. (2024, June 3). How Trump's definition of a "real" American has grabbed his audience--and what our research shows about why. *The Conversation.* https://the conversation.com/how-trumps-definition-of-a-real-american-has-grabbed-his-audience-and-what-our-research-shows-about-why-225403 (accessed January 21, 2025).

Woods, E. T., Fortier-Chouinard, A., Closen, M., Ouellet, C., and Schertzer, R. (2023). The battle for the soul of the nation: Nationalist polarization in the 2020 American presidential election and the threat to democracy. *Political Communication*, *41*(2): 173–198. https://doi.org/10.1080/ 10584609.2023.2291150 (accessed January 21, 2025).

World Economic Forum. (2024, January 10). Global risks 2024: Disinformation tops global risks 2024 as environmental threats intensify. *WEForum.* https://www.weforum.org/press/2024/01/global-risks-report-2024-press-release/ (accessed January 21, 2025).

Wratten, M. (2023, March 20). Paris Hilton addresses long history of racist, homophobic comments: "I was f****d up." *PinkNews.* https://www.thepinknews.com/2023/03/20/paris-hilton-racist-homo phobic-comments/ (accessed January 21, 2025).

Wright, D. (2016, March 16). Trump wavers on paying legal fees for violent backers. *CNN.* https:// www.cnn.com/2016/03/15/politics/donald-trump-legal-fees-supporters/index.html (accessed January 21, 2025).

Wu, M. Y., and Kurylo, A. (2010). Proverb activity: Understanding how perception and gender stereotypes are formed. *Communication Teacher, 24*: 69–73.

Wu, D. and Menn, J. (2024, November 7). After election, racist texts nationwide threaten black people with slavery. *The Washington Post.* https://www.washingtonpost.com/nation/2024/11/07/ racist-texts-slavery-election/ (accessed January 21, 2025).

Ye Hee Lee, M. (2017, August 4). President Trump's claim about immigrants 'immediately' collecting 'welfare'. *The Washington Post.* https://www.washingtonpost.com/news/fact-checker/wp/2017/08/ 04/president-trumps-claim-about-immigrants-immediately-collecting-welfare/?noredirect=on (accessed January 21, 2025).

Yen, H., Swenson, A., and Seitz, A. (2020, December 3). AP fact check: Trump's claims of vote rigging are all wrong. *Associated Press.* https://apnews.com/article/election-2020-ap-fact check-joe-biden-donald-trump-technology-49a24edd6d10888dbad61689c24b05a5 (accessed January 21, 2025).

Yilek, C. (2024, October 16). Trump campaign has spent millions on anti-trans ads. *CBS News.* https:// www.cbsnews.com/news/trump-anti-trans-ads-spending/ (accessed January 21, 2025).

Young, C. (2024, July 17). Donald Trump's violent rhetoric: A catalogue. *The Bulwark.* https://www.the bulwark.com/p/donald-trump-violent-rhetoric-catalogue (accessed January 21, 2025).

Young, R., and McMahon, S. (2021, August 18). Name discrimination study finds Lakisha and Jamal still less likely to get hired than Emily and Greg. *WBUR.* https://www.wbur.org/hereandnow/ 2021/08/18/name-discrimination-jobs (accessed January 21, 2025).

Zadrozny, B. (2024, September 13). Before Trump, neo-Nazis pushed false claims about Haitians as part of hate campaign. *NBC News.* https://www.nbcnews.com/tech/internet/trump-neo-nazis-pushed-false-claims-haitians-part-hate-campaign-rcna170796 (accessed January 21, 2025).

Zanna, M. P., and Olson, J. M. (1994). *The psychology of prejudice: The Ontario symposium.* Erlbaum.

Zaru, D. (2018, October 11). Donald Trump's fall from hip-hop grace: From rap icon to public enemy No. 1. *ABC News.* https://abcnews.go.com/Politics/donald-trumps-fall-hip-hop-grace-rap-icon/ story?id=58411276 (accessed January 21, 2025).

Zheng, L. (2019, October 28). How to show white men that diversity and inclusion efforts need them. *Harvard Business Review.* https://hbr.org/2019/10/how-to-show-white-men-that-diversity-and-inclusion-efforts-need-them (accessed January 21, 2025).

Zinoman, J. (2024, October 28). Why Trump uses comics like Tony Hinchcliffe to spread his message. *The New York Times.* https://www.nytimes.com/2024/10/28/arts/trump-tony-hinchcliffe-joe-rogan.html (accessed January 21, 2025).

Index

Note: Page numbers followed by "n" refer to notes.

https://doi.org/10.1515/9783111426327-014

www.ingramcontent.com/pod-product-compliance
Lightning Source LLC
Chambersburg PA
CBHW031128270326
41929CB00011B/1547